THE DIARY OF A WANNABE
INTERNET MILLIONAIRE

To Clare, Holly, Lucy and Fred

THE DIARY OF A WANNABE INTERNET MILLIONAIRE

SHOW ME THE MONEY

DAVID THOMAS

EBURY
PRESS

First published in Great Britain in 2000

1 3 5 7 9 10 8 6 4 2

Copyright © David Thomas 2000

David Thomas has asserted his right to be
identified as the author of this work.

Ebury Press
Random House, 20 Vauxhall Bridge Road, London SW1V 2SA

Random House Australia Pty Limited
20 Alfred Street, Milsons Point, Sydney, New South Wales 2061, Australia

Random House New Zealand Limited
18 Poland Road, Glenfield, Auckland 10, New Zealand

Random House Africa (Pty) Limited
Endulini, 5A Jubilee Road, Parktown 2193, South Africa

The Random House Group. Limited Reg. No. 954009

A CIP catalogue record for this book is available from the British Library

ISBN 0 09 187850 0

Cover design by Push

Text design by Blackjacks

Printed and bound in the UK by Biddles Ltd, Guildford and King' Lynn

Papers used by Ebury Press are natural, recyclable products
made from wood grown in sustainable forests.

ACKNOWLEDGEMENTS

Neither this book, nor the business it describes, would have been possible without my partners and colleagues Mitchell Symons, Nigel Parker, Lucien King, Dorian Silver, Stacy Mann, Adam Precious, Jonathan Fingerhut, Paul Massey, Joanna Jordan, Zac Barratt and Kit Hunter Gordon. My thanks also go to James Dyson, for his inspiration and kindness; the techies at ABC; the designers at The Attik; Danielle Nicholls, for being Cazza; Penny Smith, for the loan of her fabulous flat; the many editors at the *Daily Mail*, *Night & Day*, the *Telegraph Magazine* and the *Independent* who commissioned the stories that set me thinking in the right direction; Susan Grant, who flew me out to Paradise Island; Ted Verity, who got the point; Julian Alexander and Jake Lingwood, who had faith; my long-suffering family, who put up with yet another one of my mad schemes, and, finally, Sacha The Wonderful Waitress, for reasons that are just about to be revealed ....

WHERE IT STARTS 1998

What would it take to make you want to change your life? What would it take for you to actually do it?

For me it began with three things: a 19 year-old waitress, a 55 year-old rock star, and the sight of a 147-foot superyacht sliding into a berth on Paradise Island in the Bahamas. It then happened because of a man who spent fifteen years trying to make a better vacuum-cleaner. It may end in triumph and wealth beyond my wildest dreams. Or, much more likely, absolute disaster and the ruin of a perfectly good career. That's what happens when you roll the dice. You're just as likely to get double-one as double-six – more likely than either you'll get a score from five to eight that doesn't really take you anywhere at all.

You still go right ahead and roll.

My personal dice are stamped with a name: sho-biz.com. That's the business I'm trying to set up. It's a celebrity website, linked to an international syndication service, presenting celebrity interviews to online subscribers and then offering secondary rights to conventional media – press, radio and TV – around the world. There's a lot more too it than that, of course, but I'll spare you the details. Just think of it as a celebrity/entertainment website... that'll do.

So now, rewind back to the autumn of 1998. I am a 39-year-old journalist, living in West Sussex. I do okay. My income is a fair way down from its 1995 peak, but I'm still making a decent living. In any case, the drop's mostly due to the decision of two successive criminal courts to find John Fashanu and Bruce Grobbelaar not guilty of football corruption, thereby preventing me from publishing a book on the subject that's been four years in the works. Now that I'm off that hobbyhorse, and back to full-time journalism, things are picking up. Trouble is, while I'm working my way back to where I was a few years ago, others are racing ahead. It will be a while before I truly understand the degree to which I (and many, many others) am falling behind peers working in finance, business or the law, but I sense enough to know I might have backed the wrong professional horse.

Still, money isn't everything. My work is fun. I am paid to live like Miss World: I travel the world and meet interesting people. Better yet, I don't have to hang out with Eric and Julia Morley. In between trips, I work from home. So I never commute, I wear what I like, work when I like, make my own decisions. That must be worth something… right?

When I left London and moved down to Sussex in the summer of 1993, I made a conscious decision to put family values and quality of life ahead of careerist self-advancement. It's hard to believe it now, but that's what the Nineties were supposed to have been about – an antidote to the hyper-materialistic, Thatcherite Eighties. People used to talk about downshifting, abandoning the rat-race in search of a more contented, meaningful existence. I believed them. So, there's one trend I called wrong, for a start.

Never mind. I have a rambling old house and an acre of garden right next to a country churchyard. I am married to Clare, the same beautiful, loving woman I've been with since we met about two weeks after my 23rd birthday. We have two bright, pretty daughters, Holly and Lucy and a blue-eyed blond baby boy called Fred. We eat eggs laid by our own pedigree hens, and eat vegetables straight from the garden.

You know that old Talking Heads song, 'Once In a Lifetime'? The one that goes, 'You may find yourself in a beautiful house, with a beautiful wife / And you may ask yourself, well, how did I get here?' That's the story of my life, and by any normal person's standards it's a story with a happy ending. To do interesting, well-rewarded work; to be loved by a woman; to be blessed by children… in all cultures, through all time, these would be the signs of a man whom Fate has favoured. The two words 'smug' and 'git' come to mind.

But ours is a very peculiar culture, one in which an ordinary man's good fortune pales into insignificance next to the bounty showered upon a favoured few – the beautiful, the famous, the rich – about whose deeds he must not only continuously read, but in my case also write. I know I should be happy, I should be grateful, and most of the time I am. But somehow, it isn't enough.

I guess you would call it a mid-life crisis. It doesn't deserve a shred of sympathy from anybody. But empathy, perhaps: there are surely men like me who share a recognition of all those nagging, wee-small-hours questions: Is this it? Will I ever be the person I once thought I could be, or am I just going to keep on doing the same-old-same-old till I eventually get put out to pasture? Am I ever going to do anything else? Am I ever going to fuck anyone else?

I know you shouldn't think these things … but you do.

And then, if you're a writer, you try to turn your thoughts into prose. In early 1998, I began work on a novel, based on myself and a few amalgamated friends. It told the story of three guys in their mid-thirties who decide to blow their savings and their marriages on a wild weekend in Vegas. It was called *Wallow*, after the story that inspired it, which I was told a few years ago by an Englishman I know who works in Hollywood.

This Englishman was hired to write a film by the son of an Italian family from New Jersey who'd made a fortune in the construction business – gangster-reinforced concrete foundations being their speciality. Now this, er… family-member wanted to diversify into celluloid. The Englishman saw exactly why the Italian was interested in movies and instantly dashed off a script filled with semi-naked bimbos from the opening titles to the final credits. The guy loved it, said it was the best friggin' script he'd ever seen. (It was the only script he'd ever seen, too, but who's counting?) He wanted to meet and talk about it, so he suggested a meeting on neutral territory. How about a weekend in Las Vegas?

It turns out that Vegas is a very important city for the US construction industry, and here's why … If you want to build a shopping mall or an office block you've got to pay off all the guys from the local council, police, health and safety, and fire brigade who hand out all the approvals and certificates before work can go ahead. Plus there are unions, sub-contractors, suppliers – all sorts of people whose palms need greasing. And the grease has to be clean.

Vegas is the best laundry on earth. The way the wheels and tables are stacked, the house has a winning percentage of around three points. So if you gamble, say, five million bucks in small amounts, playing conservatively, the law of averages should ensure that you get more than four-and-a-half of it back. And it comes back to you in clean, untraceable casino cheques, which can then be handed out to anyone you like because this is America, and anyone has the right to get lucky in Vegas, right?

Better yet, the casino loves you for putting all that green stuff through their system. They love you so much that they'll fly you out by private jet, comp you a fabulous suite and throw in all the gourmet food and Cristal champagne you can handle, plus a personal butler to attend to your more exotic requirements, be they nasal, genital... whatever. The casino pays for everything wholesale, obviously. But they charge it as a tax-loss at the full retail rate, so they make a profit from Uncle Sam, thereby proving to anyone who ever doubted it that free-market capital-ism is the most brilliant system ever devised by mortal mind.

So, the Englishman flew out to Vegas to meet his contact from New Jersey and be educated in the ways of Las Vegas. He learned some of the key etiquette, like, for example: never accept a suite which has a jacuzzi in the bathroom. A Jacuzzi is no damn use to anyone unless it's in the bedroom. As he told me all this, I began to get a vague sense of wild decadence, so I asked him how the weekend went.

'I wallowed,' he said.

'Define wallow,' I replied.

'Well,' he answered, 'one of the things I learned last weekend is that when you're snorting coke off a hooker's tits, you should always make sure to snort it off the black hooker.'

'Right,' I said. 'That's a wallow.'

And yes, I know it's sexist, racist, all that stuff, too. But here's the thing: as I was sitting there in that Los Angeles diner, listening to my friend's outrageous boasting, it sounded bloody marvellous. It was a tantalising glimpse of a life beyond the confines of my tepidly respectable existence. It gnawed away at my sense that I was missing out, even if – in truth – I have never snorted coke, don't want to, and would shrivel with nerves at the very sight of a top-class Las Vegas call-girl, irrespective of her ethnicity.

This story had such a profound effect upon me, it inspired an entire novel – a lousy, useless novel that no one would ever want to publish, I grant you, but a novel nonetheless. And a sudden urge to write fiction wasn't the end of it, either. I kept wondering if there wasn't something else I could be doing. Much of this wondering was done aloud. And the person who has to listen to it was a big, chunky Jewish bloke called Mitchell Symons.

Mitch lives twenty minutes down the road in Sussex. He's two years older than me and a fair whack richer. He and I have complementary styles of ageing: he's getting fat, whereas I'm going bald. We talk every day on the phone, like a pair of superannuated schoolgirls, making silly jokes, swapping gossip, passing on information and advice. Often, Mitch's voice sounds oddly echoing and is accompanied by strange, slurping noises. This is because he is sitting in his hot-tub, from which he likes to conduct his morning business like a par-boiled walrus. We do a fair amount of work together, mostly fact-based features – lists, quizzes, that sort of thing – plus the odd quickie book. If you want an instant history of the twentieth century, knocked up in three weeks as a promo-tional tool for the National Lottery (and this is a genuine example, by the way), we're your boys. Every week or so we meet for lunch in an Arundel wine-bar called Butlers. Which is where the teenage waitress comes in.

Her name is Sacha. She has a lovely face, twinkling brown eyes, a cheeky smile, a resplendent chest and – that secret ingredient men can never resist – the gift of making you feel that she likes you. If you were being ultra-picky, you might say that her pear-shaped derrière prevents her from attaining physical perfection, but this is a minor quibble.

'An arse the size of Kansas,' says Mitch casting a loving gaze over Sacha's departing rump. This sounds like the purest male hypocrisy, since he has a gut the size of Morocco. But he's not commenting on Sacha's derrière specifically, just the way we talk about buttocks in general. Mitch cares about words: why, for example, are some words much funnier than others?

'It doesn't work with any other state but Kansas... Did you ever notice that?' he asks. 'Just try it. An arse the size of Nevada, Ohio, Illinois ... none of them work. Only Kansas. Odd that.'

I say he's wrong: Nebraska works even better than Kansas. New Mexico and Texas are almost as good. It's simply a question of rhythm and consonants. I name-drop the legendary Phil Silvers who once told me the secret of comedy: 'Hard sounds are funny. That's all you've gotta know.'

So a word with a 'K' is much funnier than one with a 'G'. 'T' trumps 'D'. And 'X' is best of all. That's why a lavatory joke with the word 'karzy' in it is much funnier than a joke with a 'loo'.

This is the sort of pointless conversation that fills our lunches. But I mention this one in particular because it embodies a bizarre contradiction. Mitchell Symons is an intelligent, successful man who doesn't have a mean bone in his body. He's generous, kind and indefatigably well-meaning. He's a loyal husband and a loving father. In short, he's a paragon... well, almost. There's just one catch: despite his fascination with the technicalities of verbal effect on a hypothetical audience, Mitch has no sense at all of the actual effect on real people of anything he says. He is a man for whom concepts like tact or subtlety are entirely alien – an embarrassment-free zone, the kind of man who starts conversations with strangers in lifts, or chats up the women at the next table in a bar, oblivious to their irritation.

For a while he had the habit, perhaps picked up during his days as a TV executive, of calling everyone 'darling'. We once bumped into each other in Chichester, the nearest big town, to which we had both been sent on shopping errands by our wives. Mitch had to go to the fishmongers. It was on my way, so I went along with him. The shop was an old-fashioned affair, opening right up onto the street, with a fish-covered trestle where the shop-window would have been. I was on the pavement side, waiting, Mitch was inside. Suddenly he called to me in a voice that echoed down the High Street. 'What do you think, darling – should I get the salmon for dinner or the shrimp?' I could not have felt more like his catamite if he'd shouted, 'You're my puppy now.'

Mitch is just as upfront with Sacha. He calls her sweetheart and darling, and tells her to 'be a good girl', when he asks her to get him his daily cup of what he calls 'poofy tea' – Mitch cannot handle caffeine, so has to drink camomile after meals. A woman sensitive to the nuances of political correctness might very well be grossly offended by the tenor of his conversation. But Sacha, being the sort of cheerily self-confident girl who knows how to keep men exactly where she wants them, always smiles, slaps him down when needed, and takes no offence, knowing that none is intended.

It is all more-or-less above board. No passes are made, no invitations proffered – we are both way too gutless to try. But we both enjoy the frisson of her company, so we keep going back to Butlers. And in between Sacha's visits to our table, we talk.

Mitch specialises in trivia and obscure information. He writes crosswords for celebrity magazines and lists for tabloid newspapers. He has a profitable sideline in TV game shows – his concept for one called *Everybody's Equal*, which was shown on ITV with Chris Tarrant as host, then syndicated around the world, is the reason he no longer has to worry about a mortgage.

That bumper pay-day aside, he has the same fundamental problem I do. As long as he works flat-out he does fine. But all he's doing is generating cash – there's nothing being stockpiled, no capital value in his business that can accumulate over time, or earn him money when he's fast asleep or lying on a beach. That's what he wants to create… but how?

We look at what we have to offer. After more than twenty years of work, Mitch has an incredible, computerised database, full of information about celebrities around the world, plus a library of reference books. I have hundreds of taped interviews with celebrities, plus a magazine collection going back more than fifteen years – thousands of copies of *Vogue*, *Rolling Stone*, *Vanity Fair*, *GQ*, *Esquire*, *Q*, *Mojo*, *The Face*, *The Spectator*, *Private Eye* … you name it.

These are all assets … but for what?

The answer, we decide, is some sort of research business, which we tentatively call Need To Know. It will be aimed at the entertainment-industry professional – broadcasters, interviewers, journalists, PRs and advertising agencies, anyone who might need specific information about individuals or groups. If a TV chat-show host wants great questions to ask a guest, plus funny, unexpected links between one guest and the others on his show we'll supply the info. Or suppose an ad agency wants to base a campaign on famous short people, or a golf hotel wants a list of fashionable celebrities who love the game: no problem, we'll have the data.

Need to Know will provide a better service than a cuttings library, because it will distil information down to what's necessary, instead of simply handing over an enormous, undigested pile of cuts. And it will improve on your average TV or agency researcher because... well because almost any sentient being with the intelligence of a newt would be better than a typical newly-graduated, clipboard-toting product of our fact-averse educational system.

So there is plan number one: Need to Know. Mitch and I think it seems like quite a decent concept, all things considered, but we have no idea what to do next. Then I get an assignment to interview Keith Richards...

27 October

New York City: Keith is late. He was due in from his house in Connecticut by lunchtime, but it's 7.00 in the evening and he still hasn't showed (although, to be fair, 7.00 *is* just about lunchtime if you're on Keith Standard Time). So I'm sitting in the bar of the Plaza Hotel, where the interview is due to take place, trying to stick to non-alcoholic drinks and limiting my visits to the Gents to one every fifteen minutes or so. It's been a long time since I was nervous about a celebrity interview, but Keith Richards is different. He's still the meanest, baddest, druggiest, scariest rock star of them all. He's Keef, for God's sake, the epitome of junkie cool, the avatar of rhythm guitar... look, I'm a fan. All right?

Actually, Keith is a sweetheart. He's a skinny little chap in a black Armani suit, with a face that looks like a shrivelled trophy atop an Amazon headhunter's pole, and scraggy blue-grey hair decorated with dangly braids, just like the ones my little girls get on their summer holidays. He sits on a sofa in his Plaza suite, half-hidden behind a line of tumblers filled with a bizarre pink liquid that may well involve significant amounts of high-proof hooch, lighting up a string of Marlboros and talking in a fey, wheezing, slurred, surprisingly posh voice that is an exact replica of that made famous by the Fast Show character Rowley Birkin, QC.

Keith's conversation staggers in and out of focus, from one sentence to another. Just when you think he's going to lose it completely, he seems to pull himself together for long enough to deliver a paragraph of coherent anecdotage or tart observation. I ask him how he lives when he isn't on the road with the Stones and he says, 'It's virtually impossible to get off the night-shift. If I have to do anything in the morning I just stay up and do two days in a row, which is no big deal. After the third day you're really somewhere else and it's a most interesting spot. That's until you finally collapse, which is the dodgy bit because you just drop and you can easily break your nose on a speaker or something. You've just got to make sure there are plenty of cushions around after the third day, just in case.'

He wants to warn me, as one father to another, about the perils of adolescence. He's been suffering from that, of late. 'You go out on the road for a couple of months, come back, and suddenly Jayne Mansfield's standing there and you're tripping over training bras. Let me tell you, that can kill you. They just fling them anywhere.'

A whole new picture of the domesticated rock god begins to emerge. 'I don't see the kids when I get up because they're at school,' gasps Keef. 'By the time they get back, I'm semi-conscious and making my breakfast. They really love my fry-ups, so I always make twice as much as I really need because I know they'll go, "Da-a-ad, can I have a bit of that?"'

Richards is very proud of his fry-ups. He has home-made sausages supplied to him in bulk by Myers of Keswick, an English grocery in Greenwich Village, New York. Sounding more like Keith Floyd than Keith Richards, he explained that, 'For a good fry-up, you've got to know your equipment, your broiler, your griddle. It's very much like writing a song: your timing is all important if you want your bangers 'n' mash to be in synch with your eggs and bacon. And you should always drink a glass of wine while you're doing it, even if it's breakfast. It does wonders.'

The old reprobate conjures up a picture of himself standing in his kitchen, a frying-pan in one hand, a wine-glass in the other, with his bangers on the go. 'I'm like any old dad. I take the dog for a walk – oh dear, it's made a mess on the carpet – light the fire. Then it's, "Hello darling, would you like a cup of tea? What do you want for dinner? When do you want to eat?" You know, the usual, and that's a pleasure for me.'

This isn't an interview so much as a really good natter, which is how these things work best. We do the proper stuff too, of course – the Stones, his relationship with Mick, the years of drug addiction, the death of one of his children, Tara, while both he and his partner Anita Pallenberg were smacked out of their brain – all that stuff. We really cover the waterfront.

We do, but not the guys who came next. Keith is promoting the Stones' latest live album and he's got half the world to cover. When I leave at around half-nine, there are still squadrons of Japanese, Norwegians, Belgians and assorted other multinational hacks, all waiting for their turn at bat.

I start wondering about those guys. Virgin Records have spent a fortune flying them in from scattered points around the globe. They all have hotel rooms and bar tabs to be paid for. But there's no way that they'll get an interview a fraction as good as I (or any other reasonably competent English journalist with a genuine interest in the Rolling Stones) have just nabbed. I went to primary school a hundred yards from the Station Hotel in Richmond, where the Stones got their first gigs. I slept rough to see them at Knebworth in '76. I only had to mention that sort of thing to get Keith reminiscing. It gave me a winning edge.

And that hasn't been the only time. Time and again, I've soothed a celebrity who's been driven nuts by an endless slew of fifteen-minute-long, English-as-a-foreign-language conversations. Stars, be they actors or musicians, hate these production-line, rent-a-quote junkets. They'll give anything for a proper conversation with someone who's actually done their research, taken some interest in their career and made some effort to entertain them, in exchange for their revelations. If they're going to spend a couple of hours talking, they'd rather do a single proper heart-to-heart than a dozen meaningless meet 'n' greets.

So why do companies bother with the dross? Wouldn't it make much more sense to do one really strong Q&A and then syndicate it into the various territories you wanted to cover? Sure, there would always be some international titles so powerful they had to generate their own material. But not many.

Back home in England, I keep turning things over in my mind, and I'm forced to confront an unpalatable truth. I care about my work. I want my pen-portraits to be good likenesses. It matters to me. But not to anyone else.

Few magazines have the slightest interest in the quality of writing they publish, nor even any ability to tell good from bad. All they want are a few decent pictures no one else has published and a couple of smutty quotes about the star's sex-life (or tragic lack of). And they want this as cheaply as possible.

British media companies are cutting editorial budgets, lowering pay-rates for freelance writers and doing everything they can to limit expenses. If I do a story in the States I have to pay my own way, or wangle free flights from record companies or film studios: publications that make millions a year will quibble over the cost of a single taxi-fare. In terms of the work I'm being offered, I'm having a fantastic year, but with word-rates if anything, lower than they were a decade ago, the only way to make money is to up ones productivity: do more and more for less and less.

In these circumstances, editors – and, more importantly, the publishers who approve their budgets – will take anything they can get, provided it's cheap enough and reaches minimal standards of quality. And that's in Britain, where the press is richer and more powerful than anywhere else on earth. In the rest of the world, anything goes.

So here I have idea number two: pile it high and sell it cheap.

I must give up on my pointless professional idealism. Stop thinking of celebrity interviews in terms of journalism or insight, start thinking in terms of product. Become a one-stop-shop for publicity-seeking entertainers. Replace journalism's myriad cottage industries – the small-time writers, photographers, PRs and syndicators – with a mass-production, mass-distribution service that radically cuts the number of interviews that stars have to undertake, while cutting costs for both originating corporations at one end of the deal and publishers at the other. Produce international pap. Put lots of people out of business. Make a fucking fortune.

Back at Butlers, I relay all this to Mitch over a couple of baked potatoes with prawns and glasses of Diet Coke. (This is our standard fare, incidentally, and I mention it by way of proof that neither of us was ever going to shag Sacha, or even try to do so: men who eat prawn jackets or drink Diet Coke are, by definition, incapable of adulterous sex.) Mitch can see the logic of my thinking, and we can both figure a way in which his idea – Need to Know – can be combined with mine – which I am by now calling the Global Celebrity Network –. to form a full-service celebrity journalism business.

But what are we ever going to do about it? The biggest problem that middle-aged men have in being innovative or risk-taking is not that they've lost the ability or imagination to have ideas in the first place. It's that they have too much at stake. At twenty-five you're free to do whatever you want. If it all goes belly-up, so what? You've lost nothing. You just dust yourself down and start again.

But at forty things are different. At forty, you have families, mortgages, standards of living that need to be maintained. You know that you'll never make really big money unless you stop doing what you're doing now and take a chance on doing something else. But you can't stop what you're doing because your whole life is geared to a certain level of income, which has to maintained. The hungry beast of your bourgeois lifestyle constantly demands to be fed. It won't let you off the treadmill.

So we are stuck. We know that there's no chance of a big payday unless we change our professional lives. But the present demands that we keep going exactly as we were. I have no means of solving this dilemma. Not at that point, anyway. But then I begin work on a series of articles that change my mind.

12 December

Paradise Island, Bahamas: I've flown to Paradise Island (which is actually an overdeveloped sand-spit, just off Nassau, and not very paradisical at all), to cover the opening of a giant casino complex called Atlantis. Michael Jackson, Leonardo DiCaprio and Julia Roberts are just three of the stars due to be in attendance. The casino-magnate's London PRs have promised me an exclusive on the party, plus the chance of one-on-one chats with the stars for – yes! – global syndication. They've promised, but, with a day to go till the party, it is rapidly becoming crystal-clear that they are in no position to deliver. There is a very real prospect of the week ending with no money and irreparable grief. I need to find another back-up feature, fast.

I go for a walk around the local marina, and I find my yarn. A vast, sleek motor-yacht called *Aspiration* is gently reversing towards me. On the stern-decks I can see a gaggle of smiling faces, many very beautiful, some very famous, toasting their outrageous good fortune in champagne.

The boat comes to a halt by the harbourside and a panel in its gleaming white stern slides noiselessly open. From within the hull comes a faint whirring sound as a telescopic gangway (a marvel of white-painted steel and spotless wooden planking) appears, swivels, and then begins extending towards dry land. As it touches down, a pair of crew-members, immaculate in white shirts and shorts, appear. They insert a series of gleaming, stainless-steel poles into the gangway. Between the poles hang black, velvety ropes, between which the beautiful people trip ashore.

They've all been for a test-drive. Aspiration is for sale, at $16.5 million – roughly £10 million. The 147-foot boat has been built on spec, but when I talk to its vendors, I discover that they're confident of finding a sale. Careful thought has gone into the design. The interior is a tastefully understated symphony of cream and pale grey fabrics, pale wood and gleaming chrome. On the top fly-deck a padded sunbathing area is protected by a wind-deflector, ensuring that any lounging babes can work on their all-over tans without mussing their bottle-blonde hair. If the tanning becomes too strenuous, it is only a few steps to a relaxing Jacuzzi. Down below, the master-bedroom has two bathrooms. The lady's has a whirlpool bath, the gentleman's a shower. Next door there is an office where he – and 99.9% of superyacht owners are, apparently, male – can work on the deals that keep him in boats. But if labour pales, a garage under the stern houses a full range of powerboats, jet-skis and windsurfers. Or 'toys', as the superyacht jargon has it.

I take a tour of the boat, interview the skipper and become instantly obsessed with the culture of superyachts and their zillionaire owners. Back home in England, I start researching the subject in earnest, hoping that readers will be equally fascinated: that I've hit on something that has some deeper, wider relevance to the way things are. The relevance of superyacht is, admittedly, hard to spot. But the stories – whose common denominators are absurd amounts of money, with lavish toppings of sex – are irresistible.

In 1980, for example, the arms dealer and international Mr Fixit Adnan Kashoggi built a magnificent, $70 million, 282-foot yacht, which he named after his daughter Nabila. The boat was mind-bogglingly extravagant. It had a discotheque, with laser beams that projected images of Kashoggi's podgy, moustachioed face. It had a complete operating theatre... and a morgue in case the operations failed. Kashoggi's bed, which slept five, was covered with a chinchilla rug. Not only were all the boat's taps gold, so were the plates and the cutlery. There were four cooks on board: a Frenchman, an Italian, an Arab and a Chinese.

There was also a stable of beautiful playmates, provided by a Côte d'Azur legend called Madame Mimi. Her girls used to call Kashoggi 'papa gateau', or sugar daddy, because his fees, tips and gifts were so lavish. His most favoured companions would return to their cabins to find diamond necklaces on their pillows. Sometimes, they would be kept aboard while Kashoggi stayed at his villa in Marbella, summoning girls by helicopter as and when required.

Aristotle Onassis seduced both Maria Callas and Jacqueline Kennedy aboard his 320-foot boat *Christina*, whose indoor pool could be converted, at the flick of a switch, to a dance floor, and whose bar-stools were upholstered with the skins of whale scrotums.

I hear of one owner who sent his Boeing 737 on a six thousand mile trip to bring a case of vintage champagne from his cellar to the yacht. Another gave his chef permission to eat $3000 dollars worth of caviar, brought in for a party but not used. A Norwegian fishing tycoon, whose yacht is under construction in Italy, has ordered a 38-seater pizzeria, complete with a proper pizza oven, quite apart from the regular galley and dining-room. He's also gone for a classical motif in the decorations, which is why the boat now contains around 240 columns. 'He started twenty years ago with absolutely nothing,' says one observer who has seen the boat. 'Now he wants absolutely everything.'

GETTING STARTED 1999

The year begins with a weird dislocation. The financial pages are filled with talk of an impending global recession, brought on by the successive collapses of the Asian economies, Russia and the Wall Street bond market. But no one's told the superyacht crowd. There are now at least 400 private boats of 115 feet or more in length – the point at which a yacht becomes, by industry convention, a superyacht – of which the largest is the 483-foot *Prince Abdul Aziz*, the royal yacht of Saudi Arabia. And the demand for bigger, faster, more expensive boats keeps increasing.

The more I report on this outrageous phenomenon, the more I want a bit of it for myself. The quiet country life seems less and less appealing. The outline proposal for my novel receives a resounding thumbs-down from every publisher to whom it has been sent. The problems of self-obsessed middle-aged white males are not a big selling-point these days, particularly when the central character – painstakingly based on all of my worst neuroses – is an unlovable, self-pitying little shit. Not so much a case of 'Wallow', then – more like 'Flounder'.

It is painfully obvious that I am living where the action isn't. As the year goes on, the mad excesses of the superyacht lifesyle begin to seem emblematic of what is happening out there in the wider economy. I keep meeting people from the same sort of background as myself, with the same sort of education, who seemed possessed of no obvious exceptional creative or intellectual gifts, who have recently, and suddenly, become – to paraphrase Harry Enfield – considerably richer than me. People like Christian Rucker, for example...

12 May

London W11: The White Company has a zero per cent recognition-rate among men of my acquaintance and 100% among women. The reason for the disparity is simple. The White Company sell linens, and whereas most men have no interest whatever in towels, blankets, sheets and pillowcases, there is some deep, atavistic nesting instinct in even the most ruthless, professional woman that makes her love the idea of something fresh and cottony in her airing cupboard. A few years ago, a twentysomething beauty journalist called Christian Rucker had the simple idea of starting up a mail-order company selling nothing but white linens. Men looked at her blankly. Women sighed, 'Yes please'. Christian Rucker made a fortune, and I was sent to report on her new London mansion by the *Telegraph* magazine.

Christian Rucker began with an £18,000 loan. The White Company now turns over more than £5 million pa. In the five years that her company has been expanding like a runaway waistline, Christian has also found time to get married (her husband has another, even bigger mail-order business of his own), have two children – Tom, who is almost three, and fifteen month-old Ella – and totally re-decorate her enormous home, just a few hundred yards from Notting Hill Gate, which is where we meet.

By chance I am also invited to a party that same evening in a house directly across the road from the Ruckers. It belongs to a couple I knew: he's a banker, she a journalist. The talk is all of hot stocks and financial coups. I chat to a man who had been a fund manager, until he tired of the responsibility of looking after other people's money. Now he runs a new fund, entirely composed of his own cash. When another man, an American, asks me what I do, I tell him I'm a writer. 'Really?' he says, as baffled as if I'd told him I was a tribal witch-doctor. 'Is there a living in that?'

The following day, back in the land of the bourgeois, I am describing the charming Ms Rucker's high-maintenance lifestyle to a friend when a look of shocked recognition crosses her face. 'Oh my God,' she squealed. 'I used to work with her. I mean, she was perfectly sweet, but I'd never have guessed she'd be so successful.'

I know just what she means. I'd felt the same way myself when I met an old university chum for the first time in several years at a charity function (a room-full of affluent fortysomethings gathered for a private movie screening, dinner and a post-prandial auction). I knew he had done well for himself in the City, but I had no idea how well until I saw the buffed and polished sheen of his skin, the perfect cut of his suit and the overwhelming self-satisfaction of his manner. 'Still writing, are you?' he condescended, from the lofty perch of his position as a senior corporate finance executive at one of New York's most famous banks.

Once again, I did my best to be upbeat. I gave a breezy account of articles, film-scripts and books. I tried to give the impression that he had grievously underestimated my not inconsiderable earning-power. Which he probably had. But not half as much as I had under-estimated his.

I was figuring my friend for the kind of guy who pulls down, say, half a million a year, maybe more when the annual bonus is a good one. Then I called Philippa Rose, the founder and managing director of the Rose Partnership, one of the City's top headhunting firms. Tell me, I said, these financial hotshots, the top guys, what kind of money are they on?

'For senior people in Europe,' said Ms Rose, 'the heads of corporate finance, mergers and acquisitions and investment banking at major institutions, you'd be looking at an annual package of between three and six million dollars. That includes everything. The base salary's often nothing at all, maybe as low as £100,000. But then there are annual bonuses, stock options and, in some cases, equity grants.'

The industry term for this kind of pay is 'a two-comma salary', and they are becoming ever more common. Here we go... Trusting my instinct, I get to work on a story about a group I call the New Plutocrats. At a time when political debate is dominated by the great pretence that we lived in an increasingly classless society, they belong to a new super-wealthy class, an urban aristocracy whose astonishingly rapid emergence seems to me to be one of the most significant, yet least-discussed social phenomena of our times.

It's all happened so fast. In 1992, the London estate agents Knight Frank analysed their major country-house sales and found that more than 60% of purchasers were foreign – Arab princelings, American super-executives, European fat cats and the like. Today, the volume of sales is rocketing up … and almost 90% involve British purchasers. 'Six years ago, we could count the deals we did over £2 million on the fingers of one hand,' said Knight Frank's Edward Rook. 'Now we're doing forty deals over £2 million. We have 2,000 people with £1 million or more to spend on our books. If you've got a salary of £200,000 and you get a bonus of £500,000, you can suddenly buy something for over £1 million. To be a millionaire these days is no big deal.'

It's even less of a deal in America, where the combination of soaring stock-markets (the Dow Jones has risen by more than 350% since 1990) and fabulous new technologies has created an explosion in personal wealth unparalleled in human history. There are now 4 million US households with a net worth over $1 million, a 33% growth since 1995. The number of billionaires has risen to 250 – of whom 60 reached that level in the last year alone. More than three-quarters of all American college students surveyed in a recent poll expect to become millionaires, and their optimism isn't entirely unfounded.

In the late 1980s, the average salary of a Wall Street broker or trader, two years out of college, was $50-70,000. Now it's $250-350,000 (call it an even £200,000). And that's at a time when the really smart brains aren't even bothering with Wall Street any more. Financial institutions and management consultancies, which used to snap up all the best Ivy League brains, are losing out to a new phenomenon. In the area to the south of San Francisco Bay, known as Silicon Valley, an entirely new industry, in fact a new economy has grown up. Companies based on the business opportunities offered by the Internet – or, e-commerce as it is being called – are springing up at astonishing rate. There seems to be a limitless amount of money available to anyone with a bright idea and vast fortunes are being made virtually overnight by entrepreneurs who are often barely into their twenties. The brilliant young stars of entertainment or sports suddenly look like paupers next to a bunch of geeks.

The blue-chip, big-money jobs to which ambitious graduates flocked during the Eighties and early Nineties seem tragically old-hat.

Now the same pattern is being repeated in Britain. When the *Sunday Times* published its first Rich List in 1989, 57% of the 1,000 richest people in Britain had inherited their wealth, there were fewer than ten tycoons who had made their money in high-tech businesses, and entry to the top 200 required a fortune of £30 million. Ten years later, less than 30% of entrants were wealth-inheritors, 96 of the self-made multi-millionaires had generated their fortunes in computers, telecoms or the Internet, and it took a £120 million stash to break into the Top 200.

Several friends of mine have married into the New Plutocracy. I can think of one college contemporary in particular – I'll call her Mary – who married a banker and settled down to the lush life in West London.

Mary spent fifteen years in a series of chic, interesting, but not particularly well-paid jobs, before getting married in her mid-thirties. When they were first engaged, her fiancée turned to her and said, 'I suppose we should have a house. Would a million pounds do it?' And this, mark you, was at the start of the decade, when a mill could still get you something decent in a posh London postcode.

As I obsess about the modern rich, I ask Mary what difference her newfound wealth has made. 'It's given me my youth back,' she says. 'I can hand the physical drudgery – washing the floors, changing the baby's nappy, rocking the baby to sleep in the small hours of the morning – to people I'm giving employment to. If I had to raise a family on a Wandsworth salary, you'd be looking at a grey-haired, knackered and maybe even divorced woman.

'I have two close friends who've married nice men on low incomes. They're trying to live that mumsy, housey, vase-in-the-right-place life and they're trapped. They're not empty-headed Sloane Rangers. They have an intellect that's not being fulfilled and they're both frustrated and miserable. But I have the sanity and the room to pursue my intellectual or professional interests, which don't have to be money-earning. I have a full-time nanny and a full-time housekeeper. And then there's someone who comes in at the weekends. So we're never without help, which means I have time for my internal life, for my relationships with my children – however I want to spend it. And I have my health. That's what money's given me.'

How, though, does Mary deal with non-plutocrats? 'It matters to me not to lose touch with old friends,' she says, with unintended condescension. 'We're already living in a socking great palace. If we throw butlers and silver cutlery at our old friends they're going to think we're toffee-nosed and they'll wonder whether the box of Black Magic they brought is good enough. It's awful to flaunt money in front of people with the same background and education. I don't think people feel I'm any different, or that they don't have access to me, but maybe I'm just insensitive and I haven't noticed.'

We discuss mutual NP friends. Like the daughter of a prominent left-wing family who'd married a global financier's son: 'She's thrilled,' says Mary. 'Now she's living in a six-storey house and she can have caviare and foie gras for Christmas dinner.' Another old friend has just bought a vast country mansion. Mary does not approve: 'It's all silver cutlery and console tables with 'important' vases on them. I don't care how many Cambridge degrees he's got. To me, that's just so Trust House Forte.'

A plutocrat wife finds herself doing all the things an Edwardian gentlewoman had to do: running a large house, managing staff, keeping everything perfect for her man. And, as Mary points out, that is a considerable task.

'A lot of people are saying that second homes are the definition of success. One entertains the idea of a second home, and children running through woodland, but actually it's a huge burden. I have all these brochures from Knight Frank sitting next to me, but I just say, "Over my dead body," because what it means is a lot more burden and pressure on the wife. She is going to have to run these places. And whether she's down on her knees, cleaning the flagstones herself, or running a fleet of staff and trying to find a housekeeper she can trust, it's work. It all becomes Upstairs bloody Downstairs. In my mind, it's just a nightmare. Book yourself into a hotel, pay five grand and walk away at the end of it.'

To Mary, the five-grand weekend is obviously now as normal as a two-pound pint might be to anyone else. But all this astonishing wealth-creation is only one side of the coin. Because what becomes painfully clear as I investigate the Plutocracy phenomenon, is that my plummeting word-rates for freelance journalism are representative of an equal and opposite phenomenon to the explosion of pay for the few: ruthless cost-suppression for the many. What it basically amounts to is this: in the global economy at the dawn of the third millennium, you are either getting much, much richer, or much, much poorer. There's precious little room for anything in between.

Which brings me back to the subject of my money-making scheme... During the early months of 1999, I make a few half-hearted attempts to bring the Global Celebrity Network to life. I speak to a couple of acquaintances who work in press syndication. I do meetings with film-company PRs and set up a trial run with a superstar actor that ends in a complicated disaster which proves, once again, that you've got to have proper connections. And I don't have them.

It also teaches me something else: stars' public relations people are much more interested in their own power to say no, than in positively advancing their clients' careers. In particular, Hollywood PRs insist on approving every single use of every word their client utters, or every photograph that is taken of them. And they want to control where those words and photographs appear. Most established freelance writers try to make extra money by selling their articles abroad through syndication agencies. Photographers – whose pictures are not only worth a thousand words, but work equally well in any language – are even more dependent on overseas sales. But the PR people's possessiveness creates a major threat to this income. You can't just put material out into the marketplace, you have to get written approval for every single title, no matter how obscure, no matter how far-flung.

This has perverse side-effects. The reaction of magazines who are denied official material is not to retire gracefully from the field, but to do anything they can to get their hands on unofficial material. So the more PRs try to restrict the flow of authorised interviews and photographs, the more they ensure the prevalence of invented quotes, cuttings-jobs and paparazzi snaps.

The ultimate example of this occurs when a friend of mine is hired to photograph one of the hottest pop stars of 1999 – a hip-swivelling sex sensation – for a London newspaper. He's sent a contract by the star's PR, without which the photo-session cannot take place. This specifies the type of lights, lenses and film stock my friend – one of London's top portrait photographers – can use. It also requires the star's approval both of the original transparencies and the computer-retouching which will apparently be required. The finished, retouched, approved photographs cannot be used for any publication other than the one for which my friend is working, thereby ensuring that the paranoid star will only be seen at his worst everywhere else.

My friend, who takes his own talent as seriously as it deserves, is appalled to be told how to take his photographs, but he has no alternative: he has to say yes. When the day of the shoot arrives, he realises why the star was so particular. He is a tall, hunky, high-cheekboned love-god all right... but his face bears the after-effects of truly appalling teenage acne.

The star says hello, then disappears into the make-up room. Now, the demands that are placed upon famous women to conform to impossible standards of beauty mean that the average female celebrity requires a minimum three hours of make-up, hair and wardrobe-styling before setting foot in front of a camera. Men, by and large, take a fraction of that time, if only because they don't like to be seen to enjoy the make-up artist's ministrations too much... even if they do.

The tragically completed superstar, though, is different. An hour goes by and he does not emerge from his dressing-room. My friend the photographer busies himself preparing lights and taking test Polaroids. Another half-hour... my friend is running out of things to do. He decides to find out what is going on.

As he approaches the dressing-room, though, he hears a strange noise, like the pumping or puttering of a low-powered diesel engine. Nervously he opens the door, and immediately sees where the noise is coming from. On the floor, a compresssor is beating away. A pipe carries compressed air from this machine to a small tank, attached to a spray-nozzle.

This, in turn, is being held by the make-up artist, who – with his own face protected by a white paper mask and clear plastic goggles – is aiming it at the superstar... and spray-painting his pock-marked face with high-density, orangey-brown slap. He isn't being made-up. He's being pebble-dashed.

With every story like that I hear, my purist journalistic scruples diminish. I have no qualms about reducing celebrities to commodity status – that's how they treat themselves. But I am stuck in the same old conundrum: I can't make big money without starting afresh. Yet I can't start afresh without risking everything I already have. Something has to happen to break that spiral – someone has to show me it is possible. And, in the event, two men do just that.

The first is a former rock PR called Neil Storey, whom I first met twenty-odd years ago, when I was a spotty student journalist and he was one half of the transcendently hip Island Records press office, with stacks of hot discs by Bob Marley, Roxy Music and Grace Jones to give away. Neil has gone into management, looking after Nigel Kennedy, but his relation-ship with the eccentric violinist has turned sour. He still has a couple of smaller clients, one of whom is an Irish girl called Cora-Venus Lunny, whom he is hoping to set up in a deal with Universal Records. He says I should meet her, maybe do a profile for someone. Sure, I say, why not?

14 July

London NW1: Cora-Venus Lunny is just seventeen and looks like a fresh-faced young Madonna Ciccone: high, broad cheekbones, tapering to a narrow chin, bright blue eyes, a devastating smile. She also possesses something even more dangerous than beauty – a charm that might cause otherwise sensible men to fall in love, as well as lust.

Neil swears that he has not been smitten, but theirs is a very chatty-flirty relationship. Perhaps it's just what Neil needs to cheer him up – he's been having a tough time of late. The Kennedy business has ended, as these things always do, with wrangles over money and unhappiness all round. Lawyers are on the case. Neil has the brittle bonhomie of a man who is up to his eyeballs in debt, praying he will eventually be paid what he believes he is owed, dreaming of big scores to come.

Maybe Cora-Venus will hit the jackpot: Universal have organised a special audition performance at the Wigmore Hall, to be attended by all their top execs. Meanwhile Neil has another project, called The Virtual Orchestra. He and his partners are planning to make synthesised back-ing-tracks to the music played by children studying Grade exams. These will be turned into CD-ROMs, along with a bundle of supporting mate-rial and booklets giving descriptions of the music the kids have to learn and the composers who wrote it.

As a father with two daughters learning piano, cello and trumpet, I can see the potential straightaway. Solo instruments played by beginners always sound lousy. But if you could set them in the context of an orchestra, string quartet or brass band, they'd immediately come to life, thereby encouraging the children. The only problem I can see is turning the music on and off when kids' hands are filled with instruments and bows. As Neil, Cora-Venus and I drive back into the centre of London in Neil's battered Renault, I suggest he should make some sort of foot-pedal, which would act as a basic control. In the meantime, can I do the text for the booklets? I can see this is going to be big and I want a piece of it.

Neil is on the way to Dover Street, to drop off a business-plan with a company called European Investment Services, or EIS. The traffic is terrible, so by the time we get there the office is closed. He finds an old brown envelope, stuffs the plan into that and bungs it through the letterbox – hardly the fanciest presentation in the world, but beggars can't be choosers.

I really hope Neil makes it. He's one of the nicest guys in the business and it would be good to believe that you don't have to be a shit to get to the top. And I admire his guts. He has a family to support, so the temptation to jack in his independence and get a corporate job must be severe. But he's hanging on for success on his own terms, no matter how tough life gets in the meantime. He's not the only one...

18 July

Charterhouse School, Godalming, Surrey: It's a Sunday, the final day of the British Open golf, but I have to drive up to Charterhouse School to see the world premiere of *A Garland For Linda* – a series of musical pieces, composed in honour of Linda McCartney. Personally, I'm amazed, and not a little nauseated by the way in which Linda McCartney, who spent much of her adult life being mocked and vilified for marrying Paul has been sanctified by dying of cancer. She wasn't a villain and she shouldn't be a saint. But the garland's been made for charity, so that's all right, I suppose. Anyway, as I pull up at Charterhouse on a perfect late summer's evening, Jean Van der Velde is just about to play his second shot, approaching the last hole of the tournament. The unknown Frenchman is miles ahead of the field. All he has to do is complete the 18th in anything less than about a dozen shots and he'll lift the trophy. I turn off the radio, knowing it's a done deal...

...so it's only when I get home, after a long, and profoundly tedious concert, that I discover that the final shots of the Open were astonishingly dramatic, not to say tragic, and that the winner was not an unknown Frenchman, but a virtually unknown Scotsman, Paul Lawrie. It turns out, though, that my journey was not entirely wasted. Sitting next to me in the pews of the school chapel, where the concert took place, was a woman called Marianne Macdonald. She's just been given a plum contract as a writer for the *Mail on Sunday*'s Night & Day magazine, and has a reputation as a writer of mercilessly brilliant celebrity profiles.

In a non-professional context, Marianne appears for all the world to be an absolute sweetheart. She's incredibly pretty in a delicate, blonde, Dresden shepherdess kind of way. Interviewees must take one look at her, decide they have nothing to fear, and open their mouths way too wide: no wonder she's so deadly. She introduces me to her partner, a chap called Dan Conaghan, who used to be a hack at the *Daily Express*. Now, he says, he works for a company called NewMedia Investors, which invests in companies starting up Internet-related businesses. 'Smart move,' I say, and he doesn't disagree.

22 September

Chelsea, London SW3: Another day, another millionaire interview. This time it's James Dyson, the vacuum-cleaner man. His professional odyssey makes Neil Storey look like a slacker. Dyson spent fifteen years trying to prove that you could make a bag-less vacuum-cleaner. He went through 5,000 prototypes, raising a family in close proximity to the breadline and amassing massive debts for year upon year, because he simply refused to abandon an idea in which he alone had faith. He lived in constant fear that his dream might turn into a disaster and he still maintains that, 'I have tremendous fear now. Fear that things aren't working. Fear that they might go badly. I think it's incredibly healthy. It stops me and everyone around me from becoming smug, or complacent, or satisfied – all those are awful things.'

I am impressed beyond words by his story. But I want to know how he, as a father and husband, had been able to do what I could not, in risking everything on the distant hope of success. What about the human side of it, the strain that must have been imposed on his family as their husband and father beavered away, without success, for year after year?

'Well, it's a corny thing to say, but I've got a very supportive wife,' says Dyson. 'She's a painter and a designer, and I'm a designer and an engineer. We both just want to create things. A lot of wives might have minded, but Dierdre didn't. Never once did she say, "You shouldn't do that." She was great at growing our own vegetables, or making our own curtains, or not having curtains at all. She gave art-classes and sold her paintings, so we managed on a relatively low income.'

Even if the Dysons could not afford a stick of furniture, they always had lovely homes, because as well as borrowing huge amounts to fund his vacuum-cleaner project, James was mortgaged to the hilt. The monthly payments often consumed half his income. He now says that it's a far better use of money to borrow as much cash as possible in the hope of getting even more, than simply squirrelling it away in savings accounts at, as he puts it, 'drippy' rates of interest. Still, the stress of his existence was considerable.

'I used to lose my temper quite easily,' Dyson recalls. 'It happens far less now, but the stress would just build up and I'd snap at people when I shouldn't, or be unreasonable.'

The more people said that his machine could never be successful, the more Dyson ploughed on. 'If lots of people put obstacles in your way, there are some people who give up. But others just get more determined. They've got a rat by the tail. And in a curious way, the more people try to put you off, the more likely your idea is to succeed, because there's a surprise, or an improbability to it – something nobody's tried before.'

So far, so inspiring. But there was a cost to be paid for this determination. 'It's like running a race, because it's getting more exciting, but more exhausting too. You start off thinking you'll have to make ten prototypes and by the tenth you're hardly scratching the surface. The overdraft is mounting and you're getting into your four thousand, five hundredth prototype, and you know you can't go on much longer. And then you know that you're too much in debt and you've got to make a deal, but when you're negotiating that deal you can't afford to get up and walk out. So the whole thing is brinkmanship and that is hugely stressful, too.'

Dyson's children were all too aware of the position their father was in. 'I haven't hidden anything from them. I told them how much we were in debt, and all that sort of thing. They used to come into my workshop and see it all going on.'

Clearly, though, they were inspired, rather than repelled by the example their father had set. Dyson is 52. He tells me that he did not pay off his overdraft until he was 48. Now, according to the most authoritative estimates, he is worth around £500 million. I leave his gorgeous Queen Anne house in one of the finest streets in Chelsea (he has other homes in Wiltshire and Provence) thinking that I've got it all wrong. It is possible to give up the comforts of cosy, middle-class life. Your family will stay with you. You just have to include them in your dream.

I am getting to the point where I'm ready to make the leap of faith. More to the point, I am beginning to realise that I have no choice.

You remember *Butch Cassidy and the Sundance Kid* – the scene where they're sitting on that ledge, looking down the canyon at the raging river below? Sundance can't swim. The fall will kill them. But in the end they have to jump because the one thing they know for sure is that if they don't take the chance on jumping, the posse that's chasing them will certainly kill them. So it's a small chance of survival versus none at all.

Well, that's the position I find myself getting into as the autumn of 1999 goes on. One magazine for whom I've worked on a regular basis since it was founded six years ago suddenly, and without warning or explanation, halves my pay-rate. For three years, I've worked at a standard fee. It has never been raised, but I didn't mind because it's guaranteed. Until now.

Then another magazine, again a frequent client, calls up to question my expenses. Now, I'm terrible about expenses. I never remember to claim them at the time I do a feature and it's only months afterwards that I go back, collect up all my paperwork and try to make sense of it all. By that stage, I've lost half my receipts and forgotten what the rest were for, so I invariably under-claim. But even so, every penny is accounted for and no one ever questions my honesty. Until now.

The managing editor is perfectly sweet about it. She is apologetic in fact. She's quite sure that I've done nothing wrong, but the accountants are forcing her to cut back. So… was I sure I had to eat that meal? Why had I taken that taxi, instead of a bus? And why, most heinously, had I taken a plane, rather than a train, to do an interview in Leeds?

I am able to explain everything, including the plane-ticket, to her satisfaction. But although I've won the battle, I know the war is lost. It is perfectly clear that I am facing the same situation as Butch and Sundance. My life cannot go on the way it is. If I stay where I am, a posse called Change is going to sweep me away, and my precious lifestyle with it. I simply have to jump. It's www, or bust.

OCTOBER 1999

2 October

I pick the *Spectator* up off the doormat and there on the cover is the head-line: 'www.getrich/quick' and the words, 'Dan Conaghan explains the secret of making money in cyberspace.' The name rings a bell. Of course – he's the bloke I met with Marianne Macdonald at the *Garland for Linda* show. So I settle down over a cup of coffee and read what he has to say. It's mind-blowing.

Conaghan begins his piece by describing two virtually-unknown companies QXL and Lastminute.com. The first is an auction site, run by a former Brussels correspondent for the *Independent*, called Tim Jackson. The latter sells airline and theatre tickets and is run by two friends called Brent Hoberman and Martha Lane-Fox. Both are expected to float on the stockmarket, making their founders incredibly rich: QXL, he says, could float for £200 million.

In the world Conaghan describes, companies can be worth millions within months of their launch – or even before their launch has happened at all. There's so much money being made so fast that no one worth their salt is hanging around in tired old businesses like banking or market consultancy. They're all heading off to the Net, stopping off at get-togethers like First Tuesday, a monthly club where people with bright ideas can meet investors with money to burn. First Tuesday has been going a year. At its first anniversary bash there were 600 websters, spinning their sites, 'And,' writes Conaghan, 'if you couldn't make your pitch in a couple of minutes flat, you weren't just history, you were biology.'

The piece takes maybe five minutes to read. By the time I've got to the end of it, I know for sure that I must either move fast, or die.

I've heard of the Internet already, of course. Part of the original Global Celebrity Network plan had involved a website, on which stories would be posted for clients around the world to buy. But now I'm struck by a screamingly obvious thought. Web technology makes my original scheme unnecessary. I don't have to worry about syndicating material to newspapers and magazines – I can cut out the middle-men and go straight to my audience, online. But how can I do that? I give Dan Conaghan a bell and pick his brains a bit more.

He, not surprisingly, is not in the business of giving information for free, even if he had the time to do so. But he does put me right about one thing. The *Spectator*, he claims, distorted the meaning of his article. It's not quite as easy to make vast piles of cash as the piece made it sound. The problem, he says, is the exit.

This, I will later realise, is where my Internet education really begins. I'm going to acquire a whole new vocabulary. Sometimes the words and phrases will be entirely new to me. Other times, familiar old words will acquire new meanings or implications. Hence 'exit', as in: the moment when you cash in your chips and leave your business with huge piles of cash.

An exit is the Holy Grail of the New Economy. And the more exits you can manage, the wealthier you become. 'People want several exits, not just one,' Conaghan says. Some entrepreneurs start one business, realise the capital assets within a very few years, and then start another. 'It's happening to several friends of mine in their late twenties and early thirties – and they will try to do it again and again,' he says.

But, there's a catch: as long as your wealth is measured only in share certificates it is completely intangible and, what's worse, liable to sudden diminution, or even disappearance if your company goes bust. Even when a start-up gets a market listing, the founding partners are liable to be tied into contracts that commit them, and much of their stock, to stay put for several years. 'Most of the people I know haven't realised their rewards yet,' says Conaghan. 'I know one guy who's 27. On paper, he's worth at least £2-3 million, but he's paying himself a modest salary and renting a £200-a-week flat in a not particularly fashionable part of London. He doesn't actually have any cash. The millions are all to come.'

Because these guys are all so young, and their wealth is so virtual, they are often a lot less flash than their peers in corporate finance, who pick up annual bonuses of real, honest-to-goodness wonga. According to Conaghan, 'I've sat in meetings with Americans who are billionaires in their early thirties and they're not toting gold Rolexes. At best it's a Swatch. Jerry Yang and David Filo, the founders of Yahoo!, are still on extended leave from their Masters courses at Stanford University in California. One of them drives the same old beaten-up BMW he had at Stanford, the other has a new BMW. Their main problem is not how to spend it all, but how to give it away, to make the most of it in constructive ways.'

I'd love a problem like that. And Mitch likes the thought of the Net, too – but for a different, more practical reason. A fanatical researcher who likes nothing more than burrowing through vast mounds of rubbish in search of choice factual nuggets, he relishes the sheer volume of accessible material, particularly since he has a BT Home Highway line that radically improves the speed at which he can work. So now our conversations move towards the idea of an online enterprise. We've already got a massive amount of potential content: all my interviews, all his trivia. There must be some way of turning it into a website.

Mitch begins working through the competition. The more he looks at what is already on offer, the more confident he becomes. He feels sure that he can use his massive Celebrity Database in ways that other people have not yet considered, so that punters can play with our information, putting it together in ways that will be entertaining – not just finding out, but having fun at the same time.

We're yakking away on the phone one day when I suddenly say, 'We've got to stop talking about this. We've got to do something.'

Mitch doesn't hang about. He picks up his other line and calls a man he knows who works for BT, but runs a Net consultancy after-hours. He sets up a meeting. And then it all begins for real…

15 October

Angmering, West Sussex: Off to Mitch's house for a meeting with his tame techie – I think I'll call him Dan. We tell him we want to do a celebrity site, based on Mitch's trivia and my interviews. Dan gets the point, and gives a brief demonstration of the sites he has set up for local customers. Then he takes us to the one that is his personal pride and joy.

It's all about Scouts. Not in a pervy, tight-shorted, woggle-waving way, you understand. Hell no.

Dan is a respectable, upstanding member of his local community who takes responsible pleasure in giving his local troop a great-looking site on which it can post news of recent events. Like, for example, their recent pot-holing expedition.

Dan shows us pics of the lads descending into dank caves, some-where in the Dales. Then he invites me to click on a flashing logo at the top-left of the page. Up pops another, previously hidden, pic. It shows the mouth of a cave shaped like... Dan giggles with anticipation... a vagina!

Apparently, the entire site is littered with secret buttons that create hyperlinks to pictures of suggestive-looking geological formations, as encountered by the Scouts. Dan points out that he could create similar fun features for us as well, but without the genital overtones, and it need-n't cost too much to do – maybe £5,000... £10,000 tops.

This is very encouraging, and it gets even better when Dan introduces us to the wonderful world of domain names (i.e. the bit between the 'www' and the 'dotcom') and – even more usefully – the sites where you can check to see whether any particular name has been taken. We even have beginners' luck. Following the lead set by the radical ice-creamers Ben and Jerry, we hit upon the idea of MitchnDave.com. We even envis-age a couple of cartoon characters loosely based on us – the fat one and the bald one – who will guide punters round the site in a jovial, lovable kind of way.

We tell Dan we'll be getting right back to him with the specifications of what we want him to build for us. Yes, we're definitely up and running.

18 October

Notting Hill, London W11: I almost never go to parties. On the rare occasions when I am invited, there invariably comes a point in the mid-afternoon when I'm sitting at home in my study and I realise that if I'm going to get to London by 7.00 I'll have go to and get changed – and probably shaved – then spend two hours driving up to town, where I won't be able to have a drink. So I stay where I am, with my family, the telly and a bottle of wine for company. Tonight though, I make an exception, go to a drinks in Notting Hill and bump into a Cambridge contemporary called Kit Hunter Gordon. When we were kids, he was one of the university dudes – handsome, upper-class, as smooth as a Brylcreemed otter. He drove around in a souped-up Ford Fiesta and shagged the girls I only lusted after, but – to do him justice – there was always a human being behind that glamorous shell.

Kit's the kind of chap I meet about once a decade, get on with pretty well, think I really ought to see more often … and then don't until the next decade comes around. I know he works in the City, but I'm not entirely sure what as. Anyway, we have a perfectly pleasant conversation debating whether the fact that my work is inherently far more enjoyable than his compensates for the fact that he probably gets paid rather more than I do.

Kit dreams of giving up the City and going back to his first love – painting. I tell him I'm thinking of changing occupations, too. I want to get into the Internet business. In fact, I say, I've got an idea for a site. 'Really?' says Kit. 'Well, if you ever want a bit of help raising money, give me a call.'

Thanks, I say, but think no more of it. Two days later, I'm flying off to Los Angeles to interview the rock star Beck. The website will just have to wait.

25 October

Virgin Atlantic: Every ad on American TV seems to be for dot-coms. Every billboard has a www address at the bottom, assuming it isn't promoting a website to begin with. However big the Internet is at home, it's infinitely more pervasive in the States. This is tomorrow calling…

Two long flights give me plenty of time to think. I begin to see how we might be able to generate serious quantities of revenue for my site. My interviews are syndicated through a company called Planet Syndication, which represents many of the top Fleet Street writers. Between the lot of us, we speak to most of the world's biggest stars. Perhaps if we put our interviews online, instead of giving them to newspapers, fans will pay to read them. And if we've got hordes of fans logging on to the site, surely they'll attract advertisers. Add in money we pick up doing research based on Mitch's database and we could start making serious dosh.

Encouraged, I get to work on what I fondly imagine is a business-plan, setting out the idea in a dozen or so pages.

27 October

I need to make some money to pay for the site, so I do what comes naturall ... sell the idea to a newspaper. The *Daily Mail* has just started a new section called e-Mail. It's run by an up-and-coming Yorkshireman called Ted Verity, for whom both Mitch and I have worked in the past. I phone him up and suggest a weekly column all about the trials and tribulations of setting up your own site.

Ted is one of those editors who gets the point fast and makes an instant decision. I've hardly finished the first stage of my pitch and I'm just about to go into the full plead-and-grovel section when he says, 'Yes – when can you start?'

He says two other things, as well. The first is that he wants to call it 'Diary of a Wannabe Internet Millionaire.' The second is that he thinks MitchnDave.com is a lousy name. It's got to go.

Yes sir, boss. Absolutely. Right away.

28 October

I have another chat with Ted Verity re. the column. He wants me to start as soon as possible, but I want to wait until I've built up a decent store of usable material. Meanwhile, there's another minor issue: what is he going to pay me?

'Me?' he says. 'Pay you? Shouldn't that be the other way around? I'm the one giving you all the free publicity.'

We settle on £350 a column. I'm prepared to bet it's the worst-paid weekly column in Fleet Street. But who am I to argue?

30 October

Clare and I do the VAT return for the third quarter of 1999. For the past six months the sheer weight of work has been so great that I got behind with all the invoicing to clients. That meant that a whole heap of money that should have been paid in the second quarter was delayed until the third. And, of course, the VAT return is calculated on total turnover, not profit (i.e. the actual income which Clare and I take from the business). But even so, there's no getting away from the fact that £55,000 is an amazing amount of money for a single quarter. And it came from a business I'm about to give up because I say it's finished. Am I completely mad?

NOVEMBER

6 November

Our neighbours, Peter and Melissa Briggs have an annual firework party on Bonfire Night. They provide the land, the monster bonfire and the mulled wine. We all contribute to the rockets and Roman candles.

So, Saturday morning, I go round to drop off my bundle of whizz-bangs (a rather feeble bundle, sadly: I've decided to start economising in view of my impending income-loss). While I'm there, I have a cup of coffee with Peter, who's an extremely nice bloke, but laid-back to the point of inertia. Now in his mid-40s, he's spent 25 years knocking about the City. But in the time that I've known him, his work seems to have become progressively less satisfying, and his general demeanour more soporific.

Until the last few months, that is. Because earlier this year, Peter started up an Internet business, helping companies create and maintain the financial areas of their sites. He's got a friend to loan him some office-space in exchange for shares in the company. He's hiring his first staff and acquiring his first clients. And suddenly, everything's changed.

The new Peter has the brimming self-confidence of a man who has taken his destiny in his own hands. He's full of encouraging stories about people who are starting from scratch and making fortunes. One of his friends has a 25-year-old son who's setting up a site selling end-of-run and surplus trainers online. He's found a backer who's given him half-a-million, valuing his company at over £5 million. Thanks to the money, he's hired a couple of senior marketing executives from M&S. Their presence has doubled the value of the company. So this kid is now sitting on a multi-million pound fortune. But the great thing is that you didn't have to be a bimbo to succeed in the new economy. Even old fogeys like us can get in on the act.

'Shall I tell you why I'm doing this?' asks Peter. 'I didn't want my grand-children to look at me in twenty years time and ask, "What did you do in the Internet revolution, grandpa?"'

Well, that's the spirit. And if Peter bloody Briggs can make a living in the Internet, I certainly can.

12 November

The City of London: A week ago I remembered the chat I'd had with Kit Hunter Gordon and sent him a copy of my plan. A couple of days later he called up and suggested we meet. He gave me directions to his office in the City. What he didn't tell me was that it really is *his* office. As in, he owns the entire building. Or rather, the private company of which he has around 50% of the shares does. Kit may be a bit more of a player than I realised.

He tells me that his company specialises in business start-ups. They like to act as true partners, he says – putting in money, but also providing legal and accounting support and bringing their financial expertise to bear. This means that entrepreneurs only have to worry about the bits they're good at, which usually excludes administration.

He suggests a number of possible ways to go. I could, for example, simply punt my idea at one of the big media companies and hope that they like it enough to give me a job starting it up. That way I would get a steady salary, with reasonable job-security and maybe a little bit of equity thrown in on top. Or his company can fund Mitch and I to get our site going, paying us salaries and providing office-space. In exchange they would expect to take 75% of our new company's equity, although they might be prepared to split profits 50–50.

Much as I like Kit, I'm not handing 75% of my company to anyone, so I suggest an alternative. I want to put my idea in front of top venture capitalists (or VCs). But I don't know these people and Kit does. If I walk into a meeting with him, they'll be reassured that I'm not a total joker. So, what if he acts as my agent? If he can broker the deal that gets me the finance I need, I'll cut him in on a fair slice of the action.

By the way, I ask, as we're walking out of Kit's office at the end of the meeting, how much money does he think we could get for my concept?

'It's impossible to tell,' he says. 'It could be nothing. Or it could be twenty million.'

16 November

My first *Daily Mail* column appears. They've given me a proper send-off – a full page on the front of the e-Mail section, complete with huge colour pic of me waving wads of tenners. Now that I've announced my intentions to the world, I feel like I'm totally committed. If I give up now, I'll be failing in front of millions of people. Plus, I have to keep moving forward in order to generate new material.

That's one of the reasons I'm doing it, of course. I need a goad to keep me from taking the easy, short-term option and sticking with the business I know. Because as much as I'm becoming increasingly excited by the potential of my site, I'm frightened too. In order to get our site to the point where we can begin to attract serious investment, Mitch and I will have to spend thousands of pounds. Meanwhile I'll be earning far less than I did before.

Even when I'm working flat-out as a hack, I'm an obsessive calcula-tor of my financial situation – forever getting old scraps of paper and jotting down all the money that I'm owed. Then I add all the jobs I have coming in and try to work out how long we could survive if I didn't get any more work. I live in perpetual dread of the day when the phone stops ringing. Nothing upsets me more than a week that begins with an empty diary, which is why I always try to be in a position where I'm over-loaded to the point of exhaustion. That way I can relax.

Now I have the very real prospect of my greatest fear coming true. There's no way I can work anything like full-time as a hack, and start an

Internet company. So I need to find money from somewhere else. I have a timeshare in Florida which I'm happy to get rid of because we never get to use it – that should fetch ten grand. Then there are two PEPs worth about the same again, plus an endowment policy, which is meant to be paying off my mortgage, which has got about 25K in it. That makes around £45,000 in total and the column will bring in about £1,400 a month. So I won't be completely potless, not for a while. But I have a life that's geared to a decent, regular income. So if I get to the end of the cash and I haven't got my site off the ground, then I'll really be in the shit. I'll have blown all my savings and spent several months out of the journalistic loop. Other writers will have nicked my work. Other editors will have arrived, with their own favourite scribes in tow. Basically, it'll be house-selling time.

Before I take the plunge, I have to clear things with Clare, because it's not just my future I'm risking, it's hers and that of our children. Although my name goes on all the articles I write, we're professional partners, too. I depend upon her for all the back-room work without which my business would fall apart – everything from handling post, banking cheques and keeping my caffeine-levels up at boiling-point, to discussing the contents and quality of half the features I write before they get anywhere near a newspaper editor. Plus, there's history that needs to be respected…

Four years ago, I got a call from Nigel Parker, an old friend who was then a partner at a firm of solicitors called Lee and Thompson, who specialise in the music industry. His famous clients included superstars like the Rolling Stones, Queen, Robbie Williams (then just another post-break-up ex-member of Take That) and the Spice Girls. For reasons I have, to this day, never quite been able to fathom, he also acquired an infamous client: Christopher Vincent, the man who first went to the *Sun*, alleging that his one-time friend Bruce Grobbelaar had been paid £40,000 to throw a match between Newcastle and Liverpool.

I remember vividly standing in Dean Street, Soho, just outside the Groucho Club, the afternoon Nigel first called to say that Vincent had a story that might just make an interesting book. I vaguely remembered Vincent's name from the news reports at the time the story first broke. He was always referred to as a 'businessman' without any actual business being specified. 'Isn't he a bit dodgy?' I asked.

Nigel was hardly going to comment on that, not with Vincent being his client. But he did point out that the case looked as though it was going to lead to a sensational trial, with three famous footballers (Grobbelaar, John Fashanu and the Wimbledon goalkeeper Hans Segers) in the dock. Anyone who had the inside track on the entire story stood to make a fortune. And I could have half of it, split with Mr Vincent.

To cut a long story short, I said, 'Yes.' Vincent came to stay at my house, because that seemed the easiest way of keeping him in one place while we conducted many hours of interviews that would form the basis for the book. He was meant to stay for a week, but ended up bringing his twenty-year-old girlfriend and making camp in my spare bedroom for the best part of two months. By the end, I had realised that Vincent was a penniless bankrupt who would take any opportunity he could get of a free bunk and regular meals. He and his girlfriend were arguing with each other and making allegations about each other to me... and Clare was going out of her mind.

Three more years of insanity followed. By the time the whole grisly saga ended, with a libel victory for Bruce Grobbelaar against the *Sun*, it had cost me tens of thousands of pounds, months of wasted work and, near as dammit, a wife.

Clare had realised within seconds of meeting Chris Vincent that this whole project was going to be nothing but trouble. From that day onwards, she did everything she could to dissuade me from taking, or proceeding with it. I refused to listen. At first, I was seduced by the amount of money I stood to make. Greed was swiftly overtaken by something far more dangerous for a writer – obsession. Quite apart from the allegations Vincent had to make, the whole saga of his involvement with Bruce Grobbelaar, and then with me, was so relentlessly bizarre that I desperately wanted to be able to tell it. I simply refused to be cheated of my book.

By this point, Clare was close to despair. She could see her husband not only flirting with disaster, but also buying it dinner and inviting it home for a coffee. She simply couldn't understand why I kept on making excuses for Vincent's behaviour. The frustration must have been unbearable as we played out yet another pointless argument – her begging me to quit, me refusing to give up. The Chris Vincent book came within a whisker of destroying our relationship and our family with it.

We survived, but my book did not. Now I'm considering another mad scheme and there is no way I can go ahead with it unless I have Clare's full support. We talk the whole thing over and at the end she simply says, 'Yes. This is going to work.' So now I can go full-speed ahead.

17 November

We've got to get a new name for our site. So Mitch comes over to my place and we spend an afternoon dreaming up ideas and then looking them up to see if they're taken. We start by going through every entertainment-related name we could possibly dream up. We perm words like 'star', 'celebrity', 'celeb' and 'stage' in every conceivable combination, but they've all gone.

We put 'mega', 'super', 'cyber' and 'ultra' before and aft – the same thing happens. We start thinking laterally. We try entertainment-industry phrases like 'red-carpet', 'access-all-areas' and 'velvet-rope' but someone has always beaten us to it.

Then we think, 'Why not go for something completely irrelevant?' If you can call a music magazine Q, or a women's glossy *Harpers and Queen*, why can't you call a celebrity website something like, 'jam', or even 'dotcom.com'?

Answer: because 'jam' is owned by a German company, Mustang Bekleidingswerke GmbH (even though they haven't yet got a site to go with it), and 'dotcom.com' belongs to a specialist name-owning company who have it up for auction, doubtless at an outrageous price.

So we're stumped. And then I have an idea that approaches, though I say so myself, pure genius. There's one crashingly obvious word that is – obviously – taken. But a tiny adjustment occurs to me, and when I check it out on register.com, I discover that no one else in the whole wide world of the Web has thought of it before.

The original word is showbiz. The adjustment is to take out the 'w', put in a hyphen and call it sho-biz. The moment I see it, I know I've beaten Bono – I've actually found what I'm looking for.

'Yeah, not bad,' says Mitch. 'But it doesn't do much for me. Let's try something else.'

21 November

Angmering, West Sussex: The more that time goes by, the more I see ways of making the site work. What if, for example, we sold more than interviews? What if we had exclusive pictures, even videos? What about screen-savers and launchers? Think of the new Bond babe, Denise Richards. What if your average oversexed male adolescent could switch on his computer in the morning and be greeted by Miss Richards' bodacious curves... and a flirty little twinkle in her eye... and a sexy little audio message in her arousingly breathy voice? He'd be prepared to pay for that... surely.

Lots of ideas are coming all at once. The concept I'm thinking about is what you might call 'digital merchandise' – anything that can be reduced to digits and sent down a wire... which is pretty well anything audible or visual.

This leads me on to another realisation – that we might be able to pay the stars.

That, in turn, solves a massive problem. Back in the spring, when my interview with the Superstar Actor went belly-up I had no leverage. But if I'd paid him to talk to me, things would have been very different.

Now we're really rocking ... except 'we' aren't. The more excited I become, the more nervous Mitch gets about the obsession with which I'm pursuing this Internet project and the more sceptical he becomes about the idea that people will pay for Internet content. He's got a mate who works as an e-commerce consultant, and he's told him people expect to get their Net-content for free. 'Look,' Mitch says, 'if people tell you that it won't work, and if these people are experts, who know what they're talking about, will you at least promise me that you'll pay attention to what they're saying and not just charge on regardless?'

My problem is that this isn't what people are saying. I've met with one of London's top syndication agents, and he's mad keen to get on board. I've had a long conversation over lunch with Neil Storey and he's enthusiastic too. Neil's previous air of barely-contained desperation has entirely vanished because he's suddenly become an Internet tycoon in waiting. Forget all that old-tech stuff about making discs and publishing books, Neil is going online. He and his partners in The Virtual Orchestra have met a bloke from Sheffield called Steve Thomas who specialises in organising Net start-ups. Steve's put them in touch with a whole bunch of investors and they're looking to raise £1.6 million to get TVO up and running. Suddenly Neil can see all his hard work paying off and his poverty coming to an end. He suggests that I should meet Steve Thomas – he'd love the celebrity-site idea.

So when Mitch keeps telling me how I'm barking up the wrong tree, it begins to piss me off. I tell him he just can't see my vision. He laughs and replies, 'Vision? You're turning into a cult leader! We're all going to turn up dead in some jungle clearing one day because you've made us commit ritual suicide.'

He has a point. I can feel the beat stirring within me, the echoes of a fanatical competitiveness I thought I'd got rid of decades ago.

You see, when I was a boy, I was a monster. At the age of eleven, I was made captain of my house at Prep school. I was already the school swot, top of every class, but now I could really go to town.

I decided that my house would win every single one of the school sports cups. In pursuit of this aim, I fixed two football matches, bowled under-arm along the ground to prevent the other side scoring more runs in the cricket final, and came to a screaming, power-crazed crescendo in a hockey match which saw me yelling abuse at a poor boy on my side who I thought had under-performed. The little boy in question was an epileptic.

The master who was refereeing the game gave me such a ticking-off that it reduced me to tears. He was a big-bellied, greasy-haired man called Cooper and when he was done, another teacher called Don Capes consoled me with the words, 'Don't worry, Thomas. You've got more intelligence in your little finger than he has in his whole body.'

It was a well-meant remark. But the problem was, Mr Cooper was right. I had been an unforgivable bastard and I knew it. For the rest of my school career, and my time at university, I did everything I could to avoid competition or power. I was never a captain or prefect of anything, never stood for election to any committee, never did anything more than was required to make academic progress. I went freelance, in other words.

In the past thirty years, Karma has had its own revenge. My sisters were both diagnosed with varying degrees of epilepsy, as was my wife.

Having fixed football matches myself, I was denied the chance to publish my book about alleged match-fixing. Now I am proposing to become an Internet tycoon and I can feel the side of my character that I have long suppressed coming back to haunt me.

Matters come to a head when we have another meeting at Mitch's place with the techies. This time it's Dan's partner, Stan, who's been sent along to speak with us.

'What's the matter with your leg?' says Mitch as Stan limps through the door.

'It's plastic,' says Stan, obviously taken aback by the total absence of any attempt to draw a discreet conversational veil over his artificial limb.

'For fuck's sake, Mitch...' I protest, amazed as ever by his absolute lack of tact.

'Look, the guy was limping,' he protests. 'I was just showing an interest.'

Stan has come to help us define exactly what we want, and to tell us how much of it is technically feasible. As long as the meeting sticks to the practicalities of database creation and management, everything is fine. Then I raise the whole subject of digital merchandise.

Mitch is convinced it won't work. He says there's too much of that sort of stuff available for free. The only thing anyone pays for is porn. 'Fine,' I say, and try to carry on talking to Stan.

Mitch won't let it lie. He keeps looking up more and more sites on his computer, trying to prove that you can get anything you want for nothing. I counter this by saying, yes, you can get anything you want. But only if all you want is crap. Then I turn back to Stan, whose embarrassment at our argument is not only palpable, but smellable too. He's sweating profusely.

I try to ask Stan, purely hypothetically, whether it's technically possible to do what I want. Still Mitch keeps going. He sits at his computer, calling up one free site after another and challenging me to argue with his contention that naked women are the Web's only saleable commodity. It's like he's on some bizarre mission to destroy every idea I have. Eventually I snap. 'Shut... the... fuck... up.'

Poor Stan is caught in the crossfire, like a dinner-guest who's walked into a marriage from hell. And I feel like the husband whose wife has suddenly started telling the guests that he's lousy in bed. When the shattered Stan has finally left I stab Mitch in the chest with my finger. 'You made me look like a cunt in front of an outsider. Don't ever do that again.'

Then I walk out, slamming the door. Kiss that partnership goodbye.

22 November

Kiss and make up time. I call Mitch. We talk. We decide that if I'm rabidly gung-ho and he isn't maybe we shouldn't be 50-50 partners any more. He makes an offer, based on the suggestion that I will do all the work in setting up our company, but he will supply the complete database. On that basis, Mitch suggests we split our business 90–10 in my favour. I agree at once – I'd been going to suggest 80–20.

Now that we're mates again, if not business partners, we decide that a visit to Butlers may be in order. A Sacha session is required.

24 November

London, W1: Right after the first Mail column appeared, I got an e-mail from a Cheshire-based company called Telinco, which acts as a host to Internet Service Providers. They were interested in my plan and wanted to get together. So I set up a meeting in London with their Sales Director, a big Mancunian called John Hyslop. He suggests a place called the Media Club, which is the in-house restaurant of an office-block just off the Euston Road, filled with new media companies.

Hyslop has a simple proposal to make. He wants to give me all the server capacity and bandwidth I need for free. This essentially means that I can have as big a site as I want, plonk it on his hard discs and then let as many people who want to download as much of it as they can. Normally you have to pay for all that, and the charges can really mount up. When big games companies put demos of their new products online for the first time – attracting a zillion game-crazed geeks, all of whom want to download twenty megabyte game-files – they can run up six-figure bandwidth bills within a matter of days. So Hyslop's making me an amazing offer, the online equivalent of offering to print and distribute a magazine, or broadcast a TV show for free. In fact, he's offering to pay me while he does all this hard work. Then he explains why...

Sending information through the World Wide Web is an incredibly chaotic business. Think of the Web as a railway map. Now imagine that you are in Glasgow, and the information you want to access is in London. Each message from you to your chosen site is like a train, composed of huge numbers of carriages, each of which is a gobbet of information. Except these carriages don't all run along in a neat line, attached to one another. On the contrary, as they enter the Web, they get broken up into individual bits and sent through the Web by entirely different routes. It's as if some carriages were going via Crewe, some via Yarmouth and some via Bognor Regis. At the end of the line, they all have to be reassembled, hopefully in the right order, so that your message gets through ok.

When you try to download information from the site back to you, the same process happens in reverse. And if the file that you're trying to download is a big one, that means that there are millions of little info-carriages all zipping round the Web by totally different routes, trying to find the way back to your computer.

As Hyslop describes all this, with the aid of a natty back-of-an-envelope diagram, I begin to understand something that is crucial to an accurate appreciation of the Internet phenomenon, to wit: the Web is not an Information Superhighway, it's an Information Spaghetti Junction... on a rainy Friday afternoon, when a petrol tanker has spilled its load across three lanes of the motorway and traffic is backed up to Wolverhampton. The Internet was not designed to be a massive commercial and media network. And its little brother the Web was not created to make people like me rich. It was created as a means by which boffins could swap information. Anything else is way beyond its basic specifications.

So mark this well: the Net is a joke. It's hopeless, the living definition of those old Irish directions: wherever you want to get to, you'd be better off not starting from here. Most of the things you want to do online, you can't. The Internet is being sold like it's this incredible, world-shattering breakthrough, but if it were a car, it wouldn't be a glossy new Ferrari. It would be a broken-down Trabant.

It's certainly Trabby-slow. Most people are still using 56K modems, at best. That means, in theory, that they can receive or transmit 56,000 bits of information every second, or 7,000 bytes (a byte being eight bits). But because the Web is a joke, and frequently overloaded; and because telecoms links are – thanks to cack-handed government regulation – about ten years behind where they would have been if things had been done properly, the average speed at which punters download info off the Web is around 33K.

In theory, this should all change with the advent of broad-bandwidth communications, known in Britain as ADSL, which will provide super-charged speeds of up to 2,000K. This, claim enthusiasts, will radically transform the whole Web experience, allowing – among other things – real-time TV broadcasts online. But, says Hyslop, it won't. If we go back to that motorway analogy, giving people ADSL is like adding about six extra lanes to the M25, and scrapping the speed-limit. For a while, it's great. There's oodles of room on the road and boy-racers are zooming along at 140 mph, having a whale of a time. But it's not long before the word gets out that the M25 is like a legal Silverstone. So more and more people start to use it. Until, of course, all the extra lanes are just as crowded and just as slow as the old ones used to be.

But don't worry, says Hyslop... he has a cunning plan. It's called drop-and-insert, and what it basically means is that if my potential customer is logged on to sho-biz.com via his regular ISP, and he decides to buy that oh-so-desirable Denise Richards download, all he has to do is press a button and he will be routed on to a new line, directly to sho-biz, missing out the Web (and thus all that chaos and confusion) altogether. Because he's on a dedicated line, he can be charged at a rate determined by us. So the downloads are paid for, not by credit-card transaction, but as if they were premium-rate line calls.

At the end of the transaction, the punter is logged back on to his ISP. He gets charged a fee for the download, which gets passed onto Telinco and split with sho-biz.com. Now I get the point: they reckon they can afford to give me all my hosting for free, because they'll make their money on the telecoms charges.

I'm thrilled by the fact that John Hyslop and Telinco obviously think that sho-biz is going to be a winner. And the fact that their conviction comes about 48 hours after I've secured 90% of the project makes me even happier.

30 November

The Groucho Club, Soho: Perhaps everyone feels this way. Perhaps there comes a point in every enterprise where the person behind it feels an extraordinary balance between fear of failure and fear of success, coupled all the time with the tantalising possibility that maybe, just maybe, your ship might be about to come in.

That thrilling but also daunting prospect comes considerably nearer when I meet Neil Storey's Internet guru Steve Thomas at the Groucho Club. He's middle-aged, very Yorkshire and he likes to drink large whiskies. As he drinks, he tells me about the package he's putting together for The Virtual Orchestra.

It looks like they've got it all figured out. A massive Japanese electronics firm is looking after all their hardware requirements. An American organisation is acting as their ISP and they've got potential backers lining up for the chance to throw money at them.

This is all very well, and very gratifying for Neil, who can now see noughts being arranged in long, deeply satisfying rows outside his bank-account, just waiting for the chance to come in. But it doesn't necessarily help me. So I ask Steve what he thinks of my idea.

He says he's read my proposal and he loves it. He reckons the Japanese electronics people and the American ISP will both leap at the chance of getting involved and his backers will all pile in too. He tells me about the sorts of people he's talking about – City players with huge sums to burn. One man he knows has put a minimum £250K into each of more than forty different projects. He reckons it'll only take one of them to come off and he's covered his entire investment. Two, and he's laughing.

Then we get down to the nub of the conversation – I ask him what the next step should be. He says I should ensure that I've lined up all the creative and technical partners I need to make my plan a reality and then look for seed capital to get the whole show on the road.

Now we're entering dangerous territory. The whole business of raising money is central to starting an Internet business, but anyone starting a website should be aware that there are massive variations in the price you pay for financial assistance.

Kit Hunter Gordon was proposing to grab a 75% slice of my corporate pie, and I've seen prospectuses put out by Internet financiers which talk seriously about leaving the founding partners of a firm with just 10% of the equity. Then again, TVO are aiming to give no more than 20% away in exchange for their £1.6 million.

Bearing that in mind, I ask Steve what he proposes. He says I should reckon to raise a couple of million quid in exchange for no more than 25% of my as-yet non-existent company. I ask him what he'd expect from me if he put all that together. 'Five percent of the company,' he says.

I start doing the sums. If 25% costs £2 million, then the company's worth £8 million all-in. If you take away the investors' share, plus Steve's, Mitch and I have 70%, or £5.6 million. Mitch's share is 10% of whatever I have (not of the company as a whole) – i.e. £560,000 – which leaves me with £5,040,000.

Bloody hell. I'm a multi-millionaire. Practically.

DECEMBER

2–6 December

New York City: The Internet business is full of former journalists, partly because we all know that our current business is getting the Big Flush and we want to escape before we get swept down the drain with the rest of it; partly because a hack's content-generating skills are instantly applicable to the Net; and partly because we have a lot of unfair advantages over regular civilians. For example, I actually get paid to interview people who may not have any obvious connection with e-commerce, but who turn out to be fantastically useful.

That's what happens in New York, where I'm doing a profile of two English guys – both 28 – called Sam Houser and Terry Donovan. Terry is the Donovan that no one's ever heard of. His father, Terence, was the great fashion photographer and martial arts expert. His elder brother Dan played keyboards in Big Audio Dynamite and married Patsy Kensit. His younger sister Daisy is the sexy co-presenter of Channel 4's *11 O'Clock Show*. *Vogue* once profiled his family, devoting acres of space to everyone else, but limiting their coverage of him to a single line which read, 'Terry Donovan is still at school.'

Donovan ends the story by saying, 'It was hilarious,' in a bone-dry, bitterly inflected tone-of-voice that suggests that the experience of such public humiliation was actually as thigh-slappingly chortlesome as a quick skim through his own death-sentence. Ten years on though, he's getting his own back, because these days he's shaven-headed, chunky-thighed and nicely on the way to becoming far, far richer than any other member of his family.

It's a mellow Sunday morning in New York City, and Donovan's sitting in his office just above the Guggenheim Museum in SoHo – about as cool a location as exists on Planet Earth – watching a PlayStation basketball game unfold on a gigantic TV monitor. Nearby, hammering away at a computer keyboard, sits his old friend and notional boss Sam Houser, another meaty fellow, whose long hair and wild beard make him seem like a strange cross-breed of Charles Manson and Winnie-the-Pooh.

The two men run a company called Rockstar Games, which is the reason I've been sent to write about them. Rockstar makes Grand Theft Auto, or GTA – one of the all-time best-selling PlayStation games – plus a bunch of other titles. Now GTA has sold more than 3 million copies and its sequel GTA2 is already heading up to 1.5. Each game retails for around 50 bucks. Well, you do the maths. These guys are coining it.

They also have a website – www.rockstargames.com – which is a mad, noisy, baffling but oddly enjoyable sea-change from your average bland corporate showpiece. This gets the subject onto the Internet, and before you know it, we're yakking away about sho-biz.com, on which Sam Houser in particular seems dead keen. The idea of the trivia data-base particularly turns him on, as does the thought that rock-stargames.com might be able to license material for its own site from us.

I, meanwhile, am wondering how I can siphon off some of their vast money-pile. And it also occurs to me that these guys must have the programming expertise – or if they don't, they employ people who do – to make my sho-biz downloads way more interesting. We could even do some kind of celebrity-related game that worked a bit like a TV soap-opera, expanding month-by-month. Soon we've completely forgotten the interview and we're merrily ranting away about how we're all going to revolutionise the Internet. Who knows? Maybe we will.

First, though, I've got lunch to sort out. Because all the while that I'm talking to Sam and Terry I'm thinking about my old pal Craig Bromberg.

He's a New York-based journalist I've known since 1983, when he came to meet me, having heard that I'd done an interview with Malcolm McLaren, on whom he was writing a book. He ended up staying at my place in Fulham for what seemed like a year-and-a-half but was probably about a month.

I'm meant to be having lunch with Craig, but the Rockstar meeting just rambles on and before we know where we are it's half-past-two. Luckily, Craig isn't too bothered when I turn up at his tiny, but highly desirable apartment on the Upper West Side about three hours after I said I would. He knows a diner that serves Sunday brunch all day, so we head out for burgers and beers.

Craig is very New York. He doesn't bother too much with extravagant displays of good manners, he just tells it like it is. Since he extends this policy to girlfriends and employers, Craig spends a lot of time as a lone wolf. But he's not stupid and he knows a hell of a lot about the Internet, having worked on e-projects for both *Time* magazine and Bertelsmann, the gigantic German conglomerate, before getting his current gig as the editor of an Internet-users' magazine. He fills me in on the (marginal) progress of bookhits.com, the literary website on which he's been working for three years or more, and which is his private passion. Then I tentatively – and with ostentatious English self-deprecation – mention that I've got, you know, a bit of an idea for a sort of entertainment-related website.

Craig is not impressed. In fact, he seems keen to dissuade me from taking things any further. There are, he says, people preparing entertainment sites in California that use technology the rest of the world doesn't even know exists. Plus entertainment is American, the Internet is American, and I'm English. Do I know anything about the technology? Can I tell the difference between Flash, Shockwave and RealPlayer? Do I have a business-plan with all my financial projection mapped out, in detail, for the next five years?

Er ... no, I don't. But, I say, I do have the format for the content worked out pretty well.

Craig looks at me with pity in his eyes. Content? What am I doing bothering with content? Do I really think any financier gives a shit about content? All they want to know about is eyeballs. How many eyeballs are you going to attract and how long are you going to keep 'em? If you get eyeballs you get advertising, and that's all the Internet is – an advertising hoarding.

Since it is now more than fifteen years since I was given my first editorship and consulted my first balance-sheet, I do have a pretty clear understanding of the revenue-generating purpose of advertising. But in my feeble Limey innocence, I'd always had the idea that you got the ads by producing the content that grabbed the readers... or their eyeballs. Craig won't have this. Having once been an equally impassioned defender of literary values, he's now a total convert to the most brutal, market-led ideology of American media.

He's spent eighteen months working on his plan and soon – six more months at the most – he'll be ready to make his play for the money he needs: half a million bucks. I'm thinking: 'Eighteen months? For a measly half-a-million?' But I don't say this because it's hard to get Craig off his stride once he's in full flow (this is, I must admit, a major case of the pot suggesting that the kettle is a tad on the black side) and if it makes him happy to think that I'm just another useless Brit, fine.

'I don't want to discourage anyone,' Craig says, leading me out of the café and down the road to Barnes and Noble, where he insists on loading me up with mounds of incredibly expensive guides to setting up your own Internet business. 'I'm only doing this because I think of you as a true friend,' he continues. 'I don't want you and your family to get hurt.'

That evening, going over what he's said, I realise that there was one nugget of pure gold in all Craig's heap of verbal slag. He's been going on about the need for a proper business-plan. 'If you don't have one, no one takes you seriously. They may say, "Nice idea, I like it," but they don't do anything until they see the numbers.'

That sounds disturbingly close to the truth. The pat on the back is easy to get. But it's a long way from there to the moment when someone gets out a chequebook, writes out a number and puts their name on the bottom. And they only do that if they think they'll get an even bigger cheque back. So I make a resolution: when I get back to England, I'm going to write a proper plan. Before I do, there's one more meeting I have planned.

Joanna Owen was eighteen when she came to the offices of Eddy Shah's *Today* newspaper on the Vauxhall Bridge Road. It was early 1986,

I'd been appointed editor of Extra, *Sunday Today*'s magazine and Jo was looking for a job as my secretary. I took one look at her and realised that there was no way on God's earth I was ever going to hire her.

You see, I was due to get married in a matter of months and Jo was one of the sexiest girls I had ever seen in my life. She had huge blue eyes, bee-stung lips and a slim, sporty figure that could – and I was later to witness this at first hand – bring entire building-sites to a total standstill. I knew that we would be working insanely long hours in close proximity and though I am, by nature, about as promiscuous as an impotent sloth, even my modest sex-drive might be dangerously inflamed by her presence. The whole marriage might collapse. I told myself to be sensible. I categorically refused to hire her.

So my deputy editor did instead.

As it turned out, all was well. I managed not to embarrass myself too drastically (since any advance would certainly have been rebuffed), my wedding went ahead, *Sunday Today* collapsed within three months of its launch and I went off to a fantastic, and relaxingly Jo-free job elsewhere on the Street of Shame.

Cut to the Big Apple, December 1999. Jo – whose energy, ambition and street-smarts are the equal of her looks – has prospered mightily over the past thirteen years. In fact, women of an envious disposition should probably not read the next sentence because Joanna Owen is now Joanna Jordan and she has turned into everything that the Bridget Jones generation dreams of becoming. She is married to a handsome, incredibly prosperous French banker, who works on Wall Street. She has one child with another on the way, she lives in a gorgeous town house in a super-chic part of downtown Manhattan and she works as a talent-booker, persuading stars to come on American TV talk-shows. Not just any old talk-shows, either. Until recently, Jo was the chief booker on the *Letterman Show*, a job for which she was awarded two Emmys. Now she has her own company, Central Talent Booking, which I want to use as the procurers of stars for sho-biz.com.

We go out to lunch and I talk through the idea. When I say that it's a website, she wrinkles her nose: there are a million websites trying to get star interviews. When I say that there'll be syndication, she wrinkles again: stars' agents hate syndication because it implies a loss of control over who gets what. But when I say, 'And I'm going to pay the stars lots of money, with royalties every time their stuff gets used,' Jo gives me her cheeriest grin.

Aaah… the m-word. Works every time. Jo agrees to join the sho-biz team. She asks me when I'm hoping to launch and I tell her the beginning of July.

'So you'll be wanting Charlie's Angels,' she says. 'No problem, I can get you Cameron, Drew and Lucy. Why don't we get Bill Murray to interview them? He's playing Bosley. And you know what would be great for you? The Victoria's Secret girls are doing a special event at Cannes in May. Nobody knows about it. I could get you an exclusive.'

What, just me and the world's most beautiful underwear models? In Cannes? Christ, this job is so tough sometimes.

On the way home I read a book that I picked up at Barnes and Noble while Craig wasn't looking. It was called *Patton on Leadership: Strategic Lessons for Corporate Warfare* and it basically tells you how to run a company the way General Patton ran an army. I particularly like the bits about slapping gutless deserters across the face with hand-tooled kidskin gloves – just the thing for improving office morale. My lust for glory increases by the hour.

7 December

I pick up an e-mail, sent by Neil Storey while I was away.

> **Meetings yesterday a great success… we feel that we may have gotten over half way already in the fundraising… we'll know for sure by early next week. Heavens.. these are seriously nervous times.**

9 December

Being an entrepreneur does weird things to you. I am, for example, increasingly incapable of doing any journalism. Even my reading habits have changed. I no longer reach for the sports-pages first thing in the morning. Instead, I obsessively scan the business sections for news of e-commerce. And as I do this, I come to a conclusion: the whole Internet business is mad. Anyone who goes into it is certifiably tonto, two bits short of a byte.

I owe this revelation to Stig Lechsly, a 28 year-old American who set up an online site dealing in antique records. Eight months later, it was bought by Amazon for $200 million (£133 million).

Stig's big sale is mentioned *en passant* in a Sunday newspaper's business-page feature about his dad, who's some kind of international corporate super-honcho. He's spent the past forty years clambering up corporate greasy poles and now he's seen his own son eclipse everything he's ever earned in a single instant deal.

Naturally, I am paralysed with jealousy. But then I start asking myself a series of pertinent questions. Like: has there ever been an antique record-selling business, in the real world, worth 100 million? Is the entire antique record-collecting business worth that much? Think about it… a bunch of sad obsessives, riffling through bins in dodgy record shops, searching for rare 78s – is that the basis of a nine-figure business? Almost certainly not.

That's mad, and it bothers me. Sooner or later, people are going to realise that Internet stock values are insane. After all, Amazon, the company that paid the $200 million, has never turned a profit. But it's worth billions.

This can't continue. Internet prices are going to plummet as fast as Dutch tulip bulbs. And then people who have ideas for sites that might actually make money – people like me for example – won't be able to get any finance because all the venture capitalists have blown their cash on antique record-selling sites.

That makes me mad, as in angry, as well as mad, as in nuts. And here's another thing: the Internet is built on a false premise – a falsehood, indeed.

The Net's big lie is that anyone can start from scratch and go all the way, that the little guy can come out on top. Yeah… right. Here's the truth about the Net – it's one more step in the relentless march of the big battalions. If anything, it's concentrating power in the hands of even fewer corporations than before.

Craig Bromberg can sit in a joint on the Upper West Side, ranting on about the need to grab eyeballs, but he's totally wasting his time. I just read a survey from some big consultancy and it revealed that the vast majority of all online advertising – over 95% in some surveys – is concentrated in the top fifty sites, almost all of them American. Financial transactions are similarly limited. And here's why.

If you walk down your local High Street, it's easy to pop in and out of most of the shops. But the Internet is like all the High Streets in the world, jumbled up together. There are millions upon millions of sites. You can't possibly enter them all.

The sheer numbers become intimidating. So what do people do? They stick with the big, international brands they trust, and ignore everyone else.

Newcomers can't make themselves known, unless they have fortunes to spend on advertising in conventional media. People say the Net is going to kill newspapers and TV, but at the moment all it's doing is pouring money into them. And what does it get in return? The vast majority of current major start-ups must be spending far, far more on announcing their existence than they are getting back in actual business.

So anyone contemplating an Internet start-up has to be crazy. Unless we really are on the brink of a revolution. A month ago, among my many millionaire interviews, I profiled a guy called Damian Aspinall, son of the late John Aspinall the casino magnate and owner of Howlett's Zoo. Damian is one of those guys who has minimal academic qualifications but maximum business savvy. Our conversation confirms something I have long suspected: that there is no connection whatsoever between the ability to pass exams at school, and the ability to succeed in the real world. For while I've been wandering around with my vast IQ getting absolutely nowhere, Damian's been getting seriously rich.

'I left school at sixteen, uneducated, and travelled around the world for four or five years,' he explains. 'I just wanted to make money. By the time I came back to England, the one thing I'd learned about myself was that I was a good salesman. And the only job you could get at that point with zero qualifications where there was any chance of making money was estate agency. And I got lucky.'

Throughout the Eighties boom, he invested in London property, making his first fortune. Then on the advice of his father's best mate, who happened to be Sir James Goldsmith, he sold all his assets before the late-Eighties crash. By the beginning of the Nineties, he was ready to make his next move.

'I had to find an English-speaking market with depressed prices where a hungry predator like myself could go and feed. And Houston, Texas, was the perfect target. I flew to Houston, spent nine months researching it. We started buying industrial, residential and commercial property.'

When the market picked up again, Aspinall prospered. 'We were doubling and trebling every year, buying properties at $3 million and selling them at $10 million.'

So there he was, making millions in property. And then, while I was devoting myself to the country life, learning to tell the difference between a lettuce and a lupin, Aspinall got bitten by the online bug. As he tells me, 'We were the first Internet investors. About three years ago, a friend of mine, Anton Bilton, and I read *The Road Ahead* by Bill Gates. We both put the book down and thought, "My God, the Internet is the play." No one was talking about it, or even knew what it was. We went and looked at about thirty different Internet companies. We found one we liked, with excellent management, called Global Internet, and effectively paid $10 million. Everyone thought we were mad. All the brokers were threatening to resign: "How can you pay $10 million for a business that's only been going six months?" We sold it three weeks ago for $253 million.'

Once the interview is over I pick Aspinall's brains on the Net. I tell him that I've been looking at some of the prices people have been putting on e-commerce businesses and they seem completely barking: aren't they bound to come crashing down? To which Aspinall replies: 'Internet valuations are loopy in some cases, but in others they're not.

'Just look at the Internet market. If you believe it's going to be the same size as the computer market – and very few people dispute that – it's currently about 5% the size of the computer market, so there's your inbuilt growth. If you believe it's going to be as big as television, there are 26 million TV sets in England. There's your market. Plus you've got music, you've got hi-fi, it's all converging into one. So I think there's huge in-built growth, but you have to make a five- or ten-year play. You can't predict short-term valuations, but you have to believe that anything you invest in will have a realistic valuation in five or ten years.'

After we've finished our conversation, Aspinall wanders through the grounds of Howlett's and pops into one of the gorilla cages for his regular Saturday afternoon tête-à-tête with Kifu, a 400lb silverback gorilla, and his family of females and kids. Aspinall doesn't bother with all that David Attenborough nonsense of sitting quietly in the undergrowth and hoping the gorillas won't pay him any attention. He goes right up to Kifu, picks some straw off the floor of the enclosure and throws it in the gigantic ape's face. Then he runs off around the cage, daring Kifu to chase him.

Now I realise why Aspinall succeeds in business. All men instinctively rank one another, to see who's the alpha male, or big swinging dick, in any social group. Then they defer to him. When they meet Damian Aspinall, they sense – even if they don't actually know – that he's the kind of guy who takes the piss out of gorillas… for fun. This gives him a massive advantage in any business negotiation.

Me, I'm not an alpha-male. I'm beta-plus… on a good day. So I shall have to rely on clever ideas and a big, cheery smile to win people over, just like I've always done. Still, let's look on the bright side. I've got another new word for the day: 'Play'. As in: 'My God, the Internet is the play.' In modern business, you don't have an idea, a concept or even a project. You have a 'play'. And when you've taken your play as far as it will go, and grabbed as many eyeballs as you can, you move towards the exit. Okay, I think I'm getting the hang of this…

13 December

Piccadilly, London: Today I meet John Hyslop's rival in the race to provide sho-biz.com with its access to the Internet. Dave Cherry works for a company called Exodus, of whom I had not heard until the guys from TVO pointed me in their direction.

Exodus, it transpires, is one of the small group of companies who do all the hidden work that makes the Internet tick. It's what's known as a 'backbone' company, because it owns the massive computers which host Yahoo!, among many others: the hidden backbone of the Net. These computers sit in a string of bomb-proof, earthquake-proof and damn-near-anything-you-can-think-of-proof rooms, scattered across America and Europe. When the world finally goes up in smoke, all that'll be left when the dust settles are cockroaches... and Exodus.

When I call to fix up a meeting, Dave says he'll be easy to spot. 'Just look for Danny de Vito, only bigger.' I suggest the Groucho. He snorts derisively and says he'll be at Henry's, a bar on Piccadilly, just down from Green Park tube.

Dave is indeed just like Danny de Vito, only bigger... and Geordie. We get the beers in and start to talk. I tell him I'm planning a celebrity site that will give punters all sorts of downloadable goodies – everything they could get from an FHM cover-story, only moving, talking, living and breathing. 'Imagine we had a shoot with Denise Richards,' I say, going into my spiel.

'Stop,' says Dave. 'You've got me right there.'

Dave explains how big Exodus is. Basically, there isn't anything it can't handle. Exodus looked after the biggest download in history – the Starr Report – and got away without a single crash. It also handled the site for the new *Star Wars* film – people were online for hours, downloading the special fifteen-minute film that Lucas posted online.

Because he works for Exodus, Backbone Dave gets to see all the big Internet proposals coming down the pike. He can't believe some of the shit that's getting financed. A few weeks ago, he was meeting with a bunch of marketing men who'd got an idea for a site – whose name he gives me, but had better stay secret. It's obvious bollocks, but they've still picked up eight million from eager-beaver investors.

He doesn't think sho-biz.com is bollocks at all. Quite the reverse, he reckons it's going to be a big hit and he wants to be part of it. So what do I need?

I tell him I need to know if it's actually going to work, and if so, how. Dave says he'll get his techies to work on my proposal – he thinks they'll enjoy it. Great, I say. And if I ever interview Denise Richards and get any saucy stuff that ends up on the cutting-room floor, I'll bung him a bootleg tape.

The meeting ends in high spirits. 'Calm down,' says Clare, when I call to tell her about it. 'You're flying.'

Yup, I'm flying, all right. Me and Icarus...

14 December

Mayfair, London: Still flushed from my meeting with Dave Cherry, I meet an executive from a Massive Multinational Electronics Company called Adam Precious. He's been helping Neil Storey with The Virtual Orchestra, but Neil has warned me he can be hard to get used to. 'Watch out. He's incredibly bullish and in-your-face. My partner Malcolm Messiter came out of our first meeting and said, "I'm never going to talk to that bastard again." But if you hang on in there, he's worth the trouble.'

With that warning in mind, I turn up at the Dover Street, Mayfair, offices of EIS – European Investment Services – the same place where Neil dropped off his tatty envelope five months ago, and where he's now on track to get £1.6 million in start-up capital. Precious has been with Neil, doing presentations to TVO investors all day. He's a stocky, middle-aged man, with short, thinning ginger hair and a grating Grimsby accent. It's now six in the evening and he's been banging the drum for TVO since breakfast, so he's knackered, pissed off, and in severe need of a cigarette. He lights the first of many Rothmans, and tells me about his life. He runs an Internet café near where he lives in Hertfordshire, which he uses as a research facility, studying the behaviour of the kids who come to work and play with his computers. He also, he says, owns a football team, which plays in the Premier league, taking on teams like Arsenal. A look of gleeful triumph crosses his face when I seem baffled – 'It's a women's team!' he exults, delighted to have caught me out.

It's this bullish, point-scoring attitude that Neil Storey warned me to expect. But then, quite unexpectedly, Precious gives away one reason why he may be the way he is. It turns out he has a son with a very rare chromosonal disorder called Cri du Chat Syndrome, one of whose side-effects is to make hair go prematurely grey. Because it's what's known as an orphan disease – one too small to make it worth a drug company's while to invest in medicinal research – there is very little data on the disease, so Precious has set up a website so that sufferers and their families can exchange information. 45,000 people from all around the world have logged on so far.

So have a lot of drug companies. They want blood samples from all the sufferers... because they want to figure out how to stop blokes going grey. 'They don't give a damn about the severe mental disability that all the kids get as well,' says Precious, adding that he's going to make the companies pay through the nose for the blood. Now I know why he's so furious – his son is handicapped and no one's doing anything about it.

Precious is full to the gunwhales with supposedly authoritative information. Contrary to everything I've ever heard or read, he says resistance to using credit cards online has all but disappeared. When I talk about the teen audience, he draws me two graphs. One shows the way boys use the Net: they sign on, rocket upwards as they surf for porn sites, then disappear again as they lose interest. Girls, he says, are different. The longer they have Net access, the more they use it. And how? Sitting in chatrooms, yakking away for hours about boys and sex, just like they would in real life.

Grown women are just the same, he says. 'I've lost my wife, she's a Netizen. She doesn't worry about what time I get home. I get in an 2.00 in the morning and she's still chatting away online.'

Precious is convinced that websites can't work if they're too up-market. He draws a little diagram, dividing society into three classes – A1, B2, C3. Then he asks me to guess what proportion of the people who shop online come from which class. I can see where he's going, so I say A1s 20%, B2s 30%, C3s 50%.

Once again, Precious grins triumphantly. Wrong, he says: the proportions are 5%, 5%, 90%. Precious wants me to understand that all Internet purchases are made by what he calls 'mongs', short for 'mongols', presumably – an interesting choice of words, given his son's condition.

'Dumb it down, dumb it down, dumb it down,' he says... 'The people are muppets!'

He describes an Internet world of sad, obsessives. He mentions, proudly, that he knows the GMTV presenter Penny Smith and seems put-out when I say that she's a good friend of mine, too. Precious says there are people out there who videotape every appearance of Penny Smith, go through them all for pervy bits – a flash of knicker, an adjusted bra-strap – then put them up on the Web. Tens of thousands of equally sad individuals log on to check out the clips and describe their sick sexual fantasies about Penny in dedicated chat-lines.

Jesus wept ... I knew that the world was full of sad bastards and I knew that celebrities had to put up with some very, very strange fans. But when you get a glimpse of what that means for someone you actually know and like, it's as depressing as it's disturbing. For a second I wonder whether sho-biz.com is going to counteract the filth or simply trade on dangerous obsessions. Then Precious is off and running again...

The way you make money on the Net, he says, is to tap into all those obsessions. There is, he says, a motion-activated camera at Crewe station, which tracks train movements in and out. Trainspotters can buy a blurry fifteen-minute download for a fiver... and 195,000 people do... every day. This would make it a £350 million business – unlikely, you might think..

Precious then mentions the Bond site 007.com. It was done by a company in Manchester that he knows, and wants to recommend for sho-biz.com. I mention that practically everyone I meet in the Internet world seems to be a northerner: what's so great about Manchester? Answer, according to Precious: that's where all the clubs are, which means that's where all the pill-heads are, which means that's where all the mad, graphic talent is. I think about making a joke about 'e'-commerce, but I'm not in the mood. An hour with Precious doesn't encourage merriment.

Particularly when he's pouring cold sick over all my bright ideas. He reckons sho-biz will attract plenty of traffic, but he can't see where the money's going to come from. The way he sees it, my idea of five- to ten-minute downloads won't work technically, and anyway kids won't want it. He reckons they want physical souvenirs to show their chums. No one ever socialises around a computer, so anything that's restricted to a computer-screen is bound to be limited in its appeal. What we need is quick, fun, easy-access ideas: how about bananas?

Sorry?

Simple, he says. The most popular thing ever shown on *Big Breakfast* was Gaby Roslin sucking an ice lolly. So try something like that. How about, every girl we interview, get her to eat a banana? Guys will love it. Make it into a little cult-y kind of thing. Charge five bucks a pop. Get the boys we interview to take their shirts off and do press-ups to get their fans excited. I have to admit this isn't an entirely crap idea (well, it is: but it's the kind of crap idea that could well make a lot of money)... I like the idea of quick-fire moving posters. Digital fast-food. Hmmm...

I end the meeting feeling way down from last night, but with plenty to think about. I've got my one and only Christmas party of the year to go to. Emma Soames, editor of the *Daily Telegraph Magazine* is having her office party at her house in Clapham. I catch a cab on Piccadilly and get the Fascist Taxi Driver From Hell. He's got a balding, shaven head, piggy face and a seriously bad attitude – just what I need after a session with Precious. I give the Taxi Fascist rough directions to the Emma Soames's street, which I've never been to in my life, and sit back to think about bananas.

Half an hour later, we're driving past Clapham Junction station, way past where we're supposed to be. I point this out as politely as possible and the Taxi Fascist starts shouting that it's not his fucking fault. I should know where the fucking street is myself. I explain, still trying to be reasonably polite, that (a) I did give rough directions – accurate directions, as it later transpires – and (b) the reason I took a cab was that cabbies are supposed to have done the knowledge and be able to get to wherever they're asked to go. But since he obviously can't do that, why not look at a map, figure out where the street is, and go there?

The map concept is completely beyond him. 'What, you want me to stop? Is that it? Why don't you just tell me where you fucking want to go?'

'I did, when I got in.'

'No you didn't. I couldn't hear a word you was fucking saying, you was all over the fucking place, stuttering and that.'

I tell him exactly what kind of a pillock I think he is, get out and start walking, all burned up with anger and frustration. When I get to the party, all anyone wants to talk about is the money people are making on the Internet. The *Telegraph*'s fashion columnists Susannah Constantine and Trinny Woodall have, apparently, done a deal for a shopping site based on their column. Apparently, they've made millions.

I wonder whether they have... From the little I know of all this – that interview with Dan Conaghan and a few conversations with Neil Storey

– most people are simply being paid in shares, which they aren't allowed to sell for quite a while. Susannah and Trinny could have made millions. Or they could simply have been given a pile of paper which might turn out to be worthless.

For the life of me, I can't see how anyone's going to sell women's fashions on the Net. If there's anything that two sisters, a bunch of girl-friends a wife and a couple of decades working for female-edited maga-zines have taught me, it's that women regard shopping as a social and psychological – even mystical – process that goes way beyond the mere act of purchase. How can anyone try on a frock online? How can they possibly know if their bum looks big in this?

Okay, so plenty of women use mail-order catalogues. Our kitchen is permanently full of them. But even then, Clare likes to sit down with a cup of coffee, flick through one catalogue, compare it with another and go back and forth between different garments on different pages, chat to me and the girls about the various things she's selected. There's no way she could do that online – not with present technology – even supposing she wanted to sit down in front of my I-Mac to begin with.

So I greet all the talk of Susannah and Trinny's millions, plus all the rumours about the amount Nigella Lawson's been paid by a food-related site, with a couple of pinches of salt. But one thing does occur to me. How many Christmas parties are there, in how many offices, where people are telling wildly exaggerated tales about the amount some colleague or another has just been given by a website, or been offered to defect to a dot-com? Everything's changing. How very pre-Millennial...

15 December

I e-mail Precious the following message detailing all the reasons why I disagree with him. If he wants a fight, he can have it...

> Dear Adam...

> This is going to be a long e-mail. But you gave me a lot to think about. Plus, I'm an argumentative little fuck at heart, I enjoy a challenge to my intellect, and I like to fight fire with fire. So...

> I took the point about the impracticality of downloading ten-
  minute chunks of full-screen video.

> Your banana idea was inspired. And it helped solve another problem
  for me, viz: what do we put in five or 10 minutes of video? That's a
  hell of a lot of screen-time in any medium, let alone the Net.

> Answer: we don't sell big chunks online (tho' they're welcome to
  buy the CD-Roms or videos). We sell Moving Posters - 15-60
  second chunks of sexy action: eating the suggestive fruit, putting
  on sun-cream... just as tho' you could actually see the girl in the
  famous poster, walking across the tennis court, idly scratching her
  behind.

> For every star, there are maybe six Moving Posters: Denise
  Richards in her bikini, romping in a pool... Boyzone telling their
  fans how much they love them... etc.

> We also sell downloadable programs.. screen-savers, launchers,
  personalised e-mails, telephone answering-machine messages,
  etc..

> Then we do some sort of partnership deal with a conventional
  merchandising company for the manufacture and distribution of
  physical merchandise sourced from our material.

> PLUS... we major on business-to-business transactions - ie. the
  syndication end of the business. Inter-corporate e-commerce is
  currently worth four times as much as consumer e-commerce... so
  let's go big with the 80%, as well as the 20%.

> PLUS... as I suggested on my business-plan, we act as a production
  company for other people, or for joint ventures with existing
  copyright-owners - record companies, film-studios, etc. Exactly
  like a video-production company... but for Net-related projects.

> So far, I'm completely on-side with you. But I totally disagree with what you said about who uses the Net and for what. Granted, porn is still the 500lb gorilla in the e-jungle, but there's still room for the rest of us. Viz...

> According to the UK Internet User Monitor – a poll of more than 50,000 respondents, rightly regarded as the best research in the field...

> The overall ratio of men: women online is 60% male vs 40% female – more even than before, when the bias was heavily skewed towards men. But among teenagers, the balance is shifting towards males. Young men have become the dominant gender (54.3%) in the below 18 years age group, a reversal from female (61%) dominance in May 1999.

> On the question of who uses the Net and buys off it ... there is no such social classification as A1, B2, C3 – it's A,B,C1,C2,D,E – and there are very few products indeed that have a market penetration skewed 90–10 in favour of Ds and Es. Even the *Sun* has enough posh readers to give it a greater ABC1 count, in absolute numerical terms, than *The Times* or *Guardian*.

> It would be extremely unlikely for e-commerce users to be so heavily skewed towards the bottom end of the market. Who owns PCs, or has access to them at work? Middle-class people in office jobs. And what's the most frequently-purchased (non-porn) item on the Net? Books.

> Mongs, as you call them, don't read books. Posh people do.

> What this amounts to is...

> You're right: I have to refine my product and tailor it better to the Net, but... I'm right: there are people out there who will spend money on high-quality, non-porn material, and... We've got to

find a way of letting them do it without reaching for their plastic.

> Hope that helps... as an aid to sleep, if nothing else...

Precious gets in touch within hours. He seems delighted by my rudeness and vulgarity. It's the kind of language he understands. He throws the entire weight of his corporation behind me. We begin a long and involved e-mail correspondence about the finer points of download technology, modem speed and CD-Rom capacity. This could be the start of a beautiful friendship.

Speaking of friendships, I bung another e-mail off to Malcolm Messiter, who's the boffin who came up with the technology for Play, the program at the heart of TVO, which actually lets people play music to a backing-track and then e-mail it to their grannies/music-teachers/ chums etc. Malcolm, I'm sure, will be able to answer the following simple question:

> How much video material of (a) a reasonable screen size and (b)
> decent picture quality can I get into a forty-minute download,
> assuming that the downloader is using a standard 56K modem,
> operating at an average 33K actual speed?

I reckon 40 minutes is the longest amount of time you can expect anyone who's actually paying for local calls (i.e. anyone in the UK) to stay online. If we can't give punters something decent in all that time, we're in trouble.

16 December

Er... we're in trouble. Because here is Messiter's reply...

> Forty minutes downloading time at 56K would give about one
> minute of Mpeg video with a quite/very small screen size and not
> great refresh rate. This may improve as technology moves on. The
> best way to judge this is to simply try it a few times. I will 'phone.
> We need to do this together I think.

> I will send a short mpeg video to you in a moment as an attachment.
> Time the arrival, and double click to play it in Windows 98.

It only takes me about 6 minutes (using a fast ISDN line, which is much, much better than your average punter's got) to download Malcolm's video. What I see, when I open it up, is a screen about four inches by three, on which a bespectacled middle-aged man can be seen leaning on a desk, in front of a PC. When I press Play, the man begins to speak in a friendly, slightly fruity voice, as follows: 'Hello David. It's Malcolm here. This is a fifteen-second Mpeg video, to give you an idea of how long fifteen seconds takes to look at and download, and also the size of the screen. I wonder if the time's nearly up yet. It will be fifteen seconds when the little red...'

Then it stops, in mid-sentence. I am greatly indebted to Messiter for the trouble he's gone to, to make this little video-demonstration, but one thing I know for sure. No one in their right mind would pay money for that, not even if Messiter were to be replaced by Denise Richards... topless... doing somersaults.

Well, okay, *that* they might just pay for. But the point remains. The whole principle behind my idea – i.e. that you can bung great quality material down the line that's good enough to pay for – is comprehensively stuffed. D'oh! d'oh! And thrice d'oh!

So, to paraphrase the old *That's Life* format, I e-mail Mr Precious and I ask him...

> Right. I get it... I can't sell more than the odd banana-munch or
> press-up on downloads. So what can I actually get onto a CD-Rom?
> My impression of your average CD-Rom encyclopaedia is that the
> movie clips are stamp-sized pieces of shit... I have this terrible
> feeling I'm going to have to deal in DVDs, which have nowhere
> near enough market-penetration at this point. What do you
> reckon?

To which he says ...

> The CD will take two hours of three-inch by three-inch plus sound
> plus screensavers plus plus. But do not waste the banana........this

can be done anon as bananaman.com....... or pressupboy.com.......
OK not wot u want to do, I know. but life sucks...... Regs Ads.....

So, it's farewell brave new world of interactive media, hello babes committing acts of fellatio upon unsuspecting bananas. Not exactly what I had in mind...

Still, there's one piece of good news. I finally did something I've been meaning to do for ages. I registered sho-biz.com. It is now my personal possession. I also own sho-biz.co.uk, sho-sport.com (because sport is the obvious next step after entertainment), sho-pro.com (which is short for Sho-Biz Professional Services: i.e. our business-to-business dealings) and sho-girl.com (just because I felt like it). I restrain myself from adding a soul and R&B site called sho-nuff. But I feel, nonetheless, as though the die has been cast. Next stop... the world!

17 December

I need a lawyer. I know a lawyer who would be perfect, since he is not only a fantastic brief who knows an enormous amount about intellectual property – sho-biz.com's would-be stock-in-trade – but is also fantastically well-connected within the record industry. There is just one problem: the lawyer in question is Nigel Parker, the man who pointed Chris Vincent in my direction.

Clare loves Nigel, but she has never forgiven him for getting me involved in that catastrophe. So she won't be 100% delighted by the idea that we're back in business together. On the other hand, I can't think of another lawyer who would suit me better, or to whom I could talk with as much confidence as Nigel. So this time I put business over marital harmony and get Nigel involved. I think the marriage should survive that minor betrayal.

Neil Storey calls. The TVO presentations have gone incredibly well. Apparently, Malcolm Messiter – who turns out to be a genius musician as well as a software demon – did this trick where he'd pull out an oboe, play along to the TVO backing-track to 'Ave Maria', mix it on-screen in front of his investors' eyes... and then e-mail it to them, so that when they got back home, the finished performance was waiting in their queue. This brilliantly simple stunt had people reaching for their wallets before the final notes of the song. So they haven't just got the £1.6 million they were looking for, they've got offers of another million or so on top. Which means that Neil can, if he chooses, sell some extra shares and the money will go to him, rather than the company. Which in turn means he can look forward to Christmas knowing he's not going to go bankrupt after all. Granted, it'll be a few weeks before he actually sees any cash, but he knows for sure that he, his family and his house are safe.

Not only that, people are saying that TVO could be ready to float by next summer, autumn at the latest, and it could be worth as much as £200 million. It sounds like a crazy figure to me, but these days who knows? So it looks like Neil's boat has come in. On the rare occasions in the past when I've discovered that a friend has hit the motherload, I've been pig-sick with poisonous envy. But knowing what Neil has gone through over the past few months, I am – for once – able to feel nothing but undiluted pleasure at someone else's good fortune. Besides, it could be me next.

Provided, of course, that I can find some way of selling anything other than bananas.

18 December

I get the flu. I lie in bed, my heart pounding, soaking three sets of sheets with my sweat. It is a very real possibility that I may die.

27 December

East Sheen, London: After a week in bed and a very, very quiet Christmas, I decide that I'm fit enough to drive up to London for a meeting with Sam Houser, who's in town spending Christmas with his family.

My business decision to interrupt the Christmas holiday is entirely justified, because the meeting goes very well. The medical decision, however, is less sensible. By the time I get back home I'm as sick as a dog. Back to bed.

28 December

Excuse the ramblings of a sick man… but I've just staggered downstairs to grab a Lemsip and a box of paper-hankies and I saw something that made me ask myself a simple question: why are there no women on the Web? Women with clothes on, that is. There are starlets by the truckload, but with the notable exception of Martha Lane-Fox, the pert frontperson of Lastminute.com, there don't seem to be too many female executives. As a feature-writer I've spent most of my career working for and with women. But in the last couple of months, as I've dipped my toe into the Internet business, it's been nothing but blokes, blokes, blokes.

Which is weird, because the Internet is constantly touted as one of the means by which women will ensure that the future is female. The theory goes that the Net is the finest communications tool ever devised, women are better communicators than men, therefore women will dominate the Net.

Me, I'd counter the notion that men are tongue-tied dunderheads with the two words 'William' and 'Shakespeare'. But maybe there is one of those atavistic hunter/gatherer sex-difference things going on here. You don't have to spend much time in the online environment to see that the Internet is still at a very macho phase. It's all about technological wizardry, nerdy computer programming, an endless craving for more size and speed – all that impersonal stuff that obsesses men and leaves women bored witless.

More than that, it's full of mad boasts and crazy risks. All those rocketing share-prices and lunatic stock-market launches, the instant fortunes, the inevitable crashes, the frenzied competition to see who's got the biggest… it's just totally a boy thing. I know it's practically illegal to make sexual generalisations (apart from, 'Men, eh? What a load of… idiots/little boys/rapists… etc'), but by and large women tend to be more risk-averse – or to put it another way, more sensible – than men, and less inclined to extreme behaviour. So men are more likely than women to be Formula One racing-drivers, but they're also a lot more likely to be careless, delusional pillocks who think they're Nigel Mansell, drive like loonies and go careering into a ditch. Businessmen are more likely to make mega-fortunes than businesswomen… but they're also more likely to go bust. And, of course, for every Michael Schumacher or Rupert Murdoch, there are a million jerks in the ditch.

I'm rambling on like this now because I've just been watching my eighteen month-old son Fred toddling around the kitchen. When Fred's sisters were his age, they would play quietly and stay in one place. But not Fred. He's just pulled a chair across the floor, climbed up onto the worksurface, grabbed a jar of peanut butter, opened it up and stuck his hand in to grab whatever's inside. Does he care that he might fall and hurt himself, or get smacked by his parents? Of course not. He's just focused on the peanut-butter.

Well, the Net's a bit like that peanut-butter jar. Lots of naughty little boys are grabbing anything they can, even if it means getting hurt. Meanwhile, the girls are quietly playing on the floor, waiting for the boys to be sent out of the room, so that they can get their peanut butter on nice, warm toast.

Eventually, the technology will fade into the background, the business will settle down, and the Net environment will become better suited to female gifts of perception, good sense and hard work. Then Internet offices will become oestrogen-rich environments, like magazines are today. So where, I wonder, will the men charge off to then?

30 December

While on the subject of sexism… I celebrate the impending Millennium (which will be greeted in very restrained style owing to the ongoing presence of that bloody flu bug) by purchasing a subscription to the *Playboy* Cyber Club. This is not at all because I am a sad, balding, middle-aged git who wants to ogle airbrushed bimbos with silicone breasts and inch-wide mohican pube-cuts. No, I have shelled out 117 bucks to check out a site which succeeds in getting punters to pay for content.

Here's the reasoning… As Mitch correctly observed, porn is the only thing on the Internet that actually gets punters to spend big money (so far). *Playboy* is as close as porn comes to respectability. In fact, it's not really porn at all. So … if I can see what *Playboy* gives its punters and then find a way of giving sho-biz.com's users the same sort of thing – only without the naughty bits – we might be able to make a few bob after all.

So here's what I've learned from my first day's perusal...

1   *Playboy* has fantastic technology for letting hairy-handed onanists get the best possible views of their fantasy-women. Not only can you get the basic centre-spread of Miss Whatever, you can also zoom in on any particular part of her photograph that takes your fancy so that you could – in theory, obviously, if you were the kind of sick jerk who would do that kind of thing – fill your entire screen with a single nipple. Or something. It's nasty, but it's brilliant. They should called it Voyeur-Vision.

2   There's just an amazing amount of stuff in the Cyber-Club archives. They seem to have virtually every article and every photo-shoot ever taken for *Playboy*. So the punter gets the feeling that it's a great-value proposition. Plus...

3   They take you behind-the-scenes. There are lots of pics and video-clips of goings-on at photo-shoots: naked lovelies checking their make-up in the mirror (so you get simultaneous boob and botty action)... photographers arranging the pose... happy giggles over the Polaroids... The subliminal vibe is, 'You're one of the gang. You're there in the studio. She really, really likes having you around.'

4   *Playboy* is very big on communicating with its customers. No sooner have you signed up than they start sending you cheery newsletters from all the guys at *Playboy*, alerting you to all the great new features they've got coming up. I've just had a message alerting me to 'New *Playboy* Pen Pals Issue!' When I clicked on the hotlink that was embedded in the message, up popped a headshot of Shae Marks (Miss May 1994), with a hand-written letter in that loopy, copper-plate script all Americans must get taught at school, telling me how, 'I went skiing for the holidays – bruised my butt! Ha, Ha!' Poor little darling. Never mind, she's going to be at the Playboy Mansion for Hef's New Millennium party and, 'That should be fun!'

5   *Playboy* cross-merchandises. By pure coincidence, that very same Millennium party is available for exclusive viewing by Cyber-Club members via a *Playboy* webcast, live from the mansion. So if you want to spend the last night of the Twentieth century hunched over your PC, Johnson in hand, watching jumpy pictures of partying playmates … you can!

6   Just like Disneyworld, the *Playboy* Cyber-Club makes you pay on the door … but once you're in, everything inside is free. Now that I've paid my dues, I can spend the next twelve months logging on for as long as I like, salivating over full-screen clitoral close-ups of as many unattainable young women as I like. I'm not going to, naturally. But I could. If I wanted.

7   Just like Disneyworld, *Playboy* Cyber-Club lets you go on the rides for free… but they've got shops everywhere. There are constant invitations to check out special playmate videos, and DVDs, and T-shirts, mugs, calendars… every conceivable form of tacky, bunny-related merchandise. So they get one lot of money off you… and then they get more.

Every single one of these business techniques has some relevance to shobiz.com. We too should have the best photo-technology. We should give the punters more than they can possibly take in at any one time. We should make them feel as if they belong to a special club that can take them to special places. We should talk to them, send messages from their favourite stars, keep in touch, let them know what's going on. And then we should extract every last dime from their pockets…

JANUARY 2000

4 January

Here's a fact that has not made me popular with my loved ones. Because I've been ill, I've been unable to speak much, and thereby have meaningful conversations with my family. I get exhausted after a few minutes of social interaction of any kind. But the one thing I can do is write.

It's always been that way. No matter how fucked-up I am, whether physically or mentally, everything is fine as long as I'm in front of a keyboard. So I write my business-plan, and thus find myself involved in the key literary form of the early Twenty-first century – the highest form of imaginative art, the most fashionable creative medium there is.

When I first started out in journalism, Channel 4 was about to go on-air. So every ambitious little go-getter in London had a C4 series proposal tucked away in their back pocket. Then the fashion changed. Soon creative types were all bashing away at blockbuster movie-scripts. You'd hear amazing tales of people who'd been penniless one day and half-a-million bucks richer the next, just because they'd dreamed up ideas that Tom or Mel had taken a fancy to.

Nowadays, everyone wants that big, fat Internet pay-off. So they've all got a business-plan where their script used to be. And oddly enough, there are several significant similarities between scripts and business-plans, the biggest of which is that neither of them are ever, ever finished.

You do a first draft of a script and you think it's brilliant – it may well be, too: several months and many rewrites later you will probably go right back to it all over again. But your opinions, as the writer, don't count. Because the director, the producer and the stars all want to put in their two penn'orth. You have endless meetings and telephone calls. New ideas are thrown into the pot, some of which are actually quite good, not to say a whole lot better than ones you first thought of. Demands are made. Realities of budget and technical limitation are faced and dealt with. Before you know where you are, your original, oh-so-perfect concept is barely recognisable.

Ditto business-plans. It is barely two months since I wrote my first, faltering attempt and already it is as dated as the *Guttenberg Bible*. But oh, what a difference now. I have refined my Value Propositions. I have listed and categorised my cost-structure, across a wide range of variables. I have calculated cash-flows and profit margins. And here's the bottom line. If I get sho-biz.com even half-way right, I'm going to make an absolute shitload of money.

But half-way right is still an awfully long way to go…

10–11 January

Mitchell Symons is the king of lists. He has lists of celebrities who believe in reincarnation, or learned to swim as adults, or never knew their father, or lost their virginity with prostitutes, or survived suicide attempts. He has celebrities who were born on the same day as one another, and celebrities who died on the same day as one another. He has men with bizarrely small feet and women with galumphingly large ones. He has medical, sexual, personal and professional trivia of every form and description, covering thousands upon thousands of people.

Mitch has been collecting this stuff for decades, patiently sifting through the papers every day, entering one fact after another into his all-encompassing database. If you were to think to yourself, 'He must be a very sad man,' I wouldn't necessarily disagree. But even though I may tease Mitch on a regular basis for being the greenest journalist in Britain – no Friend of the Earth ever recycled compost as assiduously as Mitch recycles his lists – I bow to no man in my admiration of his trivia-gathering talents. No matter how bitter our arguments may have been over the direction our website was going to take commercially, we have always agreed that Mitch's lists gave us an incredible asset creatively, because they're a brilliant way of linking one star to another.

Most showbusiness websites are based on individual star-pages, which contain a standard picture, biography and credit-list. If you're on, say Harrison Ford's page, it might tell you that he's been in all the Indiana Jones movies, thereby linking him to Steven Spielberg, who directed them, George Lucas, who produced them, and Sean Connery, who co-starred in *Indiana Jones and the Last Crusade.* But on sho-biz.com, we don't really care about Harrison Ford's directors or co-stars. Instead, we'll go for the fact that he dropped out of college, or worked as a carpenter, or had one Jewish parent. Then we'll take you to a list of all the other people of whom the same could be said. And from that list, you'll be able to go onto their pages, too. So your journey through the site will be more eccentric, but also a lot more fun.

The simplest way of describing how this is going to work is to draw a map. Mitch and I have come up with sample biographies of three stars – Brad Pitt, Bruce Willis and Sarah-Michelle Gellar, alias Buffy the Vampire Slayer – plus a collection of lists which link them all together. I draw a sketch which shows their pages as nodal points in a Web drawn by the links between them and the lists on which they all appear. This is all very well, but it's going to be hard to send it to anyone else. I need to find a way of reproducing the map using my computer, so that it's all stored digitally and I can just e-mail or fax it off to anyone who might need it.

I don't have the first idea how to do this. I use my Mac every day to write, but graphics are completely beyond me. Luckily, my ten year-old daughter Lucy has not yet gone back to school. So, for a massive £1 fee, she sits down at my desk and knocks it off in a couple of hours. Looks great, too.

17 January

It's my birthday. I am 41 today. Question: why does 41 seem so much older than 40? Somehow, actually being stuck into a decade has a far more frightening effect than any of the numbers with a nought on the end. Oh well, no time to be maudlin, I've got an Internet empire to start and it's become clear that if I want to raise the millions of pounds that are going to be necessary to fund it, I've got to have something I can show people. And that means creating a dummy or demonstration site that gives people a means of seeing and using the idea I'm writing about.

Problem: I know nothing whatever about website design. If I'd actually read, or even opened, any of the books that Craig Bromberg made me buy about the Web, many of which have invaluable, step-by-step guides to Internet proficiency, I might be a bit more clued-up. But I see no point: far better to use experts whose job it is to do this sort of thing. And luckily, I may know just the people to do it.

For the past eight years I have been a freelance journalist. I have no contracts with any magazines or newspapers anywhere. Every penny I make depends upon me either selling ideas and delivering what I've promised, or accepting commissions from editors and doing a good enough job to get asked again. So, to put it bluntly, I never say, 'No.' And once I've said, 'Yes,' I do my best to deliver what is required, when it is asked for, at the length it's been commissioned. If anyone asks me to work for them once, I do everything I can to encourage them to ask again.

Last year, though, I made an exception to that rule. Back in about February, when I was feeling a little short of work, a small-circulation business magazine asked me to write a feature about a graphic design company called The Attik, which began life in 1986, when a couple of twenty-year-olds called Simon Needham and James Sommerville, newly graduated from the graphic design course at Batley College, and set up their own design business in James's granny's attic in Huddersfield. Within a week of the commission, the phone suddenly started ringing again. As work came pouring in from big-time Fleet Street papers, I forgot about the Attik job. And whenever I remembered it, I felt a brief twinge of guilt, resolved to do something about it, and then forgot about it all over again.

Six months went by. Eventually, my conscience overcame me. I gave The Attik a call and set up a meeting and went along to their London offices, just north of Oxford Street. The first thing I saw – not surprisingly

– was a reception desk. Except this one was covered in fake fur. Day-Glo orange fake fur, to be precise.

Not far away, there was a meeting-room. It had the usual TV and video at one end, with a long table, surrounded by chairs. But the chairs were upholstered in leopardskin fabric. And in the middle of the table there were two recessed boxes. The tops of these boxes were clear perspex. The sides of the boxes were, yes, orange fake fur. And in the middle of each of these boxes was... a lemon.

Luckily, the decorative absurdity was tempered by the no-nonsense Yorkshire grit with which the business was actually run. The Attik's clients included Nike, Coca-Cola, Warner Brothers and Fox TV. It did work that was both creatively and technically dazzling and it had doubled its turnover in each of the first twelve years of its existence. How buffoon-y is that?

So I did my piece and thought no more of The Attik ... until the concept for sho-biz.com came along. Now it occurs to me that these might be the perfect people to create a hot look for sho-biz.com. I call up the London office and they tell me that all the Internet design is handled from Huddersfield. If I talk to a man called Paul Inman, he'll tell me whether it's the kind of project Attik will want to get involved with... Which is by no means a certainty, or even a likelihood. This is not a company that has to scrabble for work from un-financed start-ups. Not when they've got Nike and Coke queuing up to pay them.

But when I speak to Inman and explain the concept of sho-biz.com, he tells me it sounds like an interesting project with which his company might decide to get involved. I agree to send him a creative brief. He says he'll read it and get back to me. If he likes it, we'll have a meeting some-time next week.

18 January

Before I go any further, there's something you should know: I have never cheated on my wife. Furthermore, I am not a lech. I don't grope, I don't make lewd advances. I have never in my entire life jerked off over a porn mag. So, anyway, here is a list of the sexiest women I have ever inter-viewed, starting with a quick round-up of the ones who didn't make it.

Right off the charts, we've got Demi Moore, Naomi Campbell and Vanessa Mae. Gorgeous, all three of them. But Top 10 candidates? Not in my experience.

Bubbling just under, and frankly deserving of my praise are Joan Collins (I met her at the peak of her *Dynasty* triumph, in a hotel suite filled with lilies. One of the flowers brushed against my linen suit, leaving pollen stains across my shoulder. The way Miss Collins brushed and blew the pollen away lingers with me still) … Tina Turner and Annie Lennox. I once had dinner sandwiched between those two divas, when they were appearing on that old Channel 4 music show *The Tube*. Afterwards, I went up to Annie's room with Dave Stewart and sang Beatles songs into the early hours. Tragically, I was suffering from depression at the time (Annie and I had made friends by comparing experiences with shrinks) and so was unable to appreciate the experience.

Anyway, here are the Top 10…

10 *Lesley Garrett*. An opera singer, a wife and mother and a thoroughly respectable friend of royalty. But spend any time in her presence and you can't help noticing the wild Yorkshire lass firecracking away beneath that classical exterior. She has one of the most attractive qualities any woman can possess, the sense that time spent with her would be time spent having fun. Plus – and this is a major point in anyone's favour – she's mad about cricket.

9 *Christie Brinkley*. If you're a heterosexual man, you dream about ending up married to a woman like Christie Brinkley. I met her when I was covering Miss World in Sun City, the South African gambling resort, and despite being fifteen years older than the contestants, she was incontestably more beautiful, and infinitely more elegant. She was also in the process of dumping Billy Joel. Poor bastard. No wonder he always looks so miserable.

8 *Iman*. Astonishingly wonderful to look at – she'd be higher up the list if I wasn't so scared of her. You see, Iman was the daughter of a senior Somali government oficial when Somalia was effectively a client state of the Soviet Union. So she was sent to the USSR for education, indoctrination... and training in martial arts by the Spetznaz, the Russian equivalent of the SAS. One word out of place, and Iman could break you in two. Scary... in a good way.

7 *Paulina Prozkova.* The Eighties supermodel, who married Ric Okasek of the Cars, was the single most beautiful woman I have ever seen. This isn't a sexual observation. I'm sure that if I'd have been a woman I'd have been just as fascinated. Just a gorgeous, aesthetically flawless human being. Unlike Ric Okasek, but there you go.

6 *Jane Horrocks.* You might not think Jane Horrocks is sexy. She so often plays characters that are daft, dowdy or down on their luck ...and that foghorn accent would cut glass so much as drill through brick. But in person she turns out to be this tiny, elfin creature with delicate features and huge eyes. She's also very, very funny, and does a brilliant impersonation of a yelping dog, as you discover if ever you tread on her toes.

5 *Martie Seidel.* She's one-third of the Dixie Chicks, the country-music trio who are bigger than vast in the USA, but don't mean much on this side of the Atlantic. For those who know the band – and if you don't, you should – Martie's the violinist. I spent several days on the road with the Dixies in early '99. One night, I was mooching by the side of the stage at the New Orlean's Superdome. Martie was standing about ten feet away from me, wearing a little crop-top and a pair of skinny satin pants, fiddling away like her life depended on it. What can I say? I fell in love. It was only a ninety-minute crush and anyway we're both married. But it was great while it lasted.

4 *Katarina Witt.* A gold medal-winning skater and the sexiest, perhaps the only sexy East German athlete ever. I once saw her warming up for an ice-show. There was a curtain drawn across the arena, so that some of the ice was backstage. Katarina zoomed around it, going up to any man who was either on the ice as well, or standing near it, and gyrating around in front of them until they were paying her total, rapt attention. Once she'd warmed one up, she moved on to the next. Then, when she, and everyone else within fifty yards was thoroughly aroused, she stormed out into the arena and tore the house down. Calm down, comrade!

3 *Miss Denmark 1993.* She was the one contestant at Miss World who was even more gorgeous than Christie Brinkley. She looked like Cindy Crawford's prettier sister and was everyone's image of the ultimate beauty queen. But the Miss World judges are terrified of appearing sexist, so the title went to earnest Jamaican girl who wanted to save the world before resuming her studies as an architect. An even worse decision than the first Lewis-Holyfield fight.

After the contest, they had a party for all the girls, the media and assorted hangers-on. I was suffering from some sort of South African flu and had forgotten to bring the dinner jacket that the invitation specified. So I'm dressed in the same rank and crumpled gear I've been wearing all week, I'm covered with a slick sheen of feverish perspiration and – as the capper to it all – the disease has reduced my smooth, mellifluous speaking voice to a rasping croak that makes me sound like a kerb-crawling pervert. After dinner, at which the other guests have sensibly kept their distance from me, I realise that I have not been the only solitary buffet-muncher. Off in a corner, sitting all by herself, utterly ignored, is a disconsolate Miss Denmark, clearly trying to come to terms with the fact that she has not only failed to win, she hasn't even been crowned a Continental Queen of Beauty. Now, I'm the kind of guy who settled down as early as possible, as steadily as possible, specifically to rid his life of the need to approach mysterious, beautiful women who would almost certainly tell him to piss off. The whole idea of introducing myself and striking up a conversation, outside the comfort provided by the formalities of an interview, is completely terrifying. But by this point I'm so ill that my fear has disappeared along with my better judgement. So I go up to Miss Denmark, say hello, offer her a hot, soggy handshake and ask her to dance. To my absolute amazement, she says yes. We walk out onto the floor, I hold her heavenly body next to my germ-ridden corpse, place my moist right mitt in the flawless curve of her lower back, and stagger around in a desperate parody of a waltz. For three minutes or so I am in paradise, and she – sweetly – grants me the courtesy of waiting till the end of the song before making her excuses and running away. Later in the evening, I saw her in the arms of a beefy young hunk from one of the South African TV camera crews. When she spots me looking at her, she waves at me. Then she whispers in the young hunk's ear and they both collapse in laughter. Which is, in one gesture, the reason why marriage suits me so well.

2 *Elizabeth Hurley*. It's Los Angeles, December 1993, a month after my encounter with Miss Denmark. I'm in town to write, among other things, a piece about English girls trying to make it in Hollywood. There's this actress called Elizabeth Hurley, who's biggest break so far is a small part as the token cheesecake in a Wesley Snipes hostage-movie called *Passenger 57*. She turns up for lunch at a little restaurant on Sunset Boulevard in a pair of sneakers, skin-tight leggings and a pale green T-shirt. Her figure is a wonder of nature. There are – and this is a dirty, but oddly erotic detail – faint sweat stains under her arms. She describes, in hilarious detail, the way that Hollywood contracts specify the precise portion of nipple or buttock that an actress will reveal in any film. The fact that she is still an outsider, combined with her natural, British sense of self-mockery makes her a deliciously acute observer of the movie business. A few months later, she turns up for a movie premier in a Versace frock held together by safety pins and the woman I met in LA begins the process of transformation-by-fame into an altogether more elevated creature.

1 *Kylie Minogue*. What can I tell you? The woman is the living definition of the phrase 'small, but perfectly formed.' She's tiny, but everything's in perfect proportion: 'Honey I Shrunk the Kylie' you might say. She's also smart, funny and completely hip to her place in the great scheme of things. She once went out on to the stage of the Royal Albert Hall and recited the lyrics to 'I Should Be So

Lucky' as a piece of serious poetry, and just how cool is that? We had dinner at the Soho House. The straps of her frock kept slipping off her shoulders. She'd shrug, hook a slender finger round the silk to slide it back into place... Okay, so I'm a sad bastard... want to make something of it?

And here, finally, is the point of this prolonged digression. I need someone who can demonstrate the virtues of sho-biz.com. Someone that everyone adores. Someone who appeals to men and women, young and old, gay and straight. Someone who, if they turned up at a City presentation, would send potential investors home in a delirium of excitement. I also need someone who is not so fantastically rich and successful that they will automatically turn down any offer out of hand.

Now I love Kylie to bits, as any freeborn Englishman should. But I also know that her last album did not do quite as well as she had hoped, and that she might therefore be interested in a proposal that paid her a reasonable amount of cash, offered the chance of a whole heap more, and gave her the chance to present herself as a hip businesswoman, alive to the potential of new technology. So I trawl through my old notebooks, find her manager, Terry Blamey's number and discover from his office that he's away in Australia. No problem, I spend a fortune posting an 'Artists and Managers' document Down Under by express mail.

I know this is an old-fashioned way of doing things, but I want Blamey to receive a properly-printed, bound document, with elegant typography on good-quality paper. Something that looks like a serious proposition. But, to make sure that he knows what he's getting, I back that up by sending him the following e-mail...

> **Dear Mr Blamey,**

> **We spoke a couple of years ago when I was preparing a cover story on Kylie Minogue. I think Kylie liked the story – I certainly received a very sweet e-mail from her after it came out!**

> **I'm contacting you now because I want to make you, and Kylie, an offer you can't refuse.**

> I am setting up what I hope will be one of the major Internet launches of 2000. It's called sho-biz.com and it promises a total revolution in the way that celebrity journalism is conducted. As you will see when the 'Artists and Managers' version of my business-plan reaches you, mine is a serious proposition, with serious financial, technical and corporate backing behind it.

> Right now, I am preparing a demo of the site, and the celebrity-based digital merchandise that will be sold from it, in the form of Downloads, CD-ROMs and DVDs.

> The demo will feature a major entertainment celebrity. It will be seen, not only by venture capitalists in the City and on Wall Street, but also by every major film studio, record company and entertainment PR agency in London, New York and LA. The material from it will then be released – subject to artist's approval – on the site at its launch, and the artist will be paid a royalty on every sale of every item in which they feature.

> I would like Kylie Minogue to be our Featured Celebrity. I believe her popularity, her beauty, but above all her keen intelligence and wit make her the perfect person to illustrate what sho-biz.com can do.

> The job will require a maximum two days work in a studio, for which we would pay £15,000.

> If Kylie further agrees to participate in the corporate presentation of sho-biz.com to the UK financial community, we will, in addition, give her 1% of the initial company stock, prior to its dilution by the first round of capitalisation.

> Working in conjunction with Summit Group, a private company based in the City of London which specialises in backing start-up projects – 1999 turnover: £54.4 million – I am intending to raise £3 million for 30% of the stock, valuing sho-biz.com at £10 million.

Judging by the response to my initial Business Plan, if we can deliver a quality of product to match the quality of idea, we will have no difficulty in raising the money. At that point, a diluted 1% would be worth £70,000.

> Of course, we will only raise that £3 million if financiers are convinced that the value of their investment will be multiplied many times. So that 1% could soon be worth a very great deal of money indeed.

> In addition, Kylie could expect to earn significant royalty income from syndication and merchandising once the site is in operation. Royalties would start paying out from Penny One of income reaching sho-biz.com because the initial £15,000 will be a flat fee, not an advance against future earnings.

> The total value of the package I am offering could be worth well into six figures. It is also a chance to be in at the start of something great.

> Please call me if there is any further information that I can give you. I am sure that you receive many offers from bogus individuals. I would welcome the chance to reassure you that I am not one of them. Yours sincerely ... David Thomas

This, I feel, is a proposition that would interest anyone concerned with the promotion of an artist's career and the filling of their bank-account. I am confident of a swift reply.

19–25 January

I spend a week in feverish anticipation. I check my e-mail queue several times a day. I am very excited.

Nothing happens. I get plenty of messages, but none of them are from Terry Blamey. From him, there's naff all. Not a squeak. Back to the main story…

20 January

Sam Houser e-mails me. He caught the flu from me, that day we had lunch in East Sheen. But over it now, he's read the sho-biz plan and he thinks there's lots that Rockstar can do to help make it all happen. 'By the way,' he adds, 'there's a few pictures of my mum in *GQ* UK this month – check it out!' His mum is Geraldine Moffat, the actress who can be seen on page 103 of *GQ*, February 2000, wet from the bath and absolutely stark naked, having her breasts fondled by Michael Caine. He was playing Carter. She was the gangster's moll he screws, then locks in the boot of a Sunbeam Alpine, just before it gets dumped in the Tyne. If my mum could be seen flashing her pubic hair in a men's magazine (an unlikely concept, but you never know), I'm not sure I'd be e-mailing the fact to all and sundry. Is this some weird Oedipal thing Sam has got going on? Or is it just a healthy pride in his mother's beauty? Over to you, Dr Freud…

21 January

The City: Over the past couple of weeks I've made two or three trips up to Broadgate to meet with Kit Hunter Gordon and his partner Zac Barrett. Today's was the meeting that really mattered, so I've condensed the subject-matter of all our conversations into one entry. It's a cheat, but it simplifies everything, which – as will shortly become obvious – may not be a bad idea. Kit is tall and languid. Zac is short and bouncy. Kit comes from Inverness. Zac comes from Norfolk, where, he informs me, 'The definition of a virgin is a girl who can run faster than her uncle.' They met studying law at Trinity Hall, Cambridge and have been friends ever since. Kit's façade is his poshness. Zac's is his country-boy cheeriness. But, beware: you only have to get him started on the finer points of company law, or working out the precise mathematical implications of any suggested deal and he suddenly switches on a multi-megawatt brain.

The subject of our meetings is the funding of sho-biz.com. We have a brief preamble in which I ask them how long they think the current market can be sustained, because the thing that worries me is the Stig Lechsly factor (see 9 December): sooner or later people are going to stop paying obviously crazy prices for Internet stocks. But you can bet that when they do that, they'll stop paying sensible prices, too. It's exactly like a property boom. When things are in the manic up-phase, people buy toilets in back streets for millions. When it all crashes into the depressive down-phase you can't give away palaces in Mayfair... and I don't want to go wandering into the market just when it's suddenly gone all depressive. Kit takes the point, but sees no immediate problem: 'I think we've got about eighteen months to go yet,' he says.

That being the case, we can get down to business. There are only two questions that matter: how much money are they going to give me to get the project to the point where it can be put before investors? And how many percent am I going to have to give them?

I tell them I reckon I can get the job done for around £50,000. 'Are you sure?' says Kit. 'It looks a lot more like a hundred to me.'

But what would £100,000 buy them? In the back of my head is the thought, planted by Steve Thomas, that my idea is worth £8 million. On that basis £100,000 would buy just over 1%. Somehow, I don't think they're going to go for that.

At the front of my head is the thought that I really want the money. And that's mixed with that terrible, cringing fear, known to all free-lancers and sole traders, that if you piss your client – or benefactor – off too much, they'll simply walk out on the deal. That fear is the reason I let myself get treated like shit by tight-fisted magazines. That fear, too, is what may cause me to give too much away unless I'm very, very careful.

On the other hand, again, all I have is an idea on a few bits of paper. And these guys are seriously proposing to spend a serious amount of money, purely on the basis that they trust me to turn it into something of value. That trust is worth something, surely.

What it comes down to is this: I know I'm going to have to give large chunks of my business away to all sorts of people. I reckon, for example, that the various participants in the project – Jo, Nigel Parker, Dorian Silver and then all the hacks I hire to actually run the thing – are going to take up around 20% of the stock, and that's before we take the project off to serious investors. So I can't give up too much, too soon. Whatever happens, I tell them, I can't let them have more than another 20% of the company. That way, I figure, Mitch and I will share 60%, leaving me with

54% (i.e. 90% of our share), so I'll still have a majority stake… until the investors come in, that is.

Fine, they say. And then Kit and Zac make what seems like an eminently reasonable suggestion: why not have an arrangement that works in stages, on a sliding scale? In other words: I agree to hand over a maximum of 20% of the company, in return for a maximum of £100,000. But I don't have to take all the money, or hand over all the shares. Summit will need to have a guaranteed minimum stake – much below £50,000 and it's hardly worth their while to get involved – but beyond that point it's all down to me. So I'll be incentivised to keep costs low, knowing that every pound I save goes towards my eventual shareholding.

Well, that sounds simple enough. If 20%, or one-fifth of my company is worth £100,000, then the whole company is worth £500,000. So each 1% is worth £5,000. Except that it isn't, because I am not selling them any of my personal stake, or receiving any of the proceeds. I am, in fact, agreeing to dilute my personal stake so that additional shares in my as-yet non-existent company can be issued, and the money received from those shares be placed in the company, to be used as the company's directors see fit.

To anyone with even the faintest smattering of financial experience, let alone an MBA, that will seem pathetically obvious. But then again, I am not a financier. I am a journalist. I know how to produce copy under deadlines. I know how to extract revealing quotations from reluctant celebrities. I can organise and administer a magazine-full of journalists and keep their expenditure within a given annual budget. But share dilutions? I haven't got a chuffing clue.

So I'm completely unprepared for the voodoo mathematics that ensue. Which I think work something like this…

Suppose I have a hundred shares… I want to add more shares to my company in order to let my good friends at Summit end up with 20% of the whole, expanded enterprise.

If I issue twenty shares and give them to Summit, in exchange for £100,000, there will then be a total of 120 shares, of which they will have twenty. Which is only 16.67%, or one-sixth, of the whole thing.

So in order for Summit to end up with one-fifth of the expanded company, I have to issue 25 new shares, on top of the original 100, making a total of 125.

They then have 25, out of 125 shares, which is 20% of the whole thing.

Now comes the tricky (at least to me) bit. So, if you're as green as I am on this sort of thing here's a simple choice. You can either (a) skip straight through to the next Kylie entry (although I have to warn you that it involves no pictures, or even lavish, first-hand descriptions of the delicious Aussie moppet, merely the recitation of yet another e-mail), or (b) take a deep breath, make yourself a cup of coffee, light a fag if that's your poison, and follow through a tangled web of reasoning. This latter option involves harder work. But it has the benefit that if you manage to follow it all, you'll avoid acting like a chump, should you ever find yourself opposite a pair of clued-up City boys who are blinding you with science.

Anyway, here we go…

As you may recall, we have left the dilution of sho-biz.com nicely sorted. I will dilute sho-biz from 100 shares to 125 and give Summit 25. They will have 20% of the resulting business. If I don't take all the money, they will have fewer of the shares. That's the end of the matter. Except for one thing…

After the process is complete, we end up with a company that's worth £500,000. So – at that point – every 1% of the company is worth £5,000.

But before that hundred grand was put into sho-biz.com, the company was – obviously – worth £100,000 less. So it was worth £400,000.

Let's divide that £400,000 into 40,000 shares, each worth £10. If Summit spend the full £100,000, there will then be 50,000 shares, of which they will have 10,000. That will give them one-fifth, or 20%, of the company.

But suppose I'm careful with my spending, and I only use £50,000. That will buy Summit 5,000 shares at £10 each.

At that point, there will be the original 40,000 shares, plus their 5,000, making a total of 45,000 shares. If they have 5,000 out of 45,000 shares, they own one-ninth of the company, or 11.11%. So they've only spent half their money, but they've got more than half their total slice of the company. And I'm sorry, but that's weird.

Bear in mind that I'm piecing all this together in retrospect. At the time, sitting in Summit's office in Broadgate, I'm utterly baffled by all these percentages and dilutions. And things are about to get worse…

Because I've made another elementary boo-boo. I've said I want to end up with a 60-20-20 split. That implies that Summit will still have one-fifth of the company *after* I've given a bunch of shares to my partners, colleagues and mates.

I now discover that this, too, will be done by dilution. So, just like the last time, Summit have to have one-quarter of the company, or 25%, *before* that dilution.

Thus they pay me £100,000 for 25% of the (once-)diluted company, which values it at £400,000.

Before they give me their money sho-biz.com must be worth £100,000 less than £400,000, i.e. £300,000. So let's do the £10-a-share deal again.

The company's worth £300,000. So we start with 30,000 shares, worth £10 each. Once again, I'm careful with the cash and I only spend £50,000. Once again, that money buys Summit 5,000 shares. So now there are 35,000 shares, of which they have 5,000, which is one-seventh … or 14.28% of the company.

Got that?

I'm kind of hoping that you haven't. As much as I like my prose to be comprehensible (and I have, believe me, laboured to make it so in this case), I'd be delighted to discover that you're scratching your head just like I was.

Because, as the afternoon drags on and dusk descends, I can't for the life of me see why it's not possible to do the basic, easily-understood deal I have been expecting, whereby a set amount of dosh is exchanged for a set amount of stock, at an unchanging rate. I'm cheesed off, too, by the apparent refusal or inability of my would-be helpers to grasp what I'm after, and even more resentful of the fact that I'm too bewildered to follow their calculations, or their patient explanations of why I've missed the point.

On the other hand, I am sure that this is down to my ignorance, rather than any trickery on their part. Plus, I have to bear in mind one massively salient fact: THEY WANT TO INVEST IN MY BUSINESS.

These guys are actually prepared to get out their chequebooks and scribble. As a matter of company business, Kit and Zac have to refer any deal to Summit's board. But since theirs is a private company and they have more than half the shares between them, that's a mere formality. If they say they'll pay up, they will.

And there's another thing. The guys at TVO handed over 20% of their company to Steve Thomas and his partner Steve Smith, just in exchange for the Steves' expertise, and their help – totally successful, as it turned out – in raising the first round of finance. But the bulk of that money was actually drummed up by EIS, who took a percentage of it (quite properly) as their fee.

Now, Kit and Zac are going to provide me with all the advice that the two Steves gave TVO, and they'll put sho-biz through their in-house legal and accounting facilities, thereby ensuring that my company is kept sweet with the VAT-man, the Revenue and Companies House. Finally, they'll raise money from the City without charging a fee, because it's in their own best interest as shareholders to get the maximum return on their investment.

Most important of all, I trust them. I first met Kit and Zac in my first term at Cambridge. I had a crush on Kit's girlfriend at the time, who is now my son Fred's godmother. We all met in a punk version of *Julius Caesar*, which was directed by Nigel Parker, who was in the same college as Kit and Zac… Yes, it's your standard tale of Oxbridge Mafia incest. But it means that any one of us would have to be exceptionally shitty, and indifferent to the opinion of our friends, to shaft any one of the others. That's not to say it can't happen. It's just a bit of a disincentive.

After the meeting is over and we're walking out into the chilly January evening, I turn to Kit and say, 'Thanks. I just want you to know that I really appreciate what you're doing for me.'

'There's no need to be grateful,' he says. 'We're not giving you money out of charity. We're doing it because we think we'll make a profit.'

'I know,' I reply. 'That's the best thing about it.'

We agree to proceed in principle. But before I sign on any dotted line, I want to confab with the other people who are involved in the project, just to see what they have to say. So on that we shake, and say goodbye for the weekend.

22–23 January

The weekend is spent talking to friends and sho-biz.com partners, debating what we should do. Neil thinks £100,000 is far too little. Mitch thinks it's more than generous. When I call the most sober, restrained and well-balanced person I know, who also works in the City, he tells me that I should make sure of getting everything I could ever need now: go for a minimum £250,000. I only wish I had the guts.

24 January

London W1: It's taken a week, several phone calls and a bunch of e-mails to organise a meeting with Paul Inman. Now I meet him and a colleague called Kelvyn Collins at The Attik's London HQ. On the phone, Paul Inman had a broad Yorkshire accent that made me think of flat caps, ferrets and pints of that evil, soapy beer they like to drink up North. In person, he's a small, shave-headed groover in all-black clothes and a close-cropped goatee beard.

His colleague, Kelvyn is also black-clad and short-bearded. He's also Australian, which is a major plus in my book: I like that Aussie insistence on giving a spade its proper name, and it seems consistent with the Huddersfield ethic that underpins the way The Attik works. Their business may be the purest pink candy-floss, but there's a good strong stick running down the middle.

We go to a small meeting-room (not the flash one with the lemonsin the table) and the first thing that strikes me is that Paul and Kelvyn make no attempt whatsoever to sell themselves to me. Instead, they want to know about sho-biz.com. I try to explain the way it's going to work: the fact that it's about old media as well as new media, that we'll be trading with other businesses as well as regular consumers, and it all begins to seem a tad confused. Then I see that there's a flip-chart mounted on a tripod in one corner of the room. 'Just let me draw it,' I say.

So I stand by the flip-chart and, without any planning or forethought, try to create a diagrammatic representation of the way that all of the constituent parts of sho-biz.com link up. I do it a bit like the site-map that Lucy created for me, with circles linked by arrows. And, as I draw it, the whole thing begins to make sense. There's a real coherence to the whole thing: you can see that it all fits together.

But that's only the start of it. As the meeting progresses, Kelvyn increasingly takes the role of Chief Interrogator. I've given him the skeleton of my business, but he wants to know about its body and soul. What's the point of sho-biz.com? What are its values? Forget the money, what are the other benefits people are going to get from the company?

As he asks, I answer, drawing more and more diagrams to illustrate what I'm talking about. Key words and concepts begin to emerge. 'Trust', for example. Artists have to trust sho-biz.com to represent them fairly. Media have to trust us to provide high-quality content. And customers have to trust us to tell the truth about the stars they love.

Those customers want to get as close to their heroes and heroines as they possibly can. So add 'intimacy'. But they also want to have a distinctive experience whenever they log on to sho-biz.com, so that requires 'personality'. And then, of course, there's the whole stardust factor. Even after all these years, I still get a buzz from what I call the laminate life – the freedom that an access-all-areas press-pass gives you. I love walking into a big, empty arena and seeing the stage waiting for its performers, then looking up at the lights and the sound-system as they hang in mid-air like a spaceship counting down to blast-off. I love watching the bustle of the roadies, the cool competence of the guys behind the mixing-desk and hysteria of the crowd when their gods walk on-stage. I know all the tricks, the deceits and the inadequacies of the artists. But I still get that buzz. That's what I want sho-biz.com to communicate. So bring in words like 'glamour', 'excitement' and the prime motive force that underlies it all: 'sex'.

Suddenly, we've got a really nice, positive list: entertainment, truth, trust, intimacy and glamour – all things from which people take encouragement and pleasure. So quite apart from all the money and technology, I feel as though there's something valuable in what sho-biz.com might stand for, and it makes me feel great.

I leave the meeting buzzing with enthusiasm and energy, incredibly impressed by the way that Kelvyn has managed to create such a positive mood. It gives me the feeling that The Attik's designers are going to be filled with positive thoughts when they get down to work. As the hours go by, I calm down and realise that this is a marketing trick: by concentrating on me, The Attik have managed to sell themselves. But it's a hell of a good trick. And that's impressive in itself.

25 January

Soho, London WC1: Today I saw Stacy Mann, an encounter whose signifi-cance I can only explain by telling the story of my encounter with the Superstar Actor – the failed attempt at global syndication that was my first feeble stab at what has turned into sho-biz.com.

Back at the beginning of March 1999, I approached a number of British film companies, asking them to give me star interviews for syndi-cation in Britain, Europe and the rest of the world. This, I told them, would save huge amounts of time, aggravation and money for all concerned. One or two got the point and so, by way of a trial run, I was given the chance to interview the Superstar Actor prior to the release of his next film, which was confidently expected to be a global smash. As is almost always the case these days, the Superstar's people insisted that he was to have copy approval over the text of any articles, which had to be read and approved by him prior to their sale to any user. This, of course, destroys any remote claim to independence on the part of the press, but in my experience approval isn't too hard to get, provided that you get your facts right, reproduce quotes accurately and avoid the sort of smart-alec cattiness that has become *de rigueur* among British profile-writers. Besides which, I'm in business: if I have to sign a contract to get a deal, just hand me the pen. I won't complain.

Not so long as I can actually do business, that is. But as the interview approached, it became increasingly clear that my cunning plan might have a fatal flaw. The actor's Leading Lady had a clause in her contract giving her approval, not just of any copy written about her, but of any magazine or newspaper title, anywhere in the world, proposing to run the article. It seemed that there were still a few publications, scattered around the globe, that did not treat her with the degree of fawning admi-ration she regarded as her due. These were therefore to be punished by her absence from her pages. It did not occur to the Leading Lady, or her advisers, that the best way of bringing publications onside was to give them great material, in the forcible absence of which they would feel obliged to be more negative than ever... but never mind.

The problem was that the Superstar had the same contract-clause too. So I couldn't just give my approved articles to my syndication agent for worldwide distribution, in case they got distributed to a title of which the Superstar disapproved. Not that he would ever know, or care: this was all a means by which his People could demonstrate their power by making everyone else's life as difficult as possible. No matter: the studio couldn't let me proceed as planned. Instead, they wanted to buy out my rights and distribute the articles themselves – a politically expedient, but completely pointless exercise since even the most spavined magazine won't buy a feature about a movie from the actual studio that's made it.

I only had one question: 'How much?'

'One thousand pounds,' they said.

'You must be joking. I was expecting to make ten times that much.'

'It's all we can afford.'

'Yeah … right,' I thought, considering the tens of millions of dollars that were about to be spent on this film. So then I came up with a counter-offer. 'How about this? I'll give you the European distribution rights to my feature for a lousy grand. But I've got to be able to make a few bob for myself, so how about you let me keep the UK and Australasia?'

So that's what we agreed. The approval conditions still applied, but I couldn't see a problem. The Superstar would go ballistic if I tried to sell his story as a sex-shock exclusive to the *Sun*. But I had no intention of doing that. In fact, I'd already placed the interview as the cover of a highly-respectable Sunday supplement, which would provide several colour pages, plus around six million readers. Ideal – as the studio agreed.

I went to the five-star London hotel where the movie junket was being held and had a perfectly civil interview with the Superstar. At the end, remembering his title-approval and wishing to be courteous, I told him that I was thinking of giving the article to the Sunday supplement. I thought he'd shrug his shoulders and say, 'Sounds all right to me.' Instead he glared at me and shouted, 'I thought everyone knew that I don't talk to the British press!' Then he stormed out of the room, followed by a flock of fluttering, chirruping PR babes, three or four of whom re-appeared about five minutes later and started berating me for being so beastly to the poor Superstar.

There then followed a week of telephone calls, faxes, e-mails and increasingly intense legal threats. What it boiled down to was this: the studio had minimal legal grounds for preventing me exercising my contractual right to sell my article in the UK (or anywhere else, come to that). On the other hand, they could deluge me in writs, just for the hell of it, and cause me untold grief. So, in the end, I sold the article to them for £2,500 – the same amount I would have been paid by the colour supplement – and then watched in amazement as the star who never spoke to the British press appeared in a major glossy magazine and another Sunday supplement.

What had happened was that the Superstar's Hollywood PRs had arranged these interviews without the studio's knowledge. When it looked as though I was going to complicate their arrangements, there was a risk that they might tell the studio: if you ever want to work with our boy again, you kill this Thomas guy's article. So the article had to go. The moral of the story – so far as I was concerned – was that the studio that makes a movie has far less power than the personal publicists of the stars within that movie. Any business-proposal which involves star interviews either has to win the approval of those publicists (unlikely), or go past them, direct to the artist's management.

Oh, and there's one other thing you should know … The Superstar read my profile of him, which went into his personal and professional contradictions in considerable detail, by no means all of it flattering. And he absolutely loved it – a fact he specified, in writing, on the signed copy of the article which he checked and then sent back to me. So I was paid £2,500 not to run an article that the star really liked (and had gone to the trouble of editing) in a magazine the studio really wanted. That's showbiz.

But this is sho-biz.com. And when the time came to seek advice about the way we should approach the movie industry, who better to ask than some of the other people who had been caught up in that disastrous shitstorm? A couple of days ago I called Stacy Mann, the studio executive with whom I had exchanged most of the post-interview correspondence. I bore her no ill-will for what had happened. She had been a victim of circumstance too. But I guess she might not have expected me to take that view, especially when the opening lines of our conversation went something like this…

'Hi Stacy, it's David Thomas. How are you?'

'Er … not too good, actually. We've all just been made redundant.'

'Great!'

'Sorry …?'

'No, well, not great that you've lost your job, obviously. But great because now you can come and work with me!'

Amazingly, she did not slam the phone down in disgust. Perhaps she was just too miserable to be so decisive. Her company had just been bought by an American mega-studio, and as is often the way, many of the staff were surplus to their new owner's requirements. Now, she said, she was thinking of setting up as an independent PR on her own account. So when I said that I might be in a position to become one of her clients, this was not entirely bad news.

This evening we meet for a kiss-and-make-up drink at the Groucho Club. Now that she is no longer feeling quite so warm towards her employers, Stacy can take a more detached view of the absurdity of all our earlier dealings. And although she can see a few practical difficulties that sho-biz.com is bound to confront – the implacable opposition of the Hollywood PRs, for a start, since they will rightly see us as a threat to their power – she likes the idea and wants to get involved. Since her contact-book contains virtually all of the London film-biz, plus a hefty chunk of Hollywood, plus the producers of virtually every TV show in Europe that uses film-related material or stars (and who might, therefore, be interested in buying packages from sho-biz.com), she can open doors all over the place. Not only that, she has years of experience in dealing with stars and keeping them sweet, a skill that will be vital once we actually start to organise interview and photo-sessions.

Best of all, she's a woman. And great though all the lads who have got involved with sho-biz thus far may be, it's about time we had a female presence in the company on this side of the Atlantic. Too much undiluted testosterone in any one place is a guaranteed recipe for disaster. (The same applies to an excess of oestrogen, too, by the way – but that's not my problem). So welcome aboard, Stacy Mann.

26 January

Back on the Kylie trail, I send another e-mail…

> Dear Mr Blamey,
> re: sho-biz.com

> Did you get the Artists and Managers document I mailed you last
> week? If so... what did you think?

> We're still mad keen to make Kylie the Official Goddess of sho-
> biz.com – and to honour her with the vast, golden piles of
> sacrificial booty that her deity demands – but we need to be able
> to start making plans, one way or the other, within the next week
> or two, because the Internet business works at warp-speed.

> Would it be possible for me to meet you in London next week to
> talk the whole thing over? ... David Thomas

27 January

I get a nice message from Blamey's London office. He hasn't received my
expensively printed, bound, packaged and posted document. He's not
really sure what on earth I'm talking about. So I send him a file by e-mail
instead. Bollocks to binding, typography and paper.

And now a philosophical question for the Twenty-first century, as
expressed in an e-mail by Adam Precious...

> Why does everybody you meet have a .com idea and then insist on
> telling it to you? Answer...because they can.

> All referees are blind and stupid, I can pick a better England team,
> why do people watch soap operas and talk about them to me in
> pubs...how many beans make five?

> Enuff....u get the point...those who can are getting on with it (IE: U)
> those who can't and shouldn't, stand in pubs and talk to me about
> it...My acid test is this...Tell them to forget about the Net – it
> doesn't exist. Now ask: if they had to sell their house and build
> their idea as a traditional business, would they do it?

In other words, if it isn't a proper, money-making idea in the real world, it won't be any better in the virtual one. He's right... that *is* the acid test.

28 January

After a flurry of phone-calls and e-mails, in which the mathematical permutations become ever-more convoluted, I settle with Summit at a maximum £125,000 for up to 25% of the company. But I resolve not to spend more than £100,000, even if it means taking nothing whatever for myself. I absolutely want to keep 80% for Mitch and myself before we start diluting it all for partners and investors.

30 January

It's VAT-return day again. This time, the quarterly turnover figure was down to £32,000. Still pretty good, but a 40% drop on the previous quarter, simply because of all the time I've spent working on sho-biz.com, instead of everything else. And even then, it hides the reality of the situation, because I'm always paid in arrears. A lot of that money refers to work done in September and October, before sho-biz.com got underway. These days, the amount of paid writing I do is way, way down from that.

31 January

Paul Inman mails me with his response to our meeting. Well, up to a point... His letter reads as follows...

I have attached the meeting notes (graphical) for you to look over.

So I open up the file and discover that the lads from The Attik have been so inspired by my artistic presentation that they have managed to reduce their entire message to a series of strange, almost mystical diagrams, covered with stars, arrows, elipses and cryptic messages. The total effect is like a series of runes or wizard's spells, as if I've got Gandalf for an art director.

For example… Half a page of A4 is covered with the formula,

.//NOW + NEW

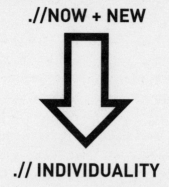

.// INDIVIDUALITY

On the next page (headlined './/PERSONALITY') there's a big blue balloon with SHO.BIZ.COM written around the top of it in capital letters. Inside the balloon it says, 'TRUTH PLEASURE ENTERTAINMENT SEX', and then around the bottom is the final word, 'PASSION'.

Underneath the blue balloon a vertical arrow, broken by the word 'DELIVERS' points down at a smaller white circle. Around the top of the circle it says, 'CONSUMER BENEFITS'. Inside the circle are the words, 'HONESTY TRUST RESPECT REALITY.'

So our passion and sex will deliver the customers' respect and reality. Fantastic. I feel like the women in the *Harry Met Sally* restaurant: just give me whatever they're having.

FEBRUARY

2 February

Berkhamsted, Herts: I take a day off from fretting over Kylie and head off round the M25 to Berkhamsted, where Adam Precious is waiting for me with a team of database boffins who can design all the software that will enable sho-biz.com to actually work. They turn out to be three blokes with beards and an unbearded lady (wife of Martin, the man with the shaggiest facial growth of all), who have devoted their lives to a world of which I know absolutely naff-all.

A keen student of facial hair, keen to determine the semiotic significance of beards, would note that the techies have very different growth-patterns – both visually, and in volume terms – from the designers at The Attik. The arty-boys use their sharply-trimmed fuzz to signify their awareness of aesthetics and the precision with which they attend to every detail of their work. But a boffiny beard like Martin's shouts that its owner is simply too bloody brainy to bother with such mundanities as buying a Gillette Mach 3.

This, then, is the hidden language of signs. And the techies have another, verbal language, too — one spoken with passionate intensity, enthusiasm and even (to judge by the chortles with which some remarks are both delivered and received) wit. We thus have an extraordinary meeting at which I define my requirements in basic, civilian English, while they reply in fluent Weblish.

The boffin who's been charged with describing their business to me is called Steve. He takes me through a database he's been creating for a rail company which enables a computer system to track whether people undertaking vital maintenance are qualified to do so. This, he says, is basically just the same, in databasing terms, as creating a system which can handle vast amounts of linked bits of trivia about the world's best-loved entertainers. He then goes into some of the principles upon which he and his colleagues have founded their business.

As far as I can understand – and I've probably got this 100% wrong – they've abandoned the Java environment for a purely HTML-based system, which can attain a remarkable degree of in-session flexibility and stickiness without any need for cookies. At one point boffins start arguing among themselves over the best way of solving some hypothetical problem that is bound to be caused by my database requirements. Adam Precious steps in decisively to restore order. 'Just go VPN over ADSL and you're done!' he proclaims, quelling all arguments with one flex of his mighty brain. To which I can only say, 'Absolutely, old boy. Just VPN your ADSL and you'll never go too far wrong.'

Funnily enough, there's one part of that sentence I vaguely recognise. If I remember rightly from my chats with John Hyslop, ADSL is one of those high-speed phone-lines that makes the Internet work at warp-speed (even if I can't remember what on earth A, D, S or L stand for) … Perhaps one day I'll be able to work out what on God's earth the rest of the boffins' conversation was about.

In the meantime, I'll just have to accept my inability to understand a word these people say as some sort of proof of their brilliance. This, of course, leaves me at a bit of a disadvantage, because they could be speaking total cyber-crap and I'd never really know. Which, as it turns out, is quite a relevant observation. Because after the bearded ones have done their dog-and-pony show, we all go off for lunch at a nearby Café Rouge, where Adam and the lads start yakking about something they call 'Six-six-six'.

This is the way that Internet security experts categorise sites, and it comes from the way they get business. Basically, they rely on a combination of 'ethical hacking' – in which you break into someone else's system… but in a good way – and blackmail. The first thing your average e-millionaire knows about any of this is when he gets a call from someone he's never met in his life who says, 'I've just hacked into your website. I've not done anything. But the next guy who gets in may not be so decent. So if you want to stay safe, you'd better let me fix everything. Here's my estimate.'

If you're one of these ethical shakedown artists, a six-minute site is one that's so easy to hack into you give up after six minutes, get on a plane to the person that owns it, and start fixing it a.s.a.p. A six-hour site is one that resists all attempts at hacking for six hours – and if you haven't got to it by then, neither you nor anyone else ever will. And six days is how long it takes to document all the holes in your average six-minute site.

Adam describes a conversation he heard about recently. It took place between a British-based Internet security expert and the boss of a US-based financial website, which is planning a billion-dollar flotation later this year. The Brit rang up the company's CEO, introduced himself, and explained that he and the lads had just hacked into the website in about two minutes flat. He then began describing exactly what this meant in terms of what other, less ethical hackers could do. As he talked, he suddenly noticed that the line seemed to be getting crackly and the signal was weak. The American CEO told him why this was: he was already en route to the airport. He'd be landing at Heathrow first thing tomorrow morning.

As we're talking, there's a document going round the table, covered in lines of script that make perfect sense to everyone there but me. It's the account of a hack on a brand-new online bank conducted without the bank's knowledge. All the way through the document someone's made little markings which indicate where the bank can be penetrated, a fact which leads to an in-depth discussion of all the various ways that some-one lying on a beach in the Cayman Islands (handy because it is both tropical and stuffed with accommodating banks) could execute the biggest theft in banking history, armed only with a bright mind, a modem and a laptop computer.

Method One – let's call it Crash and Burn – involves hacking into the operating systems of a financial website, via its 'ports', or electronic points-of-entry. Most of them are left permanently open, just as if your neighbourhood NatWest or Barclays (assuming you've still got one), kept its doors ajar, 24 hours a day. Having got in, you make the system crash – a doddle, apparently, to a competent hacker. As the institution tries to re-boot, it presents all its code, piece-by-piece, to the watching hacker. He can (a) use the code to get into the system, (b) rewrite the code with new instructions (e.g. transferring tiny, but regular amounts of money in his direction), or (c) corrupt the code so that it becomes impossible to re-open the site. Ever.

Method Two – which has actually been attempted in the USA (according to cyber-community conspiracy theorists, the guy who did it was silenced by the FBI without the bother of a publicity-attracting trial) – is Crash and Sell. This time, you begin by buying large numbers of 'put' options on a given institution – in other words, you buy the right to sell its stock at a given point in the future for the price at which it is currently trading. So you're betting the price will go down. You then crash the institution and keep it out of business long enough for its shares to tumble. On the given date you buy the optioned stock at the new, low price and sell at the old, high price... hey presto! You're rich.

Method Three is the False Front. Hack into the site and copy the opening pages, particularly those which ask customers to give their names and passwords. Place your copied pages on-line, but in front of the real bank. When punters come online, believing that they are talking to their bank, they're actually talking to you. As soon as they have entered their details, return them to the bank itself, allowing them to continue perfectly normally. Except, of course, that you have now gained access to their accounts. And you have done this from the bar at the Hotel Tropicana.

What makes these forms of theft so peculiarly beguiling is that they can be carried out without anyone at the top of the relevant banks having the first idea of what's going on. Security at conventional banks – in the old-fashioned physical environment known to Net-heads as 'meatworld' – is relatively straightforward, because anyone can grasp the concept of a great big safe, secured by the trickiest possible lock. But you can pretty well guarantee that your average bank-boss has no more idea about the finer points of computer-technology than I do. So he has no way of knowing whether his online security is any good or not. Just like me, he has to rely on guys with beards.

Mind you, that's his problem, not mine. As I drive away from Berkhamsted, I'm comforted by one warm thought: if all else goes wrong and sho-biz.com crashes to earth like a shot pheasant, I can always go into the online robbery business. So if you happen to be in the Caymans and you see this balding bloke, sitting at the bar with a glowing Powerbook and a furtive expression… that'll be me.

4 February

Fulham, London SW6: I finally get to meet the elusive Terry Blamey. He's got an office above a shop on the New King's Road. There are pictures on the wall of Kylie and his other big client … Danii Minogue. If you're in the market for a Minogue, Terry Blamey's your man.

I spend the best part of two hours giving him my most persuasive, even impassioned account of why sho-biz.com could transform the lives of entertainers around the world. And he gets it.

Blamey completely understands why artists would benefit by reducing the number of interviews they give, improving and controlling the quality and, of course, making large amounts of dosh. As far as he's concerned, I can count on Kylie to participate once the business is up and running. She's just finishing her new album and will jump at the idea of promoting it in one fell swoop, rather than endless individual sessions. But he's not so sure about whether she'll do anything before it launches. In the first place, she never works on pilots. And in the second, she doesn't do endorsements. So it might be tough to persuade her to endorse a pilot.

Fair enough, I say, but it's not entirely a pilot. After all, I really will be interviewing Kylie; we will be taking photographs, and – irrespective of the state of the website – that material can genuinely be syndicated to newspapers and magazines around the world. Plus, I'm not asking Kylie to make any public statements about sho-biz.com. I just want her to take part in what we do.

Blamey says he'll talk to Kylie. He sounds optimistic that she is open to persuasion and he hopes to have news, one way or the other, by the end of the following week, when Kylie is due to be back in England after her New Year break. I leave his office feeling absolutely chuffed to bits. I'm going to spend large amounts of other people's money, solely in order to buy time with Kylie Minogue. Isn't big business great?

7 February

I get a call from a PR who tells me about a new Net service called Homechoice, which will be offering TV programmes and films, via high-speed ADSL lines provided by British Telecom. Without really thinking, I reply (sceptically), 'Yeah? Can you do real-time, full-screen video-streaming down a 512K line? Or are they letting you have the full 2 Megs?'

The PR is stumped. He has no idea what I'm talking about. So I translate the sentence for him: 'Can you offer video-on-demand services down telephone lines at the 512 Kilobits-per-second speed at which BT are apparently saying they'll operate their ADSL lines? Or do you need the 2-Meg speed of which the lines are actually capable in order to download massive M-Peg files onto the caches in your set-top boxes?'

As the PR goes, 'Err...' I laugh: 'I can't believe I just said that.'

My time with Adam Precious and his bearded tech-men is obviously paying off. Just before the PR called, I'd been chatting to Adam about the work his lads are going to do on the sho-biz site. We'd been casually discussing XML, hyperlinks and scroll-down dialogue boxes – all concepts that were entirely foreign to me only weeks ago. Somewhere along the line I've started to learn a whole new language. 'Moi, je parle weblish.'

Amazing. Here I am, just past my 41st birthday, my hair is leaving my scalp faster than refugees quitting Kosovo ... and a whole new world is opening up in front of me.

The old world, however, chunters on as before. Another day, another e-mail to Terry Blamey...

> Dear Terry ...

> Thanks for giving me so much time on Friday. I hope I didn't rant on too much... but I feel very passionate about this project, and I am absolutely convinced that Kylie would be perfect for it.

> I take the point, of course, that she is uneasy about endorsement. So perhaps I can find two better words for what we have in mind, which are...

> 1. Consultancy, and
> 2. Participation

> I am not looking for a pretty face to parrot advertising slogans written by someone else. I want someone who can contribute intelligence and experience, who can give sho-biz.com advice about what artists want, what they need, what they will and will not do, how to make them happy, etc. That's why Kylie's top of my list and why I am, for the time being, holding off making any other arrangements.

> As I said on Friday, this is strictly a case of, 'Your mission, should you choose to accept it ...' We can, if you wish, restrict things to a paid-for interview and photo-session. But I would hope that we could come up with a broader agreement that would interest Min[*], the intelligent, professional woman, as well as Kylie, the celebrity.

> Finally there's straightforward self-interest. You heard what I have in mind. We both know what it could be worth if everything pans out as planned. I know that other people have done the same sums, because when I left your office I got a call from the multi-national electronics company that is supporting sho-biz.com

---

[*] *(Celebrity Trivia Note: 'Min' is what her friends call Kylie.)*

confirming their willingness to provide all the super-computer and server equipment the site will need (millions of pounds worth), plus database development, plus joint marketing, in exchange for a stock and royalty deal.

> **I'm offering Kylie stock ... and all she has to do is turn up!**

> **Speak to you at the end of the week ...**

11 February

Lastminute.com just announced plans for its flotation. Analysts estimate that the company will be valued at around £400 million. That, apparently, will make its founders, Brent Hoberman and Martha Lane-Fox, worth around £80 million. There were so many hits on the Lastminute site from would-be investors trying to register their interest that the servers couldn't cope. All that people saw was a cartoon of a 'maintenance monkey' carrying a wrench. They should have given the little chimp a wheelbarrow. To cart away all the money.

Meanwhile, back at sho-biz.com, it's now the end of the week, so I call Terry Blamey. His assistant tells me that he's unavailable and Kylie isn't yet back in the country, so there's no news. I send him another long e-mail. On reflection, this may be a mistake. The poor man is being buried under my manic enthusiasm. But that's what happens when you're starting something with nothing at all but your own nervous energy. The only way you can keep going is by hyping yourself up to a lunatic level of intensity. So you're bound to lose all sense of proportion. It's just a pain in the arse for everyone else, that's all.

12 February

The publicity blitz has got under way for Lastminute. Martha Lane-Fox has been listed as one of Britain's Top Ten dates, which figures. She's 27, she's the great-granddaughter of the Sixth Marquess of Anglesey, she's about to be worth £20 million and she is, according to one salivating City Page profile, 'a young blonde in a fake leopardskin coat.'

But you know what I don't understand? Last year, Lastminute turned over £195,000. Now it's worth £400 million. Well, my personal turnover was about 60% of Lastminute's. So why aren't I worth £240 million?

I reckon I'm going about this all the wrong way. I should scrap this whole sho-biz lark, change my name to davidthomas.com and float myself on the Stock Market. Maybe then I'd be one of the Top Ten dates too.

15 February

Amazing news. Terry Blamey calls to say that he's spoken to Kylie and she's interested in taking things further. Right now, they're finishing off her new album. But why don't I get in touch with the press office at her record company, speak to its boss, and sort out the details with him?

So I call the press office and the guy there is – not surprisingly – a bit cool about the idea. The last thing he wants is someone coming in and stealing Kylie's media activity from under his nose. So I make very conciliatory noises, say we're only starting up, wouldn't dream of interfering with what he's doing, just want to add to the value of it all, etc. Then I promise to send him a brief outline of what sho-biz.com is going to do.

He's still not exactly dancing in the street with delight. But so what? Terry Blamey's the man who counts. And he's on my side.

16 February

Lucien King was recommended to me by Sam Houser at Rockstar Games, who said he'd be just the ticket if I was looking for someone to help me with sho-biz.com. Lucien – who, like Sam and Terry Donovan, is 28 years old – had been one of the games-making gang at BMG Interactive before Rockstar took it over, and he'd stayed with the new company long enough to work on the creation of rockstargames.com. So he knows all about new technology. More importantly, says Houser, he's not just seriously intelligent, he's trustworthy, honest, reliable... his morals are all in the right place.

I call up Lucien and he certainly seems like a decent human being. So I fill him in a bit on the great Kylie hunt and ask him to suggest a few things we could do online if we were ever to get a proper interview with her. Let's see if he's as bright as Houser claims. It would be handy to have someone working on this project who was actually under forty...

17 February

West Sussex and Paris, France: At 11.14, I get an e-mail from Lucien King listing fifteen Kylie-related ideas, plus a series of general thoughts, as follows...

> One liner: as long as we target clearly defined groups of interest, and gain access to the people and things that interest each target group, we can tailor cool products (digital or otherwise) to satisfy them and make them pay for the things they learn and the fun they have.

> Moving forward we can work on how to allow each 'interview' or period with a star to provide info and material and opinion on the broadest possible, but relevant set of themes: food, music, travel, news, family and friends, pets, fitness, media, politics, you name it. then products can be packaged and cross-promoted by sector.

> I feel we should make the most of crossing traditional media boundaries (famous movie star on music, famous music star on Ibiza's rave scene, famous cook feeding favourite movie star etc.)

> We should move with the seasons.

> We should target international audiences with particular attention to international preferences and idiosyncrasies.

> We should cater for and speak to the widest range of age-groups. The kids are the future.

> We should look to please male and female (duh, right Lucien, less of the obvious).

> We should think up some cracking anti-perv devices.

> Looking forward to structuring this and speaking with you in greater depth on Monday.

> Let me know if this is total roobish.

> L.

I reckon that's the e-mail of someone who has got the point fast. So I'm in an excellent mood as I drive off to Gatwick for the BA flight to Paris. I'm going to interview Mandy Moore. She's the latest American pop-chick – the next one in line after Britney Spears and Christina Aguilera. On the way in from the airport, en route to the hotel, I pass endless billboards for Lastminute.com. Even France is succumbing to the power of Brent and Martha. But shouldn't that be *Derniereminute.com* ?

When I get to the Hotel California (yes, really), Mandy's busy, so I chat to her manager, Jon Leshay, who fills me in on his client's schedule. Today, Thursday, 17 February, is her 63rd consecutive working day without out a break. A couple of days ago she was in New York, shooting three TV commercials and a print campaign for Neutrogena skincare products. She flew into Paris Wednesday morning, did interviews with European press and TV all day, started again first thing the next morning.

By 4.30 she's ready for the three British media teams who've been flown out to meet her. There's a quick interview with *Top of the Pops* magazine, then a session with a cable TV music channel called The Box. They set up their gear in the brasserie. Mandy appears: tall, blonde, catwalk-slim, dressed in black vintage jeans. She chats. She sings unaccompanied – a strong voice and perfectly in tune. At the end of the interview they ask her to do a quick promo for the station – something all-American. Mandy nods. Then, seconds before the camera rolls, one of the production assistants mutters, not very distinctly, that the promo has to include the Box's slogan, 'smash hits you control.'

Mandy doesn't miss a beat. She just turns to the camera, smiles sweetly, and perkily announces, 'Hi, I'm Mandy Moore, all the way from Orlando Florida. And this is The Box … smash hits *you* control.'

It's perfect, first take. There's a brief interlude while Mandy walks up and down the street outside the hotel, so the camera can record that she was actually in Paris. She comes back inside and does our photo-session, then the interview that follows. It wraps by about 7.00. We journalists all go out to get smashed at Sony Music's expense at Man Ray – the vast basement restaurant owned by Mick Hucknall, Johnny Depp and assorted other glitterati. Mandy can't join us, because she has two more photo-sessions for Continental publications. Tomorrow it will be the same, all day. Then she'll be driven to the airport and put on a plane to New Zealand, from where she'll fly to Australia before making a whis-tle-stop tour of the Far East.

Mandy tells me she's hoping to get a break Down Under: 'Our hotel's right on the beach, I'm going to find some time to wind down.'

Oh no she isn't. While she's being photographed for my article, Jon Leshay takes a call from the States. She's been picked to sing a song on the new Kevin Costner movie. She's got to make a late-night call to the States to sing down the line so the composers of the song – which hasn't been written yet – can judge which key will suit her best. They'll knock something up and e-mail it to her in Australia, where she'll record the track between interviews. Leshay whispers to me, 'Mandy doesn't know this yet.'

Once she's finished the single, she's got more promo to do in the Far East and Japan, followed by work at home in the States and a return to Europe in time for the release of her first single 'Candy' in the spring.

Mandy Moore will turn sixteen on 10 April. If I needed one good reason why sho-biz.com is going to change artists' lives out of all recog-nition, she would be it. We could save her an enormous amount of aggra-vation, simply by syndicating material to all the people who are now getting it for themselves. But since she's still schlepping round the world, I pass one piece of advice to her, just before I go to dine and she goes back to work. It was first given to my mum – a Liberal politician – by an American senator called Bob Packwood. He told her that there was only one thing to remember when you were on the campaign trail: 'Whatever you do, never turn down an opportunity to eat, sleep or piss.' Senator Packwood was later caught up in a particularly messy sexual harassment case, so I guess there may have been a few other things he did at every opportunity, too. But, with due deference to Mandy's tender years, I leave out that bit ... and I don't say 'piss', either. 'Use the bathroom' will do just fine.

18 February

Brent Cross, London: I get picked up at Gatwick by a limo from Homechoice, the video-on-demand TV service. I've got an 11.00 meeting with its founder, Simon Hochhauser. The company operates out of a grim industrial estate just opposite the Brent Cross shopping centre. Hochhauser is 47. He has an enthusiastic but unassuming, almost gentle manner and a round face that makes him look a bit like Elton John, only with natural brown hair instead of an orange wig. Within half an hour of meeting him it becomes perfectly obvious to me that he is about to become fantastically, mind-bendingly, wallet-droppingly rich.

Hochhauser comes from a family of musical impresarios, but he trained as a scientist. He got a doctorate in optical fibre physics at Imperial College, but by the end of the course he'd had it with academia, so he went off to Wall Street to make some money. He came back to London in 1983 and was hired by Jacob Rothschild to run a venture capital fund, backing science-based start-ups – anything from cellular phones to biotechnology. So by the end of the Eighties, he's about as clued-up on finance and new technology as it's possible to be.

Then, one day in 1990, Hochhauser's looking at his CD collection. He's got hundreds of classical discs, but that's still only a tiny fraction of what is actually available. He starts thinking that it would be wonderful if he could somehow access and listen to all the music that he doesn't own – just order it up whenever he wanted from some sort of central library. But it takes until 1992 before the technology is available to give him the slightest chance of turning his idea into an actual business.

And now a quick historical sidetrack... Back in the late '80s/early '90s, the big idea in new media was the so-called Information Superhighway. This was to the Internet what herpes was to AIDS – the massive public hype that disappears completely when an even bigger hype comes along. The point about the Information Superhighway was that it was inspired by the arrival of fibre-optic cable, which enabled vast amounts of information to be pumped into consumer's homes through upgraded telephone lines. People quickly realised that this would enable TV companies to offer a massive choice of programming, all of which could be ordered à la carte by viewers as and when they pleased, along with all sorts of shopping options, which could be controlled from a set-top box on TV sets.

This, they decided, was how the future would work. So a bunch of huge American media companies set up trial systems in the States, and BT wired up Chelmsford, or Colchester or some such place with all the superfast cable that would – as John Hyslop told me a couple of months ago – have made the UK a world leader in telecoms if BT and the government hadn't had a spat which made BT pull out of the whole thing in a huff. But (and this seems to me to be a point worth noting) no one could make any money out of it all. Hundreds of millions were spent dragging punters into the Twenty-first century … and the punters decided to stay where they were. Then the Internet came along and everyone forgot about the Information Superhighway. A nagging little voice at the back of my mind wonders whether it doesn't have a lesson for us all today.

Anyway, that's enough history, back to Simon Hochhauser …

He spends four years putting together a team that creates compression and communications software that will enable him to send audio and video signals down high-speed telephone wires. He knows it all has to go down landlines because satellites will never be big enough to handle all the bandwidth required by millions of consumers simultaneously accessing their own private programmes: even with Sky Digital you mostly have to watch what they give you, when they give you it.

Hochhauser is funding the idea with the money he'd saved during his banking years. The years pass and every bit of it is spent, but he keeps going. 'I'd seen how to build businesses,' he tells me. 'You have to stick with what you do for as long as it makes sense. If you feel you have something and people are responding positively, you have to stick with it. People always tell you why things can't work. I'm telling you that it can.'

His faith pays off. In the last three or four years he's begun to attract some serious investors. In 1999 alone, he raised £60 million from people like Bernard Arnault, the French tycoon who runs Moet Hennessey-

Louis Vuitton, and the former Foreign Secretary David Owen. He'd have got a few million from me, too, if I had them, because as soon as Hochhauser describes what the years of research have bought him, the whole play begins to make serious sense.

When I was talking to the Homechoice PR, I'd assumed that the system worked like a conventional download, just at a much higher speed. In other words, you pull down a file from the Internet, store it on your hard-drive and use it as and when you need. But that's not it at all...

Homechoice has the rights to 700 movies. It will have 3,000 by the end of the year and 5,000 by the end of 2001. You rent a movie just like you would a video from Blockbuster: a first-run hit costs around £3.00 a day, but it's much less for oldies. You can also watch TV shows – *Walking With Dinosaurs* will go out at £1 an episode – sports or music vids, which are free. Plus there are all the regular TV channels to access as and when you want.

When you sign up to Homechoice, which costs £12.99 a month for the full service, you get an ADSL line free. BT are proposing to charge users £49.00 a month for the line, all by itself, so this has to rank as the deal of the century. Since Homechoice are paying the difference, they must either be reckoning to drive BT's price way, way down, or to make up the gap from the money punters spend renting videos... or both. And the chances are that they will, because the service is incredible.

When you order a video, you are effectively buying the right to access it for 24 hours. At the end of that period, the access just shuts off, so it's goodbye to the fortunes we all pay for videos we forget to take back on the day they're due. In the meantime, you can play it any time you want and it behaves just like a tape – or, to be pedantic, like a DVD. You can fast-forward, rewind and pause. You can even go straight to a specific point in the movie.

And, of course, it doesn't have to be a movie. If you've got people coming to dinner and you need to make a recipe, you can just order up a Delia Smith episode and follow the blessed Delia through – say – her Oven-Baked Chicken With Garlic and Parmesan from the Summer Collection, stopping to check her every move as you go. To the customer, it feels like you're controlling something that is actually in your TV's set-top box. In fact, you're sending instructions down the line to a

Homechoice server, which sends the appropriate signal straight back. To show me how it works, Hochhauser leads me into a chilled warehouse at the back of the Homechoice HQ. It's mostly empty at the moment, except for a couple of racks of servers. Pretty soon, though, it will be filled with identical racks, and there'll be other rooms just like it all over the country, zinging programmes back and forth to the three million homes he's hoping to have signed-up within the next five years.

When we get back to his office, Hochhauser excuses himself for a moment to go and talk to a colleague who's demanding his attention. While he's gone I get out my notebook and do some quick calculations…

Say he's got three million subscribers and they each pay £15 a month, which is less than one first-run film a month on top of their subscription. That comes to £540 million per annum.

But let's get real here. If you can get the latest vids just by pressing a button, you're going to do that more than once a month. If every house spends £20 a month, that makes £720 million pa revenue to Homechoice. If they all spend £30, Homechoice generates a turnover of £1.08 billion.

Well now… Lastminute turns over a few hundred grand, if it's lucky, and all the City analysts reckon it's worth £400 million. Last week, the auction site QXL – the one started by the journalist Tim Jackson – reported third-quarter revenues down from £1.9 million to £1.5 million. It said its losses rose from £8.1 million to £10.7 million last year… and the market responded by sending its shares up 115p to £14.28, valuing the company at £1.625 billion, which is more than seven times its valuation when it floated last October.

These companies are losing big money on tiny turnovers and they're reckoned to be worth nine or ten-figure sums. On that basis, if Homechoice generates a billion quid per annum it's going to be another Microsoft.

I make two resolutions. One: I've got to find a way of buying some of this action. And two: I've got to get into business with Simon Hochhauser. When he comes back to the room I ask him if he can spare me five more minutes, so I can tell him about my business. He says yes, so I give him an instant sho-biz.com pitch, emphasising what a fantastic fit there could be between all his films and music videos and all my celebrity interviews, information and trivia. You could wrap all my stuff around his stuff, like the extra tracks they have on a DVD. Punters could see the movie… then check out the exclusive chat with its star. Or they could click on the babe… and buy her dress. The possibilities are endless.

Hochhauser sees them too. 'Send me a business-plan,' he says, and agrees we must meet again.

Yessss!

19 February

The Attik have appointed a project-manager on the sho-biz.com design-job. She's called Liz Walton – so that's another woman on the sho-biz case – and she seems to be pretty together. We've been talking over the past week or so, as a result of which she's now come up with a site-map for sho-biz.com and a schedule detailing the development of the dummy site. It should be complete by 31 March, leaving us with plenty of time to sort out any glitches before going to the City in mid-April. We'll send out the business plan just before Easter, with a view to having a series of presentations to investors in the weeks afterwards: we should get the money by June.

The Attik's estimate comes to £25,000 for the whole job, but that includes around £5,000 for corrections and changes. Liz's calculations presume that an Attik graphic designer is charged out at £1,000 a day, while the HTML programmer who turns those designs into an actual working website costs £1,200. It only confirms my suspicion that I've gone for the wrong job. As a writer, right at the top of my profession, I can just about make £500 a day, if I'm working flat-out, in a really good year. But I could buy virtually any freelance journalist in London for the promise of a guaranteed £300 a day. So an experienced scribe costs a quarter as much as a 22-year-old HTML programmer. And they wonder why kids don't bother to learn how to read or write…

Still, there's no arguing with the market. The Internet rules and anyone who works within it can charge top-dollar. The Attik's rates, amazingly, aren't any higher than any other blue-chip company. I accept Liz Walton's estimate, with the caveat that I have every intention of being extremely detailed in my specifications of what I want, so I very much doubt that we'll be spending the cash she's set aside for corrections.

In the meantime, The Attik need a down-payment to pay for their first designs, which are going to cost £7,500. So I agree to send them £3,750, plus VAT, just as soon as my corporate bank-account has been set up, which should be any day now.

21 February

Lucien King comes down to Sussex for our first face-to-face encounter. He's easy to spot, getting off the London train at Chichester Station – he's the only shaven-headed, parka-wearing dude, shambling along the platform with his undone trainer-laces trailing along the ground. Once we get home, there's a minor hitch when he says no to virtually all of the lunch I had thoughtfully (I reckoned) bought that morning at M&S. It takes me a while to twig that this is not because he's rude, or dismissive of my efforts, but because I've been loading up on cold ham and smoked salmon and Lucien is a vegetarian. Smart work, David.

After I've eaten and Lucien has sat there politely nibbling the cold lentils and bean salad that happened to be lurking around in the back of the fridge, we get down to work, talking about the site and how it should be organised. As with the Attik meeting, the easiest means of doing this is graphically. But I don't have a flip-chart or white-board, so the only way we can get a big enough expanse of paper is to find an old roll of Laura Ashley wallpaper and scrawl site-architecture diagrams on the back of that.

Lucien seems remarkably laid-back, given the rampant absurdity of the situation. But as we talk, there's something that's bugging me. I've always been fascinated by accents and used to drive Clare nuts (until she made it plain that her continued participation in our relationship was conditional on me stopping at once) by imitating anyone on TV who had any sort of interesting voice. It may be something to do with a writer's interest in and sensitivity to words, their meaning, and the way that they are delivered. But I can come away from an interview with a pitch-perfect sense of the way my interviewee sounded, yet absolutely no recollection of the details of their appearance. As a result I have to force myself to take notes of everything I see before I begin a conversation (I frequently take a Polaroid, too, by way of insurance), because I know that once we start talking I'll be all ears and no eyes.

Now I'm trying to figure out the origins of Lucien King's voice. If I had to place it anywhere in the United Kingdom, I'd say middle-class lowland Scots. But there's a slightly sing-song intonation to it, mixed (as you might expect, given his street-credible career) with a smattering of white homeboy slang: this is a man who can call you 'Dude' without the slightest self-consciousness.

So I ask him, 'Look, I know this is a weird question, but I'm trying to figure out your accent… Where does it come from?'

Lucien looks at me: 'Is that a way of asking where I come from?'

'Yeah …I guess.'

'My father's Scottish, my mother's Indian.'

Right. That explains the intonation, then. My journalistic curiosity has been satisfied. We get back to talking about sho-biz.com till it's time for Lucien to take the train back to London. When I get back from the station I ask Clare what she made of him. I'm desperate to avoid another Chris Vincent debacle.

'I like him,' she says. That, believe me, is one hell of a recommendation.

22 February

Lucien sends me an e-mail containing what he calls his 'proposition commerciale' – as I shall discover, when in doubt, he slips into French. He's not asking for an outrageous amount of money or stock, so that shouldn't be a problem. With his terms comes a CV, detailing his professional and academic history.

He has ten Grade A O-Levels, four Grade A A-Levels, two Grade 1 S-Levels and a Special/1st Class degree. That essentially means that the examiners couldn't decide whether to fail him or hail him. They simply didn't know whether he was a lunatic or a genius.

When I look at the names of the establishments that taught young Lucien en route to his O's, A's and S's I laugh out loud. Funky-Parka-Trainer Boy went to school at Winchester College before taking his degree at King's Cambridge. I love the idea of him, Houser and Donovan – a Whykamist and two Paulines, with about four hundred grand's worth of private education between the three of them – creating their hardcore games company, whose two chief titles are a psychotically violent, urban-nightmare shoot-'em-up and a skateboard game done in conjunction with *Thrasher* magazine, which writes about boards and thrash metal music. Still, he can't be all bad if he's a Kingsman. After all, it was my college, too.

24 February

The paperwork is complete. I am now the proud owner of 33,750 shares in Sho-Corp Ltd, the parent company of sho-biz.com. Mitch has 3,750. Out of the goodness of our hearts we have – as the board minutes reveal – agreed to dilute our shareholding by issuing a further 6,250 shares, each valued at £10, which have been bought by Summit Group Ltd. The total purchase price of £62,500 constitutes the working capital which will pay for the first phase of sho-biz.com's development. We can, if we wish, issue a further 6,250 shares – again at £10 apiece – which Summit will buy. This would leave me with 33,750, Mitch with 3,750 and Summit with 12,500 (i.e. one-quarter of the 50,000 shares issued up to that point). I understand these maths because, as of now, I am a proper, grown-up businessman. Allegedly.

28 February

Barnet and Berkhamsted: I finally clap eyes on the other two members of the TVO quartet as Neil Storey and I go to Barnet to meet Malcom Messiter and John Lenehan. Messiter lives in a small, modern, semi-detached house in Barnet. It doesn't look much like the home of a man who's about to become a multi-squillionaire. But the Net seems to be some sort of real-life fairy godmother that comes up to people in the most unlikely circumstances, taps them on the shoulder and says, 'You shall go to the ball.' Or, in this case, the Footsie.

Messiter does most of the talking (which, I suspect, is par for the course). He's big, burly and bubbling up with a sort of hearty, jovial energy that seems to mask a fair amount of inner nervousness. At the back of the house he's got what was once a garage, but is now an office packed with computers and electronic keyboards. This is where the

Virtual Orchestra was born, and Messiter begins the story of how that happened by popping into his office and returning with a CD. On it's cover there's a lurid picture of a palm tree swaying in front of a purple sunset – like the wall decorations of the Tiki-Tiki lounge in a cheesey old hotel, somewhere like Akron, Ohio or Des Moines, Iowa (in whose bus-station I was propositioned for a little rent-boy action – me being the prospective rent-boy – at 4.00 am one morning in 1977… but that's a whole other story).

Anyway, Messiter puts this CD on his serious hi-fi-buff's stereo, plays a track called 'The Road to Provence', and bugger me if it isn't a really artificial bit of muzak that sounds like the backing-track to the kind of Rothman's ads they used to show at cinemas – the ones with a male-model dressed as an airline pilot driving down the French Riviera with some hot-panted tottie looking on admiringly as he sucked on his gasper. This is not what I have expected at all, since the whole point of the Virtual Orchestra is supposed to be its ability to simulate the sound of a mighty orchestra with uncanny accuracy, and I don't do a totally A-plus job of disguising my disappointment.

Messiter doesn't seem too bothered. Having established that the track he's just played me was the very first thing he and John Lenehan ever did together, back in 1997, he leads us all into the garage-cum-office, rummages around his computers and finds another CD, which he slides into a PC that's been wired up to some heavy-duty speakers. This, he says, is a little something he and John have just completed. It's Tchaikovsky's First Piano Concerto… and it's absolutely incredible. You'd swear the room was filled with blokes in tail-coats plinking, fiddling and tooting for all they were worth. Suddenly the gobsmack-factor has come right back into play. These guys are going to make a packet.

Which is just as well, given how totally skint they've been. Because what I haven't realised until now was that everyone involved in the TVO had been just as stoney as Neil Storey. 'We were all being terribly British,' says Messiter. 'I was living on home-made bread and lentils. There were a lot of John Mills-type stiff-upper-lips.'

Like Neil, he'd had it all and then lost it, because as well as being a world-class oboeist, he'd also been a successful software entrepreneur until both his business and his marriage simultaneously fell apart in the late 1990s. By the summer of 1999, having sold his S-Class V8 Mercedes – 'Yeah, the car I got rid of was a Mercedes, too,' Neil inserts at this point – he had reached the point where his money had simply run out. 'I was having to borrow to buy the ink to write my music. One morning my neighbour noticed I was pushing my car down the road. I told her the battery wasn't working. She said, "Why don't you buy a new one?" I told her that it would cost £100 and I couldn't afford it. So she bought one for me.'

Lenehan, meanwhile, had built up a career as a top accompanist, playing piano behind stars like Nigel Kennedy – which is how he got to know Neil – and got naff all to show for it. 'I'd got to the stage of having played for twenty years, having a good reputation, and always being broke. And I'd got bored of it.'

As the men talk, they start to open up and Neil reveals things he's never previously told me about how drastic things had become after he had ceased being Nigel Kennedy's manager. 'I was completely unemployed. I fled to France and spent two weeks in Brittany, sitting and looking at the sea. When I got back home I had estate agents round valuing the house in case we had to sell it. You find yourself owing money to the bank, the taxman and the credit-card company. There's some serious ingenuity needed.'

It was ingenuity of another sort that had earned Neil his place within TVO. Because when Messiter first played him his demo disc, in early '99, Neil had said, 'Gosh, it's virtually an orchestra.' Which is where they got the name. And when Messiter and Lenehan explained that they knew that their technology was going to be good for some sort of commercial application, but they couldn't think what it might be, it was Neil who'd come up with the original idea of making CD-ROMs for kids practising for Grade exams.

So we sit in the garage as the guys swap war-stories about the bad old days, like the way there'd always be one of them who'd have to buy all the drinks in the pub… because he'd be the only one with any money at all. And then there came the happy ending, the story of how they and their partners had spent a fantastic Millennium Eve at Malcolm's place, just bursting with the promise of success and hope after all the months of poverty and frustration.

Neil describes how hard it had been to believe the good news that TVO had got all the money it needed... and then some. 'I had a bottle of champagne in the fridge. It took me three days to open it because I couldn't believe what had happened.' He pauses for a moment. 'No, that's wrong. I still haven't opened it. The thing is, we never set this up to make huge chunks of money. We did it so that we could all have a bit of a living, and it's grown organically from there. What matters most is the emotional support I've received from Malcolm and John – you can't measure that sort of thing.'

By now I've got to leave because I've got a meeting with the techies in Berkhamsted. So I drive up to the M25, wondering whether I'll have stories like Neil's to tell someday. Will I ever have to sink so low? Will I get the chance to rise so high?

An hour later, I'm sat in the Café Rouge in Berkhamsted, figuring out the best way to structure the database that will run the syndication side of sho-biz.com with Toni, the wife of Martin-the-shaggy-bearded-techie. We've got to find a way in which editors from all over the world can log onto the site, find out what's on offer and be able to buy what they need in total confidence that none of their competitors can ever buy the same thing, in the same territory. This raises all sorts of issues. How will we sort material? How will we ensure that user-passwords are classified to allow access to some parts of the site, but not to others? And how can we be certain that anyone who wants to make a purchase is actually entitled to do so? Luckily, Toni's the kind of person whose mind seems to run on smoothly oiled rails of pure logic. If ever there's a flaw in my reasoning, she quietly spots it, suggests a correction and sets the process moving forward again. This makes working with her an intellectually stimulating, yet oddly soothing business. There's no tension or neurosis... just the gentle purring of brain-cells.

By the end of a 90-minute meeting the parameters of our database have been established. If Steve and Martin can program the database to deliver the service Toni and I have envisaged, it will be a world-beating proposition. I drive back to Sussex with a song in my heart. What a bloody wonderful day.

MARCH

2 March

London W1: It's a big, big day ... the first showing of The Attik's provisional designs for sho-biz.com. I agree to meet Lucien King at Victoria Station (his flat is nearby), then we'll go on to The Attik together, meeting Adam Precious and the techies Steve and Martin, there. But when I get off the train and look around, Lucien's shaven head is nowhere to be seen. Then a grinning, heavily-bearded figure in a baby-blue Peruvian knitted cap that looks worryingly like a tea-cosy appears beside me, sticks out a hand and says, 'Hi dude.'

This is Lucien. He pulls off his hat to reveal that his head, which was barely more than be-stubbled ten days ago, now has a thick coating of silvery hair. 'It's my Indian blood,' he explains. 'I can grow hair at incredible speed.' He explains that he works on a fortnightly cycle of shaving and re-growth, all of it moderated by the constant wearing of hats (this one, he feels, is particularly fine). Okay, I think to myself, he's a tad eccentric. Nothing wrong with that.

Lucien does, at least, remove his distinctive chapeau before the meeting begins. Liz Walton and Paul Inman stand at the far end of the boardroom-table (the one with the lemons in it, this time), open up a plastic portfolio-case and pull out ... a throbbing pink penis.

Well, that's what it looks like from my end of the table, anyway. On closer inspection, it turns out to be a Tintin-style rocket, flying through space, whose vivid magenta tip looks exactly like a circumcised todger. I raise this point – as it were – as politely as I can, while we all try not to titter. Liz and Paul then go through a series of further pages in which the rocket is the basis for very bright, colourful designs, all based on the puntastic concept of flying to the stars.

Knowing that I have a terrible tendency to open my big mouth far too wide and too often, I restrain all the comments that immediately come to mind (apart from the phallic symbolism) while the Attik mob come on to Option Two. This time, the feel is Las Vegas, 1960: the pages look like they could be menus from a funky diner. But there's quite a nice idea for an animation on the opening page: lots of groovy celebrities dancing inside a graphic that resembles one of those big neon billboards outside a Vegas casino.

Overall, though, the rocket wins by a mile. If we can get rid of its willie-ness it will make a perfect logo that can be used on anything from websites to business-cards to giveaway T-shirts. As the conversation whizzes round the table, the rocket provokes a moment of genuine inspiration. It's not really possible to say who comes up with which parts of the idea, but the general reasoning goes something like this…

Rockets need fuel if they're going to get to the stars… So maybe Rocket Fuel could be what our punters use to buy the products which get them close to their favourite stars. Instead of buying a subscription, or using credit-cards or phone-charging for each and every purchase on the sho-biz.com site, punters could fill up their Rocket Fuel tanks, just like they re-charge their phone-cards. The designers and the techies swap indecipherable opinions across the table and agree that it's all technically possible. Users could be given a fuel-gauge when they register with the site, showing them how much fuel they had at any one time. They could buy more whenever they wanted to. Or, more to the point, they could get their credit card-carrying parents to buy it for them.

That's excellent, as is the way that the designers have used different colourways to differentiate between the various areas of the site. But there are a few problems. For example, there's no indication of what punters are going to buy, where they're going to buy it, or how we're going to take them to the purchase point. Nor does any of the text bear any relation to the actual copy – or style of copy – we are planning to use. Nor is there any sense that anyone has thought about the way that lists are going to be used to take users from one star to another.

What makes this extra-galling is the fact that I have supplied The Attik with everything they need for the first sample pages: all the copy for the stars, all the lists that link them and a series of detailed maps (thank you, Lucy) showing exactly how those links join up. I've sent this material on both paper, for ease of reading, and disc, for ease of inclusion in a computer-generated design. AND NONE OF IT HAS BEEN USED.

Now, just as rugby forwards think that three-quarters are all a bunch of big girls' blouses, and builders are certain that most architects couldn't successfully erect a Wendy-house, so I – as a writer and editor – have long been convinced that designers don't actually read a word that's put in front of them. It's fantastic to find one who can grasp the intellectual substance of a concept, see its internal logic and work out the practicalities of delivering it in the most effective way, but it's also painfully rare. Deep in my wordsmith's soul, I suspect that graphic designers, as a tribe, are engaged in a secret war against the written word. But I'm paying £1,000 a day here... and now I'm going to have to pay another few grand for them to do the work that I'd asked for in the first place. All of which comes as a blow, particularly given the fantastic impression Kelvyn Collins had made on the day we met. And speaking of which ... where is he?

'Probably off meeting another new client,' says Lucien, as we leave the meeting. 'All these companies work the same way. They've got a small bunch of super-bright people who set everything up. Then they hand you over to their mates and you hardly ever see them again. Didn't you know that?'

Oddly enough, no – not in so many words. And, to be fair, both Paul and Liz are a lot further up the evolutionary scale than your average designer chimp. But I take Lucien's point. And in future I'll definitely bear it in mind.

5 March

Trafalgar Square, London: An exhibition opens at the National Portrait Gallery featuring 'The New Masters of the Economic Universe'. Brent and Martha are, of course, featured in it, as are two Swedes called Ernst Malmstein and Kajsa Leander, who've got the clothing e-tailer Boo.com. That's the one with TV ads filled with grainy, hand-held shots of loonies dancing on the New York subway.

The exhibition has been organised by Rufus Olins, editor of *Management Today*, who is quoted by the press thus: 'I do think we are living in a time very much the cult of youth. It is seen as an advantage, whereas in the past being young was seen as a disadvantage.'

In the past, being unable to construct a decent sentence was seen as a disadvantage, too. Now we are living in a time very much the cult of crap syntax. Yeah, I know. I'm old, I'm crusty and I've reached the age when I wince every time I see or hear a grammatical howler. What chance have I got in the exciting world of the Internet?

7 March

Things are getting worryingly quiet on the Kylie front. The last time I spoke to Terry Blamey, he explained that Kylie's recording sessions had gone on a bit longer than had been anticipated, so she might not be able to do anything till the end of March. I can just about live with that, provided I've got something to show investors by the time we present to them in late April, but time is getting tight. Perhaps we'd better consider an alternative…

Lucien King has a bright idea. His girlfriend Emily is an executive at MTV. She knows all the girls who present their shows – girls like Cat Deeley, for example, who is endlessly coming top of lad-mag polls to find the world's sexiest babe. The great thing about MTV, though, is that it doesn't pay its presenters a huge sum of money: they do the work for the exposure (in every sense of the word). That makes them open to sensible commercial propositions. So why don't we go for Cat, instead? We draft a letter to her agent, offering her a guaranteed £10,000, just for turning up to a photo-session, plus 1% of the company if it all goes well.

8 March

Lucien speaks to Cat's agent's assistant. The e-mail has been received. It has been passed on. They'll get back to us.

Meanwhile, with my cash running dangerously low, I surrender two endowment policies which I've had since 1986. I've been paying around £100 a month for fourteen years – a total of around £16,800. The Stock Market has gone up by about 500% in that time, but my useless endowment has gained about one-tenth as much. Still, £24,578.36 will come in very handy indeed, given the current state of my overdraft, and if it pays for me to survive long enough to launch sho-biz.com, I'm not knocking it.

9 March

The City of London: A message from the agent's assistant: Cat will take a look at our proposal over the weekend. She'll let us know. Meanwhile, I have weightier matters on my mind. Neil Storey has fixed a meeting for himself, Lucien King and me at a small, but perfectly formed bank called English Trust, whose headquarters are in a gorgeous Georgian house in Charterhouse Square, on the western edge of the City. The partners each have one of the main rooms as their office: very civilised.

I sent them a copy of the business-plan earlier in the week, so they're familiar with the bare bones of the business – now I've got to flesh it all in. We sit down around a polished antique table, hand out the tea and biccies and begin. There are three English Trust directors at the meeting. The one who takes the lead is the head honcho – a man called Jasper Allen, who comes across as very much an old-style, public-school banker (except, that is for a passionate love of computer games, which he admits to an impressed Lucien), but very sharp.

I get the impression quite early in the meeting that they're definitely interested in working with us. The question is: how? I reckon I need four or five million (the figure keeps going up and up) to fund sho-biz.com properly. In Jasper Allen's view, I should not be hanging around, waiting till everything is ready before I approach investors. Instead, I should be seeking out every source of private finance I can, trying to put together a portfolio of backers. This is bound to take a lot of time, so I might as well get started now. That way, the market will be nicely warmed-up just as I'm ready to meet it. Once we get the first tranche of private finance – a process which he would be only too happy to speed along, via his own contacts – the next key step is to move towards a Stock Market listing, perhaps in the late autumn of this year, or early 2001. English Trust would be ready to handle it all.

That's all clear enough, but as Neil lets me know over lunch, getting the money is just the start of one's problems. Neil is going through another tough time. He's gone back into management, working with Nitin Sawhney, the brilliant British Asian musician who just won a South Bank Award for his album *Beyond Skin*. Neil thinks he could do for Asian music what Bob Marley did for reggae. But his career is temporarily on hold while Neil tries to sort out a legal wrangle with his old record company, which he now wants to leave. Meanwhile, things aren't going well for him at TVO. Steve Thomas and his partner Steve Smith have brought in a big-time City player called Tony Caplin to be the company Chairman. I get the feeling that the new guy and Neil don't get on. He seems very depressed about the whole thing. He's supposed to have a consultancy deal with TVO, but that presumes that anyone wants to consult him. The only recent contact he's had with the company has been a conversation telling him he can't buy some computer equipment which he thought had been approved months ago. He still owns 18% of TVO, but it doesn't seem to have done him much good. He feels as though he's been frozen out.

Which is a point worth bearing in mind as Lucien and I set out on part two of the day's money-safari. We're due for a meeting at Summit, to review the way things are going. I tell Kit and Zac about what happened at Summit and they talk through the way they see things going. Essentially, it's the exact opposite of the English Trust approach. They want to go for City institutions, not private investors, because in their experience the pros are easier to deal with. Plus there tend to be fewer of them, which makes corporate communications a lot easier. Once they've picked their targets they want to give them a short, sharp shock: here's the deal, go for it now, or miss the boat. But for that to work, everything has to be in place, and glitch-free, well in advance. So don't worry about the money, concentrate on your plan, your dummy site and your partners.

Whom should I believe? Clearly, both English Trust and Summit have their own agendas. ET want the business, Summit don't want to lose it. Equally clearly, they're both run by intelligent, highly competent individuals giving honest and – as they see it – good advice. It just happens to be directly contradictory. Finally, there's the whole question of going for a Stock Market listing. I know it's the be-all and end-all of Internet start-ups, but (as I told Kit Hunter Gordon right at the start of all this), I'm not in business to become the CEO of a listed company, endlessly at the mercy of institutional investors, my share-price and government regulators. If I'm going to sell out, I'd rather do it in one big go to a company that wants to take sho-biz.com over. That way, best of all, I can take the money and run. But if I'm going to stay and watch the company grow, I want to do it on my own terms – and that means staying private. Kit won't object to that – it's exactly what he's done. And he's got the large country house to prove what a good idea it was.

10 March

Lastminute's shares have just been hiked by 67%. They were going to go on sale at between 190-230 pence a share. But the demand has been so phenomenal that Morgan Stanley have upped the price to a spread of 320–380 pence. This will make Brent worth £50 million, while Top Ten Date Martha's dowry now tops £35 million. The papers are full of columns by green-eyed hacks (not remotely like me, of course), detailing all the reasons why we now hate Martha.

According to Lastminute's latest figures, it has more than a million registered users, but only 5% of them actually buy anything. Last year it lost £6 million. It hopes to make a profit by 2004. Maybe.

Meanwhile the Chancellor of the Exchequer, Gordon Brown has advised private investors to be cautious when buying high-tech stocks.

Down in sleepy Sussex, where we don't really like to invest in anything riskier than a new lawnmower, an e-mail arrives out of the blue from a man called Michael Magoulias,who says he's the Publishing Director of Britannica.co.uk. He's working on the launch of the UK version of Britannica.com, the online face of the Encyclopaedia Britannica. He writes that 'Michael May suggested that I contact you to explore the possibility of collaborating with Britannica to provide either a private-label or co-branded entertainment channel targeting the UK and European markets.'

First question: who is Michael May? The only person I can think of called that is a surgeon in Harley Street who specialises in hair-transplants. I interviewed him for a big feature I wrote a few years ago about male vanity. Maybe this Magoulias guy is a closet slaphead who got into a conversation with his doc while the plugs were being popped into his scalp … But what do I care? This could be an amazing opportunity. I call him up straight away – he's American, extremely courteous, sounds like a nice bloke – and fix a meeting. It's next Thursday, 3.00 pm, at his office in Golden Square, just north of Piccadilly Circus. I'll meet Magoulias and his hair then.

11 March

Neil and I talked for ages yesterday about the two options facing me when financing sho-biz.com. Today he sums up his thoughts in an e-mail, whose ten points are a sort of primer for anyone thinking of raising money to fund a start-up. By the way, when he's talking about 'due diligence' what he means is the process potential investors go through of checking every single aspect of your business, down to the tiniest detail, to make sure they're not being sold a pup. So here goes…

> 1. I seriously believe you have all you need in your business plan – barring a few revisions etc, – before you present it to investors.

> 2. Stop fine tuning your business–plan. One can go on ad infinitum… which a) promotes more head–spin and b) can be an endless process – one has to have a cut off point.

> 3. We discovered that there is a figure above which investors (of whatever variety) get twitchy… I'd say anything over 3.5 million (UK). Below this and you should be comfortable. Above it, and you'll find so much due diligence in your way that the entire fundraising process will be ghastly.

> 4. You need to go to the market (investors) pronto, otherwise you'll be in cash-flow probs.

> 5. If you go with a handful of investors (most likely serious VC funds) then the due diligence you'll go through will be extreme. If you take the route of (say) thirty or so investors bringing in the figure you require, each individual portion is that much lower and due diligence is a bit easier on your brain.

> 6. The serious VC people will – no matter what anyone says – want a lot from you, be it equity or a seat on the board. You might get into a situation of losing creative control when you don't want to. Big money speaks loud.

> 7. Get a Board... I'm not sure how finalised it is, but would advise that this needs pulling together fairly quickly.

> 8. I'd really seriously analyse your figures... do you really need as much money as you think?

> 9. One can always fund in two stages... for example... to bring in 2- or 2-and-a-half right now would (in my view) be a doddle – the idea, the plan and the proposition is all there. It may be that that figure keeps you going toward trading for (say) nine months. Once you start trading and the site is up and running and showing success (doesn't have to be immense) then going to the market for major money injection (say another five) would not be a problem.

> 10. Staying private, floating, being bought out... at this stage, it doesn't really make that many odds. Who can predict the future? Personally, I think you're wise to aim to stay private but, if 'the digger' comes in with a barrel load of cash... will you? I think it's unlikely...!!!

I think about all this and decide to do precisely nothing. Or rather, nothing new. I've made my bed with Summit. I might as well lie in it until they actually kick me out. Then again, I'm not actually going to tell English Trust to get lost. It's nice to think that I've got them as a backstop if the Summit deal goes wrong.

And there's a little bonus at the end of Neil's e-mail. He has, through means I have never quite been able to fathom, acquired a colleague-cum-assistant who is – how can I put this? – fantastically well-connected. She's the Girl Who Knows Everyone and she has an address-book that goes all the way to Windsor Castle. It includes the name of Prince Rupert Loewenstein, financial advisor to the Rolling Stones. Neil feels that the Prince might be interested in sho-biz.com. He has asked the girl to make discreet inquiries. More news will follow as and when...

13 March

A new version of the sho-biz.com business-plan has been completed and sent to Summit. It's got all the design specifications included, a lot more technical details, an outline of the Rocket Fuel concept. And it's also got a full-page copy of our logo – the Flying Dick.

Meanwhile, Lucien has called Cat Deeley's agent's assistant, but not got any answer. I have tried to call Cat's agent herself, but been rebuffed, even when I did my bigtime journalist number. Whole posses of lovers and chums have been despatched to track down Cat Deeley at the MTV studios, but no contact has been made.

This is very weird. We have just offered someone £10,000 in cash... and they haven't even bothered to say, 'No'. Maybe she's making more than we thought.

14 March

The City of London: Lastminute.com is launching on the Stock Market. Advance trading suggests its value might be pushed up beyond the billion-pound mark. I still have not been able to find a single person, in any business remotely connected with the Internet, or its finance, who can explain to me why a company which makes its money off the cut it gets from hotels and airlines from selling their surplus rooms and seats –

i.e. the stuff nobody actually wants – can possibly be worth that kind of money. But maybe I'm just thick.

Either that, or a lot of other people are. Lastminute launches at a share-price of 380p. It rockets up to 555 and ends the day at 487.5. That gives it a valuation of £732 million, bigger – as the FT observes – than the food firm Unigate, which last year made profits of £155 million. As of this evening, Brent is worth £68 million and Martha's making do on a measly £45m.

16 March

Oxford Street and Soho, London: Because I live in Sussex, I try to make sure that I always have more than one thing to do whenever I come up to London. This means that I run around like the proverbial fly with an azure anus, but it also has the effect of creating days that turn into miniature guided tours to the Internet business. Like today, for example.

It begins with a get-together at The Attik. I'm late and made later by the fact that just as I'm about to go through the front door of the office-block, just north of Oxford Street, where the Attik mob hang out, the phone goes. It's Kit Hunter Gordon. He's read the latest version of the plan, and he's very happy with it. But it just needs a few extra ingredients.

First: whenever I use a statistic or an opinion-poll or a piece of consumer-research, I've got to provide a reference, just to prove that I haven't made it up. (Of course, the people I got it off might have made it up, but that's not my problem.) Next, in a similar vein, I've got to provide written confirmation of every agreement in the plan. If I say I'm going to be working with a particular company, the deal's got to be in writing and stuck in an appendix at the end of the plan. If I say that a CD-ROM costs $3.50 to produce, I've got to prove it. And, while I'm at it, could I please provide some concrete examples of potential syndication revenue?

Third point: marketing. I don't specify what sort of advertising and promotion I have planned. Or not, at any rate, in the necessary detail. Kit needs descriptions of both strategy and tactics – what we want to achieve and how we're going to do it, medium-by-medium – alongside precise figures, names of agencies and everything else that's required to sell a website to the general public. He wants to see phrases like interactivity and viral marketing – buzzwords that will excite investors. In fact, he wants to make the site so interactive and so virally welcoming to users that it generates viral building – in which the contributions of punters and their pals actually provide our content. For free. In fact, since the presence of punters on-site means that we can make money from advertising, they'll actually be paying to build sho-biz.com for us. The money people will love that.

Finally, there are the numbers. If this is going to go out to VCs and investment funds, we'll need detailed, year-by-year, even month-by-month projections for the first few years of operation. That's Zac's department. As soon as I've got everything else ready, all I have to do is lob the whole lot over to Zac, he'll put it all through Summit's computers and – as if by magic – investor-ready spreadsheets will appear.

That all seems achievable, particularly if there's several million pounds at the end of it. I tell Kit I'll get on the case and head into the meeting, to find the groovy-bearded designers talking to the hairy-bearded techies with Lucien holding the ring for me, Liz representing The Attik … and not a lot appears to have been achieved. Since we last met, I feel like everyone's been waiting for the other guys to take the initiative.

The issue is this: the final site is going to be database-driven, which is to say that pages will be created from an active database that will automatically sort out lists, create links and handle commercial transactions. But how are we going to work the demo? After all, one of the reasons we need money is to pay for the actual database construction – so what's the procedure in the meantime? The designers say they haven't been able to do any finished work because the techies haven't given them the database specifications. The techies haven't done any database work because they're waiting for design details. I'm not sufficiently Net-literate to bang heads and sort out a properly prioritised schedule because I'd almost certainly get it wrong. There are fifteen days to go before the supposed deadline and we're busy going nowhere.

Which is, of course, what happens when you're first starting out and relying on a whole bunch of different people, scattered all over the place, none of whom rely on you. They've all got something more important to do at any one time. It only takes one person to miss one delivery date by a single day to throw the whole schedule out, all the way down the line. The fact that we haven't got Kylie, or a replacement, for example, means that there's a whole bunch of stuff that The Attik simply can't do, because I haven't given them the raw materials. So late days become late weeks. Timetables dissolve into thin air. I'm supposed to be doing the rounds of the entertainment industry in less than one month's time, and as matters stand I've got bugger all to show them.

By the time I leave, some progress seems to have been made in sorting out who'll do what first, who'll talk to whom and when this might all happen. But much as I'd like to spend another couple of hours sitting around The Attik's boardroom table, seething with frustration and pent-up rage, I have another appointment. One which, given Kit's insistence on marketing plans, couldn't be better timed.

Happy Dog are a happening gang of hip-tastic young advertising whiz kids. Or something like that. Well, that's what their PR claims, anyway. When she calls to fix up the meeting, I ask what the gang are called. 'Toby, Nick, Scott and Daisy,' she replies.

It sounds like something out of Enid Blyton: 'Four Go Mad Online':

> *'I say, Toby, let's start an exciting new media ad agency.'*
> *'Gosh, Scott, that's a spiffing wheeze. Don't forget to bring the*
> *sandwiches, Daisy … and oodles of pop!'*

That's how I imagine Happy Dog … and that's remarkably close to how they actually are. When I get to their building in Dean Street, Soho, just up the road from the Groucho Club, Nick is in a bit of a frazzle. A rubber-ball type of character in his mid-twenties, with an untucked purple shirt, rosy cheeks and frantic curly hair, he's having to cope with a major situation.

At the foot of the stairs, half-a-dozen burly furniture-shifters are trying to find a way of getting a large and back-breakingly heavy object up the stairs. This, it transpires, is Happy Dog's air-hockey table. As Nick explains, it's no ordinary air-hockey table. It's a classic, reconditioned Seventies model, bought online via e-Bay (they paid 1400 bucks, he says proudly: it would have cost £4000 in England) and then shipped from Texas to Soho.

There's just one problem. When they bought this table, they neglected to consider its dimensions, relative to the size of the stairwell. Specifically, they ignored the possibility that it might just be too damn big to go upstairs. Nick hovers about, trying to resolve the situation while the movers cast him looks which suggest that they are less than impressed by the situation. Me, I'm delighted. The idea that these guys are actually paying for a machine powered by hot air. Brilliant!

More seriously, I'm wondering, based on my own experience, how the partners in a brand-new e-commerce company find the time and money to worry about amusement arcade items when they're barely four months into their operations. But maybe I'm just too old to understand…

Finally, we go upstairs – even if the air-hockey table doesn't – and Nick leads me into a vast and almost entirely empty open-plan office. At one end of the room there is a table around which a group of young women are working. Halfway along is another table at which there are two more men: Toby and Scott, I presume. In the far corner, there's a groovy chill-out zone with bean-bags and a telly. The whole place is littered with little toy dogs. An actual dog, called Pippa, is scooting about the place, yapping occasionally. The company logo, however, does not feature a dog. It shows a Forties-style plane flying over a skyscraper. 'We didn't want a dog,' says Nick. 'That would be too obvious.'

Before we start, the boys call for Daisy. One of the women gets up from the far table and comes to join us. Or so I suppose. In fact, she's merely despatched to get some drinks and sort out the table-hockey situation. Good to know that women are playing an active, leading role in the new economy. So different from the old one, eh?

We get down to the meeting. I explain my situation, tell them what sho-biz.com is planning to do (reproducing the diagram I first drew at Attik a few weeks ago) and outline the general marketing strategy that I want them to plan and perhaps even execute. The key to the whole thing, I explain, is that I don't want to go down the standard Lastminute route of a massive spend on conventional media, because I won't need to. Stars sell themselves. If we're filling the papers with stories about our interviewees, all of them credited to sho-biz.com, that's more effective than any advert. Plus, the people who want to know about stars online are already logging on to fan-sites and chatrooms. The key thing is finding them and making sure they know about us, and can link to our site with maximum ease. How can Happy Dog help me achieve that?

The three lads begin their corporate pitch. Next to Nick, Toby is older, thinner and calmer in his conversation, but still every inch a London ad-boy. At the far end of the table, Scott is a dry, almost dour Kiwi – but he seems the least caught up in the company's own hype.

It turns out they all used to work for a much bigger called (deep breath) TBWAGGT Simons Palmer, which was itself part of a multi-national corporation, Omnicom. But, says Nick, 'We were working for clients who didn't care about their brands. We cared more than they did. As far as they were concerned, they had two years to go until they got their next job and they couldn't be bothered.'

So the boys began dreaming about something new, something different, something more in tune with the digital revolution. Rather than let them go, TBWAGGTSP agreed to give the trio a sort of permanent secondment, fund their new enterprise, and split the shares of the new company 60–40 in the founders' favour. So Happy Dog had the freedom of an independent start-up, with the security of big-time corporate backing, while their former bosses had the reassurance of knowing that if the project worked, they still owned a decent chunk of it.

For, it now emerges, Happy Dog is not a conventional agency. They get involved right from the start of a new company's life. As Toby puts it, 'We have clients who say, 'I know nothing about this, but I have a great idea, and someone's given me £5 million.'

'Most of them come from the City, management consultancy and PR,' adds Nick. 'We turn away people who just want to be rich. Passion and energy are our criteria. We distil their drive and commitment and turn them into a fantastic brand.'

To do this, they get all the key people involved in a new company to attend a 'one-day passion-focusing workshop'. This draws out the emotional, financial and conceptual soul of the new company. Nick and the gang go away and spend two weeks chewing over everything that comes out of the first session, then they have a second meeting, to go over the specific issues that they have distilled from it. 'A week later,' says Nick, 'we come back with a brand manifesto.'

'If you're building a company,' Scott explains, 'you've got to be able to get up every day and know why you're doing it.'

That manifesto marks the end of Stage One of the Happy Dog process. In Stage Two, they devise a communications strategy, setting out the ideas that the company should be putting across through all the media channels on which it sells its message. Then they charge you £18,000.

By this point, I'm beginning to notice that Happy Dog is an ad agency that doesn't actually make any ads. Nor does it buy airtime or ad-space. It will point you in the direction of people whom it recommends to do those things, which is nice, but Nick and the gang have got better things to do than write copy or art-direct photo-shoots. 'We are an ideas company,' says Nick. 'We don't actually execute. We don't have a product. We're not in the business of outcomes. We're in the business of possibilities.'

How fabulously virtual. And how handy, since this absence of vulgar product leaves room for the nicer things in life. For their own corporate manifesto not only gives Happy Dog's employees 25 days holiday, but also adds another ten days of 'scratching and sniffing'. The scratching is five days of personal development: things you've always wanted to learn, skills you want to master... that sort of thing. And the sniffing is a week at one of the other companies with which Happy Dog works – the kind that actually make ads, for example – learning how they do their jobs.

As I listen, and look around at this empty space, scattered with bright young bourgeois things, I realise that I have finally entered into the glowing, beating heart of the Internet revolution. In all the months that I've been working on sho-biz.com, the vast majority of the people I've met have been sober, middle-aged businessmen and technicians, making money out of this new phenomenon, just like they did out of all the old ones. But here, at Happy Dog, I get a taste of the dot-com world, as portrayed in all the articles I've read about teenage tycoons and snazzy young entrepreneurs.

Yet, at the very same time, I'm overwhelmed by déjà vu. These ambitious Happy Puppies remind me of my own youth as a thrusting little Thatcherite, back in the Eighties, right at the very dawn of the capitalist counter-revolution. Oh, those happy days when the coke on the Groucho loo-seats was as clean and fresh as virgin snow; when the BMW 3-series was a novelty rather than a cliché; when cappuccinos were a rarity, an Armani suit a thrill, and a chap could buy a two-storey flat in a fine Fulham street and still have change from a hundred grand.

Still there's something quite sweet about people who can seriously boast about having the first 'Internet-enabled' research facility in London. Think about this for a second. A research facility is just a room with a two-way mirror, behind which people with clipboards can make notes on the ramblings of focus-groups nattering away on the far side of the glass. As for 'Internet-enabled'… my kitchen is Internet-enabled. So are my bedroom, my living-room, my study and (with a swift call to BT) any other room in the house. Because all you need to be Internet enabled is a telephone-jack. Plug in a laptop, click on the Internet Explorer or Netscape logo and… yes! You're enabled, too.

Nick, Toby and Scott look almost downcast when this is pointed out. But their high spirits cannot be suppressed for long. They go on at some length about the virtues of viral marketing, 'We call it word-of-mouse,' says Toby, who also adds that, 'Branding isn't the icing on the cake. It's the yeast that makes it rise.'

God, I love these guys. I'm not going to spend a single penny of my Summit money on their corporate manifesto, let alone their scratching or sniffing. But I love 'em. And I'd love a go on their air-hockey table, too.

I've got one last meeting, with the mysterious Michael Magoulias, who isn't suffering in the slightest bit from male-pattern baldness (and no, it isn't just a fantastic rug-job). In fact, he has a thick head of almost black hair. His manner is quiet, almost diffident, not at all what you might expect from a go-getting American e-publisher. But then, as he explains, he's spent the past decade in England, on and off, so perhaps he's been infected with British bashfulness.

Once he starts explaining Britannica.com, though, any hesitation disappears and I'm not surprised – it's a brilliant concept. 'We've been a start-up for 250 years,' he says, pointing out that Britannica has been indexing and categorising the world since the mid-Eighteenth century. They've got 73,000 articles, containing 44 million words, about every subject under the sun, all cross-referenced by every possible criterion, all the way from a-k (an ancient form of Asian music) to a town in Poland called Zywiec. Now all of that ordered information is being turned into the basis for a Web portal. 'It's perfect for electronic media,' says Magoulias.

Damn right it is. Magoulias demonstrates Britannica's search facility. Every other search-engine I've ever seen just spits out a random selection of websites, which may or may not have something remotely relevant to what you're actually looking for. But a Britannica search ends with a page on which are listed the ten most appropriate sites, as chosen by Britannica; a list of relevant articles in the site's own database; recent magazine and newspaper articles relating to the subject, and a list of different, but related subjects. It's fantastic – an instant crib-sheet on any subject under the sun.

As soon as punters get to hear about this, they're going to come running. Britannica are planning to roll out their service in Australia in May, followed by a soft launch (i.e. a trial run with minimal promotion) in the UK in July. There's only one catch. Britannica's research indicates that it has all sorts of positive brand-values. People think of the Encyclopaedia Britannica as authoritative, unbiased and reliable. But it has negatives, too. It's considered stodgy, not fun, too bookish, purely academic. So the key task Magoulias has to accomplish is to bring a bit of fun to the business. And I am just the boy to help him do it.

Just like I did with Happy Dog, I use my magic diagram to describe sho-biz.com, emphasising the fact that our deals with syndication agencies will mean a steady stream of hot interviews, right from the off. Plus, of course, there's Mitchy's amazing trivia database, in which all the facts are as scrupulously checked as those in the encyclopaedia … it's just that Britannica tends not to reveal the common link between Marilyn Monroe and Gianluca Vialli (both were born with 11 toes), or to know that Dustin Hoffman lost his virginity to a girl who thought she was sleeping with his brother. Now, is that fun, or what?

Michael Magoulias certainly thinks so. Pretty soon we're talking about making sho-biz.com the official provider of entertainment news and features to Britannica.co.uk. In fact, he's so enthused by my presentation, he doesn't just want to work with sho-biz.com … he wants to own it. Well, *he* doesn't. But he knows a man who might.

Britannica is owned by a man called Jacob 'Jackie' Safra, who bought it in 1996 for a rumoured $500 million. Jackie can afford it. He's a billionaire.

His uncle was Edmond Safra, an international financier who was also a billionaire and who died back in December in a mysterious fire at his Monte Carlo apartment. Jackie, though, is very much alive, and – as Michael Magoulias puts it – he likes buying things. And sho-biz.com might very well be just the sort of thing that Jackie would like to buy.

I tell Michael to pass a message on to Jackie: when billionaires want to buy me, I am only too happy to sell. There'll be a business-plan in the post tomorrow morning.

17 March

I call Michael Magoulias to thank him for the meeting. He has already spoken to his boss, who'll be the person who speaks to Jackie Safra. This is why Americans rule the world. They don't waste time hanging about. They just go right ahead and buy you.

But while that door opens, another slams in my face. An e-mail arrives from Terry Blamey. The second line reads, 'Kylie & I are worried that if we keep you on hold we'll really throw you out, so we'd best pass at this stage.'

Evidently her recording-sessions are still dragging on and she still doesn't have a single or a finished album. Obviously, that has to come first. 'Sorry for any inconvenience I may have caused,' says Blamey. 'Hopefully we'll be able to be there later in the year when you are up and running! (Would have been nice to have a small per cent in Lastminute.com – hopefully you'll do as well!)'

Well, I guess that can't be helped. But bugger.

Bugger, bugger, bugger, bugger.

And Cat Deeley hasn't got back to us, either. What are we going to do?

20 March

Chiswick, London W4: I visit a company called Now. They work out of one of those anonymous identikit, commercial sheds that could be anywhere, though it happens to be in a business-park next to the A4 in Chiswick. Inside the faceless exterior there's an extraordinary site – a vision of the future. Two hundred young reporters, producers and computer technologists are working in a PC-strewn environment, criss-crossed by black rubber cables. At one end of the great, open space is a tented café zone where metal tables were dotted beneath multi-coloured spotlights, rigged on trusses like a rock 'n' roll stage-show. That's where I meet Now's boss, Michael Johnson.

He's one of those bulky, middle-aged men who seem to exude testosterone and power. This is potentially his third multi-billion-dollar start-up, the first two being the Hong Kong-based broadcasting plays, Star TV and AsiaSat. His official job-title is 'Senior Advisor to the Chairman's Office, Pacific Century Group.' What that meant, informally, is that he's right-hand man to Richard Li, a 32-year-old businessman who is currently investing more than £300 million in a bold attempt to create a worldwide Internet and TV channel, Now.com (Now being an acronym for Network of the World). Johnson tells me about how he and his team are creating a visionary fusion of PC and TV that will enable subscribers to watch live broadcasts online, while simultaneously surfing the Net (via a 3-D browser), or chatting to their e-friends about the football match that's playing in one corner of their screens.

Johnson's an amazing character who blasts out rapid-fire quotations, descriptions and glittering imagery. One second he's drawing the link between this project and the shamanistic rituals of primitive cave-paintings, the next he's declaring that, 'My mental model for this is the Moscow Arts Theatre. That was a point in time when a group of artists, actors and even painters were given the task of adapting the new technology of moving pictures to the objectives of the Soviet revolution. What we've got to do here is to examine the role our technology can play and ask ourselves: how will the stories of the future be told?'

'This is a perpetual emotion machine,' enthuses Johnson. 'It's creating an environment that allows passive inter-action, active inter-action, sharing illusion and sharing information. Hah! We've rediscovered society.'

This man would make a brilliant holy-rolling preacher. But amidst all the hoopla, and the astonishing technology – Now claim to be able to provide live video-streaming through a basic 28K modem, which is a bit like saying you can deliver full-colour, surround-sound home cinema through a twelve-inch black-and-white telly – one phrase stands out above all. Johnson uses it in passing. Halfway through a sentence he refers to 'what we used to call the Web'. I almost drop my pen. Here are the rest of us still struggling to get to grips with an entirely new phenomenon... and the serious players are already one step beyond.

22 March

In the continued absence of any communication from la Deeley or her advisors, I go for the nuclear option. I'll forget about the lot of them. Instead, I'll create my own, fictional superstar and do with her as I please. In order to do this, however, I need a real human being. I could simply hire a model, but the chances are she won't be able to act out a character, which she has to be able to do if the interview extracts are going to work. I could hire an actress, but I don't have time to organise proper auditions, even if I knew how to. So I do what any other idle bastard in my position would do. I ring a mate.

Alex Armitage has a special place in my affections because he held the party, 25 years ago (Jesus!) where I met my first really serious girlfriend. Since then, he has taken over the family business, a talent-agency called the Noel Gay Organisation, whose clients have included Sir David Frost, Esther Rantzen, Rowan Atkinson and Richard Littlejohn. So I give Alex a bell and explain my situation: I need a beautiful young woman. Does he have any on his books?

Naturally, he has. And the one whom he believes would best suit my needs is called Danielle Nicholls. She's cute, bubbly, and presents Children's ITV. As if this were not enough, she's ambitious, hard-working and gets the point fast. A picture, he says, will be in the post tonight, and she's on the telly this Friday: two days' time.

23 March

The picture arrives, as promised. Miss Nicholls is, as advertised, a pretty, perky little thing with a big smile, bright eyes and a nice-looking figure. That's what I think. The women of my family beg to differ. 'Urghhh! She's awful,' exclaims my eldest daughter, Holly, to her sister Lucy's strong agreement. 'She's on CITV and she has this weird accent. It's so-o-o gross.'

Then they and their mother begin a serious examination of the picture. Danielle's eyes, they agree, are piggy. Her calves appear too large. Her outfit is a disaster-area. She looks common. No... she just won't do.

I take another look at the picture. As I thought, it clearly shows a perfectly nice-looking young woman, in a printed top and skirt (knee-length, incidentally), smiling sweetly. I completely disagree with their assessment. Plus, which is more important, this girl looks exactly like the character I'm devising in the deep recesses of my twisted mind.

24 March

At last! The first sho-biz.com pages are secretly posted on The Attik's website. There's a landing-page, homepage, gossip page, search-page and a Brad Pitt star page. The good news is that they're very bright, very eye-catching and very suggestive of fun: they're about entertainment. The not-so-good news is that they're also a bit messy and that too many of the elements have been cobbled together from the designers' imaginations and free pics pulled down off the Web, instead of from material we have created for ourselves. But I can hardly blame them for that – it's my fault for not sorting out the babe crisis a great deal sooner.

When the kids come home from school, I show them the pages and receive the ultimate compliment: 'That is so-o-o-o cool!' Which is a lot better than being so gross.

And while we're on that subject, I check out Danielle Nicholls on CITV. She's not, it must be admitted, a classical, fine-boned, aristocratic beauty. She's got a big, round face and a Manchester accent so broad it makes Liam Gallagher sound like Lord Snooty. But she's also full of energy and life. She could definitely be turned into an interesting fictional character. So I agree to pay Alex Armitage £5,000 for two days of her time (an outrageous price, given her lack of star status, but I want her thinking that she's making big money, not counting the minutes till she can knock off) and start putting wheels in motion for a photo-session. Lucien King appears to agree: 'I think you got a game one there in Danielle,' he mails me. 'Thanks man, I feel like we are back doing the good stuff.'

26 March

Meet Cassandra Clark – known to the world simply as Cazza – the sho-biz.com cyber-star, whose biography I wrote this afternoon...

> **Date of Birth**:   27.10.78
> **Place of Birth**: Manchester
> **Star Sign**:   Scorpio

> **Key Credits**:
> *Znep da Brosh!* (Bulgarian TV), *Chix Rool!* (Sugarchix album), Sugarchix the Movie, 'Walk on the Wild Side' (solo single), *Cazzamania* (forthcoming solo album)

> **Biog**:
> Born in the Moss Side area of Manchester, Cassandra Clark never met her twin brother, who died at birth, nor her father, who was jailed for arson, burglary and grievous bodily harm, before being stabbed to death during the legendary Strangeways riots. Cassandra's Philippine-born mother Bonita worked as a hospital cleaner to put Cassandra through dance-lessons, though these were of little use as she went through a number of unusual jobs, including *Coronation Street* tour guide and singing telegram, before getting her first break as a hostess on a prime-time Bulgarian quiz-show. On a weekend break back in England, she forced her way into the auditions for a new girl-group and so impressed the group's managers with her go-getting attitude that they hired her on the spot. Cassandra Clark – or Cazza, as the tabloids instantly christened her – became the mouthpiece of the go-getting Sugarchix as they stormed to the top of the charts, becoming worldwide sensations and inspiring their young, female fans with their slogan Chix Rool! Yet, little more than a year after the band's breakthrough, Cassandra had left the group, citing a row with their

Svengali-like manager Nigel Sheridan, plus the stress caused by endless newspaper gossip about her weight problems and her rumoured on-off affairs with Mike Tyson, Stan Collymore and Prince Albert of Monaco. Now she's back with a new single (a cover of the Lou Reed classic 'Walk on the Wild Side'), a new boyfriend (Danish soccer star Kurt Bohansen) and plans for a new career in Hollywood.

Essential Trivia:
Cassandra Clark... is the celebrity twin of Vanessa Mae (born on the same day, month and year)... uses her mother's maiden name... has dated a Prince... lost her virginity at fifteen... has a tattoo of a rose on her left buttock ... has been refused entry to the Royal Enclosure at Ascot ... has denied rumours of plastic surgery... has a dog named Bozo... has admitted using Prozac... has bungee-jumped for charity and is a self-confessed chocaholic.

Mitch has lists for people who share Cazza's birthday; for people whose twin brothers died at birth (Come on down, Oscar Wilde and Elvis Presley!); people whose parents were jailbirds; who had unusual jobs before achieving stardom; who have suffered gossip about eating disorders and who conform to every single one of the criteria laid down in the Essential Trivia column. What kind of mad genius is this man?

28 March

It's been more than three months since I met Adam Precious, more than two since he first gave me verbal confirmation that his company would provide all the hardware sho-biz.com would ever need. Today, he's finally put pen to paper, or finger to keyboard, and came up with the goods. Across two, closely-packed spreadsheets he's given exact price and specification details for the 288 bits of hardware, plus supporting Oracle database technology that will together form a state-of-the-art set-up allowing sho-biz.com to expand from a small-time start-up to a mega-site handling up to one million hits-per-day. Sold to me at a cost-plus basis for a cool half-million, to be paid from revenue as and when it arises.

What this deal essentially means, in its payment-structure as well as its content, is that Adam and his employers have taken the view that they will render sho-biz.com as failure proof as they can possibly make it. We are guaranteed the capacity to succeed, whether or not we can guarantee the capacity to pay for it. They want to be in business with us and they are going to do everything they can to make sure that we are in business.

And we are in business, sort of, because our Cazza/Danielle shoot is now set for 5 and 6 April. The photographer will be Paul Massey, one of the best snappers in town (four times winner of the Nikon Showbusiness Photographer of the Year Award, no less). He's a man I can absolutely trust, having worked with him on a bunch of stories over the years, starting with the Hot d'Or Porn Awards in Cannes and working up from there (you truly have not lived until you have heard a tearful starlet thank the jury for granting her the top prize in that coveted category 'Best Gang-Bang'). He'll sort out a studio.

I've got a stylist, who'll get in all the clothes and hire the hair and make-up artist. Lucien is getting a video-cameraman/director (a moonlighting whiz-kid from MTV). I've got a deal at the knee-tremblingly hip St Martin's Lane Hotel which is giving us cheap rooms for all the people who aren't based in London and need a place to crash. I'm tracking down a friend who has a stunning Notting Hill Gate apartment where we can shoot Cazza's at-home feature. I'll soon have a minute-by-minute schedule for the entire two-day shoot – absolutely essential if we're going to get anything like enough done. So it's all tickety-boo apart from one minor detail. I still haven't met Cazza.

29 March

In between creating pretend superstars, I've been spending the past few days on the line to The Attik, trying to sort out the changes I want made to the site. Meanwhile the cost is rising. The pages that have been done aren't yet as good as I want them. We still haven't begun work on

Cazza's page, or any of the vital sales-pages that will spin off it, showing all the pics, games and interviews that people would be able to buy. And the price has, as of today, gone £500 past the original estimate.

As Kit warned me, more than two months ago, building a business is like building a house. No matter how much time and money you allow, it always takes twice as long and costs three times as much.

30 March

Brent Cross and Soho, London: In the afternoon I meet Simon Hochhauser at Homechoice, along with his Head of Production, an ex-BBC exec called Hugh Williams. We agree that it would be a good thing to start work to see what sho-biz.com can provide for Homechoice. But there's going to be a slight delay because I'm going to France on holiday in April and Hugh's doing three weeks in Australia. When we're all back in the same place again, we'll meet and get specific. So we're making progress. It's slow… but it's happening.

That sorted, I head back to Soho for a meeting at the Groucho with Danielle Nicholls and Rebecca, her agent at Noel Gay. Danielle is wearing tight jeans and a fitted red leather jacket, which she removes to reveal a black bustier decorated with sequins. Probably just as well that Clare and the girls aren't here, all in all.

In the flesh, Danielle is no more classically pretty than she appeared on TV. In fact, there are times when she almost seems plain. But her face lights up when she's animated, which she is for most of the time. This is not the sort of girl who'd spend a date moping over a limp leaf, whining about her problems. This is a girl who'd have a good time. Not to put too fine a point on it, she's fucking sexy, a fact that is rapidly demonstrated twice over. First she charms Nigel Planer, who's wandered over to say hello, and is rapidly reduced to gazing in Danielle's direction with a blissful smile on his happy face. Then, as we leave, she's set upon by a bunch of young execs, out on the piss, who recognise her from the telly and beg for an autograph. They get that and a peck on the cheek too, in exchange they happily let Danielle have the cab that they were about to take, leaving her looking as delighted by the deal as they obviously are.

As Rebecca and I get on the tube – her to go home, me en route to

Victoria and the train back to Sussex – I become uncomfortably aware that I'm babbling at her in an incredibly incoherent, hyper way, as if I'm paralytically drunk. In fact I've not touched a drop of alcohol all evening.

'I'm sorry,' I say. 'Do I seem a bit crazy?'

'Well,' says Rebecca, hesitantly, 'I wasn't going to say anything, but ...'

'I know. I'm raving. It's just relief. I've spent the past week getting more and more tense, wondering whether I've made the right decision, staking what could be my company's entire future on Danielle. And tonight I realised that I have. So now I'm unwinding, right here in front of you. Don't worry, I'll be fine in the morning.'

And then we pulled into Victoria and I got off, leaving one very bemused agent standing in the tube-train behind me.

31 March

Arundel, West Sussex: It really is remarkable, the effect money can have. Mitch and I got to Butlers to pay hommage to Sacha, like we do. She's standing behind the bar when we arrive, chatting to her mum. Once I've said hello I ask her whether she likes to be known, officially, by her married or maiden name. She looks at me suspiciously and asks me why I want to know. 'Because,' I say, 'I'm going to have to put your name on a share-certificate and I've got to get it right.'

Sacha's still not sure what the hell I'm going on about, so I explain. 'You know that Internet company I've started...'

'Oh great,' moans Mitch, 'It's his company now. He has a partner, you know...'

'Okay, that company *we* started, but which *I* own nine times as much of as he does... Well, the thing is, we'd never have had the idea for it if we hadn't come here for lunch. And the reason we came to lunch here was you. So you deserve a share. So we're giving you one-tenth of one per cent, which may not sound like much, but if the company takes off, who knows? It could be worth a fortune.'

Sacha looks at me. 'This was your idea, wasn't it?'

'Er ... yeah. It was.'

'Thought so.'

And then an amazing thing happens. Now, don't get me wrong, I'm not making any improper suggestions, nor making any undue claims. Sacha is both married and pregnant. She loves her husband like any new bride should. Plus she comes from the kind of good, Catholic family where they takes these things seriously. So that's not what this is about...

But...

Within the last few moments Sacha has discovered that I may – however improbably – make a fortune. Furthermore, I have the power to bestow some of that fortune on her. And for the next hour this changes everything. Suddenly, she's on my side. She's always treated us royally, but now I'm getting even more attention (point of evidence: she gives me a free helping of prawns to go with my salmon and avocado salad), mixed with a distinct element of respect, even – dare I say it? – deference.

If this is what happens when you only *might* be rich, think what the effect of actual money and power must be like. Now I understand what makes men work so hard.

APRIL

3 April

Here's what always happens with designers. You end up doing it all yourself. I haven't been able to get the sho-biz.com homepage looking the way I want it using words, whether written or spoken. So now I sit down at my computer, do my best to recall the graphic skills I picked up watching Lucy make her diagrams, and draw the page, and the elements within it, in the way that I want. Then I write a fantastically savage, sarcasm-laden memo explaining, for the benefit of any moron who can actually read, that if you want to create a page that looks like a riot of non-stop action, but that can be instantly updated through a database-driven system, it's absolutely vital to give it a strong, coherent structure. The punter won't know it's there, but we have to.

Then I press 'delete' and send a nice polite note, thanking everyone for the amazing progress made so far (which, to be fair, is actually the case) and suggesting in the nicest possible way that they might follow a few of my suggestions, as amateurish and cack-handed as they are. Because, after all, I've only been laying out pages professionally, as an editor, since 1982... so what do I know?

Ooops... a little sarcasm got past the censor.

4 April

Wall Street, New York City, USA: The party's over. The long-awaited Internet crash has finally, and indisputably arrived.

In New York, NASDAQ loses 14% in a single day. They're calling it Turbulent Tuesday. James Cramer, the professional Wall Street investor and journalist whose website TheStreet.com has also made him an Internet guru (and hero to those who worship the Net's overnight zillionaires) pooh-poohs all the unrepentant optimists who say this is just a correction or a temporary decline. 'If you sat at my turret, stared at my computers and heard the voices on my phones you would know that crash might have been too sweet a word for the carnage wrought by the massive pileups of sellers packed into that tiny NASDAQ off-ramp.'

Writing in *New York* magazine, he lists all the stocks that have lost more than 85% of their value in the past couple of months. So what do people need to see before they'll admit that this is a crash: do the shares have to fall below zero? And then, speaking with all the rueful wisdom of a man whose own company's stock was launched at $19, raced up to $71 *on the first day* and is now slumped at 'five bucks and change', he makes the definitive announcement, 'The dot-com gold rush is over.'

Now he tells me.

5–6 April

Clerkenwell, Soho and Notting Hill, London: Finally, we get to the shoot that I've been thinking about for the past three months, the shoot that will finally prove that sho-biz.com is a viable proposition – presuming that the great ship *e-Commerce* isn't terminally holed below the waterline, that is.

After all the aggravation and uncertainty that's gone before, it proceeds with an almost eerie smoothness and we get a fantastic amount done. On day one, working in a stunning photo-studio on the top floor of a Clerkenwell warehouse building, we manage to shoot a cool, upmarket fashion layout, in beige suede and cream-coloured wool; a slightly funkier denim look; a bright and bubbly, hair-in-girly-bunches teen look; a mid-market women's-mag look and a sexy knickers 'n' vest lad-mag look. There is a minor moment of wobble when Danielle says no to being shot in her bra and pants, but we can live with that. By the end of the day, we have everything in the can that we need and we've barely broken sweat. Danielle heads off at the end of the day to meet a man about panto: she's gunning for Cinderella in Manchester.

Day two begins with a few shots in Danielle's bedroom at the St Martin's Lane Hotel – or Cazza's exclusive hideaway, as it will shortly become. Then we do a bunch of mini-interviews to gather material for the site. Our story is that Cazza has just quit her girlband, the Sugarchix, and is now heading off to Hollywood to seek her fortune in the movies. This is like falling off a log for Danielle: her own horror-stories of life on the road with the Chix are all entirely truthful accounts of her pop career, while the Hollywood stuff is exactly what she really dreams of. She may not have the porcelain complexion or matchstick thighs of a proper supermodel, but she's got about a million megawatts more oomph than your average mannequin.

While we're at the hotel, we film a rock-video sequence, set to Cazza's latest single, which is a cover of Lou Reed's 1972 classic 'Walk on the Wild Side'. The cover is so faithful that it is, in fact, Lou Reed's actual version. But Lucien King swears he'll knock up a new version in the studio he owns down in Wimbledon (where, he proudly informs me, he recorded two computer-games soundtracks that won BAFTA awards. No, I didn't know you could get them for that kind of thing, either).

We break for lunch, then head off to Notting Hill to shoot Cazza at home with her Danish footballer lover Kurt Bohansen – or MTV camera-man Ben Hall, as 'Kurt' actually is. By half-past five we're done and dusted. Can it really be that simple?

7 April

No, of course not. At around 3.00 in the afternoon, Paul Massey rings up from the laboratory he has been using to process his stuff for well over a decade. There's been a problem. Their machines went haywire... with all our films inside. No one's quite sure how many of the films have been damaged, or how much.

At 4.00, Paul calls again. It doesn't look too bad. A couple of rolls of 35mm film have been wrecked, but all the large-format stuff he used for the studio shots seems to have survived. That's not what he's telling the lab, of course. As far as they're concerned, we lost the vital frames and the whole thing is a disaster. So can we have the processing for free … please?

5.30: the developed films have all been put in the last post and are on the way to me.

8 April

I rip open the package, I flick through the pictures… and I panic.

I hate them. The girls were right. I've just wasted somewhere in the region of £10,000.

I take another, closer look. Okay, so some of the shots aren't as perfect as they need to be to satisfy someone who's spent too many years working in the editorial departments of super-snooty magazines, where every imperfection, no matter how tiny, is ruthlessly removed by whatever means – from minor retouching to full reshooting – necessary. But actually, there are plenty of really great photographs which will certainly suffice to cover everything we could possibly need. So get a grip, Thomas, and stop being so ridiculously queeny.

10 April

I call Neil Storey. He has good news and bad news. The good news is that Nitin Sawhney's shows supporting Sting at the Albert Hall went brilliantly. Madonna came… twice. And if Madge thinks you're hot, that's the record industry's answer to the *Good Housekeeping* seal of approval.

The bad news is bad. There's a total lack of progress re. Lowenstein and the Stones. Neil's been calling The Girl Who Knows Everyone all week and, er … she doesn't want to know him. Well, she hasn't got back to him, anyway. Not that he's particularly bothered by that, its often her way he says. Yet, while that may be the way it works, it doesn't ease my mind at all.

There's worse. Last month, he now confesses, it was suggested by the suits who control his company that he should fall graciously on his sword. Three weeks ago, he resigned from the Board of The Virtual

Orchestra on the basis that he'd remain as a consultant to the company. Since then, there's been not a word from Malcolm Messiter. Nor from Steve Thomas. Nor John Lenehan. Nitin Sawhney may be flourishing, but Neil Storey's stuck in his garage-office near Camberley rightly or wrongly feeling left out by the very people whose friendship sustained him through the chaos and poverty of the past twelve months.

And right or wrong, there's nothing he can do about it.

11 April

The City and Islington, London: Imagine you had a fantastic idea for a movie, and you found yourself at dinner next to Steven Spielberg. Or suppose you wanted to be a professional footballer, and you were playing in a Sunday morning park game, and Sir Alex Ferguson just happened to walk by ... and stayed for the entire match. Well, if you're in the business of starting up an Internet firm, that's how amazing it is to find yourself in Geoffrey Chamberlain's office and to be given his undivided attention.

Chamberlain is the Chairman and Chief Executive of a City institution called Durlacher, which was the first British investment house to specialise in the Internet and new technology. The company began life in September 1995 with a share price of 38p. By December 1999, when Chamberlain made £3.7 million by cashing in a bunch of options that had been granted to him at 5p each, the price was over £16. That, though, disguised the true strength of the shares, because the company had earlier issued a bonus of fourteen shares for every existing one. Had it not done so, the actual share price would have been around £246. By February, at the peak of the Internet gold rush, even the diluted shares had gone up to the best part of £40, so Durlacher diluted them again, issuing a bonus of eight new shares for every one that investors already held. Anyone who possessed one Durlacher share at the beginning of 1999, now had 23 – and every one of those 23 shares was worth more than the single one they had started out with.

If investors were doing well, Chamberlain was really rocking. After he'd sold his options in December, he was left with 16% of the company. That stake was then worth £136 million. Two months later, the shares had risen so steeply that his holding was up to £330 million. And why not? His chairman's report revealed that in the six months to 31 December 1999, the company's turnover was up 125% on the corresponding period for 1998, profits were up 853%, net assets were up 640% and earnings per share up 717%. In June 1999, Durlacher was valued at £141 million. By February 2000 it was over £2 billion.

Now we're in April and things aren't looking quite so peachy-keen. Just after the final share issue, Durlacher stood at 441. By yesterday morning, it had slumped to 227. During the course of the day, it crashed another 24 points to 203. So it's not quite the wonder-stock that it was. But what the heck, Geoffrey Chamberlain is still the finance king of the British Internet, and I've got an appointment to interview him, pick his brains … and, even more important, pitch sho-biz.com. I've got to be on tip-top form.

It's still reasonably bright when I leave home at eight, but by the time I reach central London, two hours later, thick grey clouds are billowing overhead. Just as I walk out of Liverpool Street tube, a steady penetrating rain starts to fall... and guess who hasn't got an umbrella? I try to figure out the way to Durlacher's offices in Chiswell Street from the map in my pocket-size *A-Z*, but nothing seems quite where it ought to be. My sense of direction is one of the more reassuringly reliable aspects of my personality, and there are some parts of London where I'm as well-versed as a cabbie, but the City is still completely alien territory: the money's all waiting there, but I don't know where to find it.

I get to Durlacher soaking wet and with seconds to spare before my 10.30 appointment. There's just time to dive into the Gents and rub a couple of paper towels over my face before Geoffrey Chamberlain appears in the reception area, shakes hands, leads me to his office (note: there's no snooty secretary doing the honours, just to remind me of her boss's importance – this is a low-bullshit individual) and the working day begins.

Chamberlain is 57. He's a few inches shorter than me – say, five-nine or ten – with a slim build, fat-free face, silver hair (thinning in the middle) scraped back off his forehead. He has quite a light speaking voice and an obviously quick mind. He'll leave sentences unfinished as he moves straight from one part of an argument to another – it's down to me to be bright enough to fill in the gaps and keep up with where he's going.

His office, which is reasonably big, but certainly not flashy or ostentatious, is decorated with antique stock and bond certificates, one for the Chinese government, another for South American gold-mines. Those memories of previous booms and busts seem all too appropriate as the market in technology stocks keeps falling through the floor.

Chamberlain doesn't seem too bothered by losing the best part of £150 million in four weeks flat. 'What is money?' he asks, rhetorically. 'It's paper. It comes and goes. Whatever you see in the Rich Lists can change dramatically within three days of publication.'

He's keeping a cool front in the face of the market meltdown. He calls it, 'A little period of panic, which will be healthy to arrest some of the rather more obvious facets of greed, greed, a little bit of fear and more greed. That needed to be tempered. A bucket of ice needed to be poured on that and it has now.'

Sure, he says, there are plenty of 'graveyard companies' littering the marketplace – e-commerce start-ups which were once worth hundreds of millions of dollars, now running into the ground as their cash dries up and their long-expected revenues fail to materialise. But the way Chamberlain sees it, the failures of weak companies are part of a natural evolutionary process in which stronger, fitter businesses will survive: 'We're in a period where the men are being sorted from the boys.'

Of one thing he's certain: the Internet revolution isn't going to go away. 'What worries me,' Chamberlain says, 'is when I go to business meetings or dinners and hear old-economy CEO's asking me, "When will the bubble burst?" and not, "How can I get to grips with the technological change that's going on?" They're talking as if this will go away. But it won't go away. There's a seismic change going on.'

I get the feeling he prefers it when the going gets tough, when you have to be a pro to survive, and the hordes of day-traders are sent packing back to the real world with their mice between their legs. Where was the challenge when the market was a one-way upward bet? 'It was like Christmas had come early,' he says. 'People didn't have to think about it. They could just leave their jobs and become day-traders. There was a steady roll-out of companies into a frenzied market-place. It looked like very easy money. But I've never seen any such thing in my life. I've always had to work extremely hard.'

So then he tells me his personal history. For all his present-day polish, Chamberlain is not typical of his generation of City players. He comes from a modest, northern background and supported himself through his business studies at Manchester University by working midnight shifts at local bakeries. He retains an unquenchable drive to prove himself and to test those around him. When, for example his local rugby-club in Buckinghamshire asked him to coach the seven year-olds' mini-rugby team (Chamberlain was a useful fly-half in his day), Chamberlain replied that he would do the job, but only on certain conditions.

'I'm not very good with small children because what I see is chaos, which I can't stand. So I said they'd have to do things my way and that parents would have to buy into that, too. There's to be no missing training on Sundays to go and have lunch with granny.'

Chamberlain took his team of little boys and made them literally unbeatable. In five years, they never lost a game. 'I always tried to set them new challenges,' Chamberlain recalled. 'By the third or fourth year I asked them if they could go through the entire season without conceding a single point. I recognised then that I'd gone over the top.'

His ex-wife and family could have told him that. Chamberlain admits he lost his marriage to his overwork, but the experience hasn't made him alter his ways. He leaves home at 6.30am, is at his desk before 7.00, doesn't quit the office till 8.00pm and goes straight to a working dinner. Saturday, he takes off. But by Sunday evening he's on the phone to his partners and Monday morning the circle starts rolling again.

Confronted by that schedule, I feel like a total slacker. I'm just not working hard enough. Which reminds me ... back in '83, when I was just starting out as a journalist, I interviewed my teenage hero, David Bowie, just before he released 'Let's Dance'. At one point I asked him if he still took a travelling library with him wherever he went.

'How did you know about that?' he asked, with a tone of genuine amazement in his voice.

'Because when I was a teenager I read just about every single magazine article about you ever written,' I replied.

'Good Lord,' he said, chuckling at my artless flattery. He then told me a story about going down to New Mexico in 1975 to film *The Man Who Fell To Earth*, directed by Nicholas Roeg. 'I took with me hundreds and hundreds of books, all kept in boxes like the ones amplifiers get packed up in. I was trying to find a book for Nic to refer to on alchemy or something, and all these books were just pouring all over the floor, there were just mountains of books. Nic was sitting there watching me and he said, "Your problem, David, is that you just don't read enough." And I didn't even think it was funny until months later. I was so gung-ho that I really thought he was serious. I just felt depressed and wondered, "What *else* should I read?" I don't travel with those books any more. Although I must say that because of that period...' and here Bowie paused for a beat before adding ... 'I do have an extraordinarily good collection of books.'

I've been looking back at that interview a lot recently, if only to remember what it meant to me then, and what it has to tell me about my ideas for sho-biz.com today. When I told David Bowie that I'd read everything ever written about him, I wasn't joking. I spent most of my teens as a devoted Bowie fan, buying every new album on the day of release; covering my bedroom walls with his photograph; imitating his every image (a lunatic idea, given (a) what his Seventies images actually looked like, and (b) the fact that I neither bore nor bear any visual resemblance whatever to Bowie himself), and buying any book or magazine which even hinted at some new interview with or information about the man himself.

The interview was given at Claridges Hotel, in Mayfair. Bowie had taken a suite for the day and was meeting reporters in its sitting-room. Just before being led into his presence, I was escorted up from the hotel lobby, where I had spent the morning in an increasingly fevered state of anticipation, and left to await his summons in the suite's bedroom. I sat there for about half-a-minute before nerves overcame me and I dashed for an emergency pee in the bathroom. Another five-minute wait... another slash. By now every pore in my body had opened up and sweat was flooding out of me. I became fixated by the wetness of my palms: here I was, about to meet my hero, and I wouldn't be giving him a handshake, so much as a hand-splash.

I looked around in panic for something on which to wipe my molten hands and noticed a tissue-dispenser, just beside the bed. So I grabbed as many tissues as I could, scrunching them all into two great balls, which I clenched in my fists, to soak up all the moisture.

My whole body was clenched, too – curled up in an almost foetal position on the edge of a chair, with my head gazing down at my bunched-up fingers. So I didn't see the door open, or the trim, blonde-haired man walk in until he was just a few feet away from me, holding out his right hand and saying, 'Hi, I'm David Bowie.'

I gazed up in total horror, then leapt to my feet with my hands still wrapped around their Kleenex sweat-absorbers. By now I was in a state of total panic, far beyond the realm of rational thought. As Bowie stood there, with his hand stretched out, waiting for me to take it, I flung my own arms wide and opened my hands, showering the room with moist paper-products. Then I grinned manically and said, 'Hi, I'm David Thomas.'

My humiliation was total, my journalistic credibility shattered. Bowie burst out laughing. Then he gave me what remains one of the two or three best interviews I have ever had in my life.

When I think of the kids who will one day log onto sho-biz.com, I think of the force of that devotion, the intensity of emotional identification which kids have towards their heroes and heroines. I look at the way my daughters devour every episode of *Buffy the Vampire Slayer*, watching it again and again until every line, every movement has been committed to their memory. No matter what technical or financial issues I have to consider, I must never let myself forget the psychological motivations that underpin the entire project.

But perhaps those adolescent passions never go away – they just get diverted somewhere else. Geoffrey Chamberlain's a multi-millionaire less than three years away from his 60th birthday, but he talks about the Internet the way my kids talk about Buffy. There's that same all-embracing fascination. The same determination to convey every last ounce of its importance.

And just like the young David Bowie, Chamberlain reads obsessively, too. That's where he gets the information from which he's derived another Bowie-esque quality – the knack of spotting opportunities early and getting in ahead of the game. Back in the early Seventies, he saw that there were people in Chicago creating whole new categories of tradable securities – options and derivatives that enabled traders to use money far more efficiently (and also more riskily), using leverage to buy much bigger positions with their cash. The City and Wall Street booms of the past quarter-century have been powered by the juice that derivative trading provides, and Chamberlain was one of the very first people on this side of the Atlantic to understand the way it worked. He literally wrote the book: the first British textbook on the subject.

He began thinking about the Internet and the World Wide Web in 1993, and he found himself unable to shake the idea that these innovations were about to have an impact of historical significance. Silicon Valley, he realised, was the Klondike of our age. 'I'd be going to America on business and my body would be in New York, but my mind was on the West Coast. I'm passionate about ideas that I believe in. I'm not Italian in the demonstration of that passion, but the passion runs deep. It's a bit like Magnus Magnusson. I've started, so I'll finish.'

He had no pressing need to reinvent his career – three decades of uninterrupted success in the City had left him financially secure – but having spent his working life within other people's institutions, he felt a powerful urge to create a business of his own, by which he might be remembered. 'I had finally escaped from major corporations and I vowed I would never go back.'

So he gathered a group of partners and took over an unexceptional stockbroking firm called Durlacher. Then he and his colleagues spent the next twelve months doing nothing but researching the new technology market. 'It was all expenditure and no revenue,' he recalls. 'People considered it a very strange business-model.'

But the research paid off. Durlacher established itself as the City firm that knew more about technology stocks than anyone else. As the Internet bubble expanded, Durlacher went along for the ride. Five years down the road, Chamberlain admits he's travelling 'blindfolded, without a map.' But he remains convinced he's making the right journey. 'In another ten years time, what are you going to say to yourself? Did you have a go? Did you try to put into practice some of the beliefs, some of the theories, some of the let's-do-it-differently that either circumstance or a powerful corporation once prevented you from doing? Basically do you have the guts?

'This has been the most exhilarating phase of my life. There are so many challenges, so many things to do. I have never known days and months and years fly by so quickly. How could one possibly waste this period of time we're living through now? There is so much to do. Over the past six-to-nine months it's almost as if a little chip off the West Coast of America has landed here. It's too fascinating a period in history not to put in the time and effort to try to understand it and help it along.'

Oh yes, quite so, I murmur agreeably, delighted by the way things are going. Here I am in Geoffrey Chamberlain's office and our twenty-minute scheduled interview has turned into well over an hour's conversation. We've got a nice mood going, with just the right level of mutual respect, within an overall atmosphere of mild deference to Chamberlain's experience and status. I've had one dodgy moment when Chamberlain referred to the process of disintermediation and I had to ask him to spell it, thereby revealing my total ignorance of a term that must be some sort of basic bankers' jargon. But aside from that minor slip, I'm doing fine. Chamberlain's perfectly primed. All I've got to do now is make my pitch and I could be off to the races.

Now, just as I digressed for a moment on the subject of David Bowie, so I should now make another Ronnie Corbett-style swing away from the main thrust of the story to point out one other essential fact. I am a brilliant pitcher.

That's not very modest, I know, but it's true. I've spent most of the past decade as an uncontracted freelance journalist. My entire living has depended upon an ability to sum up an idea and sell it to an editor, day after day, week after week, year after year. Ask anyone who knows me, I can talk for Britain. Above all, I've got passion. People look at me and they think, 'This bloke may be nuts. And I wish he'd shut up. But he's definitely got ideas and energy to spare.'

Yet when it comes to pitching sho-biz.com to Geoffrey Chamberlain, everything goes pear-shaped, right from the off. Instead of going straight in with a direct appeal to his business interests, I try to be clever, flattering his ego by asking for advice. I've got this idea, I say, and I'm not sure which way to take it: perhaps he can help? Well, that puts me on the defensive, right from the off. I'm not a passionate salesman, I'm a clueless jerk. Plus, I'm a clueless jerk who isn't getting any response, and that is seriously bad news.

For me, a pitch is a form of performance and I need an audience reaction. Chamberlain, though, is one of those people who just sits there, listening to what you say, storing it away in his planet-sized brain and saying precisely nothing. It's like playing tennis with someone who absolutely refuses to hit the ball back at you. Which would be okay, if it wasn't for something else. As I'm going through my sho-biz story for the umpty-third time, I suddenly realise that my emotional batteries are completely flat. The ups and downs of the past couple of weeks have finally caught up with me. The tank is empty. The Duracell bunny's just stopped drumming. Here I am, about to give the most important sho-biz spiel of my concept's short life... and I'm all out of juice.

The upshot of it all is that I say my piece, and Chamberlain looks about as involved as a man who's just turned on the radio hoping to hear something interesting, and found the shipping forecast instead. Distinctly unimpressed, would be two words that summed up his reaction. So I drag us back to the interview and try to carry on as though nothing has happened. Because nothing has in fact happened. Which is precisely my problem.

After the meeting is over, I take a cab through the pouring rain to Islington, where Lucien and I are due to be meeting Oyster, the company that designed the Rockstargames.com site and which Lucien would clearly have preferred for sho-biz.com. I call Lucien en route, and he seems on good form, given that he's just got in from New York, travelling at the back of the bus. He says he spent plenty of time with Sam Houser, who should now be able to draft some kind of letter confirming Rockstar's interest in working with sho-biz.com. He also hung out with some of his old music-biz contacts, all of whom had the same message: sho-biz.com can definitely work, but there's no chance of persuading Americans to buy into it without a strong US presence and demonstrable proof that the concept is already working on this side of the Atlantic. We can't just turn up and expect them to take us seriously.

By now the cab is pulling up outside Oyster, where Lucien is waiting for me. Cue a classic Y2K moment: I'm still blathering into the mobile as I'm paying off the driver, Lucien is chattering back to me... and we're standing ten yards apart. We keep talking, by way of regular, technology-free conversation, once we get inside. Oyster's base is a big old warehouse, packed with young groovers and computers – your classic new media outfit, in other words. In the lobby, they've got a couple of funky Hitachi TVs from the Seventies – round, bright orange, late Twentieth century antiques. Apparently they belong to Hugo, one of Oyster's partners, who's got a vintage Porsche 911 to match. Eventually Hugo turns up: big, burly, panda-eyed and sweatshirt-dressed. He says he spent the weekend driving his Porsche round a racetrack in Anglesey, a classic rich-lad's anecdote, which he tempers with a nice new-man, new-economy touch. It wasn't the speed he enjoyed, he says. It was the satisfaction he got from learning how to take his car round corners with maximum precision and grace.

As we walk through the office, he apologises for the chaos and over-crowding. They've only been there a year or so, but the business is grow-ing so fast that they've already got to move out. One of the partners, Hugo, says they're thinking of relocating... to Bombay. India's just packed with brilliant programmers, paid a fraction of UK wages. Plus they've got a huge middle-class market, right on their doorstep. Lucien is delighted by this vote of confidence in the sub-continent and flashes me a triumphant grin as if to say, 'See, dude? Isn't that what I've been telling you?'

Once we get down to the business of the day, I give the sort of snappy, incisive, desire-inducing introduction to sho-biz.com that I should have provided for Geoffrey Chamberlain. Hugo leaves most of the talking to his partner Anil, who's very smooth, very plausible, very Oxbridge. As Anil describes the multi-level functions that Oyster have within their company – site-design, database-enabling, strategic plan-ning, the whole kit'n'caboodle – he casually refers to the crucial process of disintermediation.

I stop him. 'That's the second time I've heard that word today. What the hell does it mean?'

Anil takes pity on my aged cluelessness (I'm a good dozen years older than anyone else in the room) and explains: disintermediation is just a fancy name for the process by which a new business, or new tech-nology cuts out a bunch of middle-men, or intermediates.

I'm delighted. That's exactly what sho-biz.com plans to do. We're going to disintermediate the relationship between artists and the media via our syndication site, by removing all those interfering journalists and TV crews. And then we're going to disintermediate the relationship between artists and their fans by putting entire interviews and photo-sessions up for sale on sho-biz.com. Except, of course, we're going to put ourselves in where all the other intermediates used to be.

'That's called "reintermediation",' says Anil, approvingly.

It turns out that, in bankers' eyes, sho-biz.com will be seen as a disintermediation-reintermediation play. This is evidently a good thing. So I'll have to rewrite the first line of my business-plan's Financial Headlines one more time, just to get the point across as early as possible.

We leave Oyster promising to stay in touch. But Lucien's words about how hip young companies work are echoing round my head. Hugo and Anil obviously have brains. But here's the big question: how do I know that the rest of Oyster aren't monkeys?

I ponder that as we take the tube back to Pimlico. At Lucien's flat I pull out all the Cassandra Clark shots. Not being a hypercritical ex-magazine editor, Lucien sees them with considerably less cynical eyes than mine. As far as he's concerned, they look fine, and he knows a designer who'll be able to turn them into covers and layouts. We do a rough edit and I give him a series of assignments. Just having someone else to share the workload improves my mood enormously. Perhaps we'll make it after all.

12 April

Geoffrey Chamberlain may have cold-shouldered sho-biz.com, but what does he know? Durlacher were off another 20 yesterday to 183. Which is, coincidentally, almost exactly the same price as Lastminute.com. Its share-price has dipped to 186.5 – thereby taking it below 50% of its launch price in less than a month. Dear Mr Guinness, Is this a record?

Other companies, however, seem to have brighter prospects. At 10.48 I receive the following e-mail from Adam Precious: 'David, attached is my spreadsheet. Look on the right and there are some assumptions for years one, two and three. Just change the numbers to get a profit figure. I think my assumptions are quite reasonable. Perhaps year three is optimistic.'

I open up the attachment and try to make sense of the columns of numbers that pop up on the screen. Precious has taken the cost and revenue assumptions given for Downloads, CD-ROMs and DVDs in the latest version of my business-plan. He's then extrapolated into the future, to see what would happen if we did more interviews and sold more copies of each, creating a compound effect.

Now, spreadsheets are hardly my speciality, and my girls could certainly create them more effectively than I ever could, because that's the sort of thing they learn in school these days, instead of the dates of battles or the capitals of foreign countries. But even I know how to find the bottom line of a profit-and-loss calculation. And when I look there, this is what I find ...

Year One: $943,550 net revenues
              ... pretty much as I'd calculated in my plan.

Year Two: $6,160,250 net revenues
              *... just a million shy of covering the costs for the
              entire operation.*

Year Three: $196,733,500 net revenues
              ... holy shit.

I call up Adam Precious who is, not unreasonably, very pleased with himself and his calculations. But as we talk, and look at the numbers more closely, it becomes clear that there's been some sort of fundamental miscalculation, because the columns don't add up as they should. Temporarily deflated Precious, hangs up, saying he's going to play around with the numbers and get back to me.

At 11.48, I get another message, called 'Sorry, New Model.' This time, the numbers read as follows ...

Year One: $943, 550 net revenue
              ... well, we're all agreed on that one.

Year Two: $4,336,875
              ... more than half our operating costs.

Year Three: $15,321 750
              ... a palpable profit.

Year Four: $43,705,875

                ... a serious business, by anyone's standards.

Year Five: $99,872,000

                ... time to order the yacht.

Yesterday my personal graph was plunging. Today's it's rocketing. Paul Simon once sang that there was a 'girl in New York City who called herself the human trampoline'. There's an old boy in West Sussex who feels pretty much the same way.

Once I've calmed down, I take another look at the stats. Adam has assumed that the number of interviews carried out by sho-biz.com will rise from 21 in the first year of operation to 510 by the fifth. A minor problem: there aren't 510 stars in the world whose interviews could reasonably be expected to generate enough money to justify a full-on interview, photo and video-session. So I have another go, working more modestly.

Say we get twenty interviews in Year One. That's not too unreasonable. I did twice as many myself last year. Then add another ten for every succeeding year, up to sixty interviews in Year Five. Then assume that half of all the stock you have in any one year continues to earn a little bit of money in the next: not a lot, just ticking over. You end up with something like this...

Year	New Interviews	Archive Interviews	Total
One	20	0	20
Two	30	10	40
Three	40	20	60
Four	50	30	80
Five	60	40	100

Now, if I put those numbers through Adam's spreadsheets, being a bit more modest in my expectations of the money we're likely to make from any one interview, we end up with the following projections...

Year One: $921,000

                ... pretty much the same-old same-old

Year Two: $4,165,000
               ... *still on the same path*

Year Three: $14,871,000
               ... *beginning to drop back a fraction*

Year Four: $22,040,000
               ... *distinctly modest by comparison*

Year Five: $28,710,000
               ...

Now, imagine someone said that you could own a business which, in five years time would make nearly £20 millions worth of net revenue, thereby turning in profits of around £4 million. Then consider that typical new media multiples of 80 would make it worth around £320 million... Would you say, 'No'?

Precisely. Neither would I.

13 April

I get a video-tape in the post. It contains the best bits of the Cazza tapes, edited down by Ben Hall, so that we can use them onsite, or for promotional and presentational purposes. They look great. A second copy of the tape has already been sent up to The Attik in Huddersfield, so all I have to do is choose four mini-extracts from the interview sections and e-mail the timecodes for the start and finish of each section up to The Attik. They can then extract the vital moments and bung them onto the world-exclusive Cazza interview page.

Neil Storey calls. He's finally spoken to the powers-that-be at TVO and found out why he's been having problems. It all seems to have been a pointless misunderstanding. He had promised to give a share in the company to the Girl Who Knows Everyone. The gang at TVO got the impression that he was doling out their stock behind their back. In fact, he was simply going to give the Girl some of his own holding. Wires got crossed, communications broke down. No one made a simple telephone call to ask, 'What the hell's going on?' and sort the whole thing out.

The whole thing is crazy, but it's a typical example of the way money can bring more problems than adversity. Rock bands are just the same. When everyone's piled into the same Transit van, schlepping from one dingy club to another, living off grease and chips, they're all bound together by the common sense of 'us against the world'. Then they get the first hit single, the first platinum album, the first hotel suites. All of a sudden, the drummer and the bassist are pissed-off because the lead singer's getting all the attention and most of the songwriting royalties. The singer's exploding because he has to go to every bloody interview because no one wants to speak to the rhythm section, who can sit around the hotel pool getting pissed instead. And the guitarist is shoving his half of the publishing money straight up his nose.

Same with a business. When there's no money, there's nothing to fight over. When the first coins drop into the pot of gold, everyone starts figuring that they deserve a bit more than they're currently getting. New people arrive who want their share, too. Fights break out. And people like Neil Storey end up sitting by the side of the corporate road, wondering what hit them.

Apparently, Steve Thomas did his best to cheer Neil up by telling him not to worry: he was going to be fantastically rich in a couple of months. I wouldn't be so sure about that. Do the words Lastminute.com mean nothing to them? Have they not checked the markets recently? Any hope of punting TVO onto the market at some wildly inflated price evaporated weeks ago, assuming it was ever there to begin with.

My advice to Neil is to forget TVO completely. Either it'll make him rich, or it won't. There's bugger-all he can do about it now. Besides which, what does he care? He's got a second chance of making his fortune with Nitin Sawhney. And there, at least, the news is all good. Neil tells me how he was hanging out at the side of the stage at the last Albert Hall show and saw another bloke, standing a few feet away in the semi-darkness, really getting into the music. It took a few minutes to realise that it was Sting, who stayed there till the end of the set and gave Nitin a hug and a big thumbs-up as he came off-stage. Sting has asked Nitin to support him on a whole bunch of European dates, and has expressed a serious interest in recording with him.

He's not the only one. Nitin's been doing some mixing work for Paul McCartney, who recently dropped in for tea *chez* Sawhney. Nitin had a few hours notice, so he frantically tidied up the flat, in honour of the great man's arrival. Macca turned up in a chauffeur-driven Merc and had a cuppa with Nitin, who finally gave in to overwhelming temptation, handed the great man an acoustic guitar and asked him if he could possibly, as a huge favour, play 'Yesterday'.

McCartney flipped the guitar upside-down so he could play it left-handed and duly obliged, leaving super-hip Nitin Sawhney, the red-hot young standard-bearer for cutting-edge Asian culture sitting opposite him with all the gobsmacked, jaw-dropped awe I felt as a baby reporter in the presence of David Bowie. Well, how would you feel with a genuine Beatle sitting on your sofa, playing 'Yesterday'?

14 April

Just when you think that the markets have hit rock-bottom, they crash again. In New York, NASDAQ plunges down 354 points – losing another 10% – to 3321. On this side of the Atlantic, I'm off for a week's pre-Easter break in France tomorrow, so the day is spent on corporate housekeeping, making sure everyone has everything they need, to do everything I want while I'm away. There has, for example, been an eerie silence from Britannica.com. So I send Michael Magoulias an e-mail, just to remind him that we need to meet to talk through the Britannia/sho-biz.com deal.

Meanwhile, Lucien has found a graphic designer to create around twenty magazine covers, all featuring Cazza, while Attik are putting the Cazza pics, biog and interview online, and doing a hunch of extra pages. Stacy Mann, the film PR, has just called to say that she is due to have dinner with her dear friend Karin Smith on Wednesday. Karin Smith is High Grant and Liz Hurley's personal publicist. Who knows? Maybe they might be interested in a business concept which promises the chance to gain maximum publicity with minimum effort and total control. 'Have the dinner on me,' I say. 'And sell sho-biz.com hard.'

Great. Everything's sorted. I'm off.

15 April

En route to Dieppe, France: There's a Force eight gale all the way to France. In between trips to the head, I check the *FT*. Durlacher has been losing ground all week. It was down another 22 points yesterday and now stands at 155.

16 April

Cry-sur-Armancon, France: We've rented a country house in Burgundy, a little south of Chablis, and a little north of Beaune: bang in the centre of wine country, in other words. The landscape is lush and rolling, the food is incredible, and the weather's getting better. We've got a fantastic cook, Michelle, who prepares vast buffet spreads for lunch and four-course feasts for dinner. Best of all, we're sharing the place with some really close friends and their kids, so the cost per head to live in the lap of Gallic luxury is roughly £300 for seven nights, including rental, food, drink, service and even ferry tickets – not that much more than a nasty package trip to the Costas, but an immeasurably nicer experience.

Anyway, I'm sitting in the drawing-room by a roaring fire, drinking a glass of Chablis, reading *Tender Is the Night*, and looking up from time to time to watch all the kids as they play a game of Cluedo. This, I realise, is why I'm spending so much time and energy on sho-biz.com. It's not because I want to become obscenely rich, fly private jets, or hang out with movie-stars (even though I'm not immune to the charms of any of those ideas). It's simply that I want to protect what I've already got, and I don't want to give my family less in the future than I have done in the past. Lord alone knows how I'm going to do that if this business doesn't come off.

The 'obscenely rich' option looks less and less likely by the minute, anyway. In London, YesTV, a video-on-demand service that is competing with Homechoice, has just announced that it may abandon its Stock Market float, planned for this week. Yes had been hoping to set a share-price that would value the company at £800 million. Now they may be taking 25% off and going for £600 million. If they float at all.

17 April

Cry: *Tender is the Night* is just about the dumbest book I could possibly have read, given the current circumstances. Not only does the quality of Scott Fitzgerald's prose serve as a crushing reminder of why I will never be a great writer, but the subject matter targets my personal and professional insecurities as unerringly as a Patriot missile.

The book follows the decline and fall of a man called (appropriately, and deliberately) Dick Diver. His career never lives up to its early promise. He starts to drink to excess. His once-legendary charm gives way to bitterness and cynicism. By the end of the book, he has lost his wife and children, declining into penury and obscurity in the backwoods of New York State.

I read all the Fitzgerald novels in my mid-teens. Even then, I was fascinated, and terrified by Dick Diver's arc of descent. All my working life, I have lived in dread of slipping off the ladder and falling back down to the bottom of the pile. And all the time, too, I've had to fight to ward off the weakness which, in the end, does for Dick Diver: in the end, he can no longer persuade himself. He can't suspend his disbelief. He sees through the pointlessness of what he does. He can't, to be crude, persuade himself to give a fuck.

I lie awake, late into the night, gripped by Fitzgerald's hymn to self-destruction. By the end, my reaction is not so much intellectual, or even emotional, as primal. Sleep is impossible. I resolve to read something cheerier in the morning.

18 April

Cry: Bugger that resolution. I get to work on *The Great Gatsby*.

24 April

A survey has just been released by a consultancy company called Rubus which claims that seven out of ten Internet companies will not last out the year.

The weekly update from Forrester Research leads with its latest report: 'The Demise of Dot-Com Retailer,' whose basic findings are that dot-coms spend far too much on advertising, give too little thought to customer service, don't pay any attention whatever to the basic laws of finance and are liable to go bust in droves.

So… are we going to be one of the survivors when the dot-com dust has settled? Or am I just totally deluding myself? I haven't the foggiest idea.

25 April

Stacy didn't have her dinner. Karin couldn't make it. They're rescheduling. Damn.

I check out the sho-biz.com demo site. Bugger-all difference.

What has everyone been up to while I'm away?

Hello? Hello-o-o-o?!!

Oh hang on, here's something. One magazine cover has been completed. It's *Company* and it's got Cazza looking very cute in a pale purple skirt and sequinned boob-tube. On one side of her head it says, 'Cazza reveals all!' On the other it says, 'I killed Meg and Noel's tropical fish!' Along the bottom there's a strap-line promoting a sixteen-page special on the fifty most eligible batchelors in Britain. Now that's value, in anyone's book.

26 April

The Attik have just posted the fully-updated sho-biz.com site, complete with all the Cazza material that was put together while I was in France. And they've done a great job – it looks absolutely bloody brilliant. We may be running more than a month late, and there are still a few small details to deal with, but we've finally cracked it. Thank God.

A message is forwarded to me from… well, I'd better draw a veil over that. Its subject is, 'This is what I get up to behind closed doors.' And it reads…

> This is what I get up to behind closed doors. I'm 28, and love to
> strip naked while being watched. I've attached a pic for you. If you
> want to see more go to my website here [and there follows a URL]

So of course I click on the link. Up pops a series of pages featuring shots of a woman, dressed in spike heels, stockings and black knickers. She's kneeling on a bed. All the photographs are shot from behind so that you can't see her face. But you can see her hand, which is stuck between her legs.

The photographs are arranged in two strips at the top and bottom of the page. Between them is another strip of text, which shuffles back and forth across the screen. It says things like, 'I am a young, horny redhead. If you want to see more, click here.'

So you click, and there are more pictures, still semi-clothed, and another line of text. 'Why do I do this? Because I enjoy it.'

The next page has a close-up and an invitation to see much, much more on the next page, which has… a credit-card form, on which to subscribe to the chance to see the horny redhead have sex.

Just forget, for a moment, the politics or ethics of what I have just described. It's an absolutely brilliant tease, and a fantastic sales-tool. Because even though I do not fill out the form – I'm neither that sick, nor that mad – I instantly bung the message on to Mitch.

This is viral marketing at its best. Now, suppose that the initial message was not a tease from a tart but a message that said, 'Hi, it's Robbie Williams here! I'm about to go on my world tour. If you want to come with me, just go to my website…'

When you got to the site, there would be pictures of Robbie – or Britney, or Boyzone, or whoever – walking through the backstage area at a giant arena, towards the dressing-room. As they walked and you clicked from one page to another, messages would tell you all about their tour, and how you could get daily reports from the road on what was going on, what songs were played last night, what the hotel was like, who came backstage… 'All that good stuff,' as Adam Precious would say. And then, just as the star was about to disappear into his/her/their dressing-room … Bang! Up comes the form which lets you subscribe.

If you're a mad-keen fan you sign on at once, because you'd love to be that close to your hero. And also, we're not a porn site, run by gangsters, so we won't take a credit-card number for a $5 monthly subscription which you are then – surprise surprise – unable to unsubscribe, because the site contains no mechanism for you to do so and you're hardly going to go to your credit-card company and say you've been ripped-off buying filth on the Net.

So here is the moral of the story… If you want to make money from the Net, don't be ashamed to learn from people of whom you heartily disapprove. This isn't a right-on consciousness-raising session. This is business.

27 April

London NW1: Stacy had dinner with Karin Smith – Hugh and Liz's PR – last night. She didn't make any sort of commitment, but she promised to read the business-plan and get right back to us.

28 April

Toronto, Canada: I should be in Ireland. One of my oldest friends is getting married this weekend, just outside Dublin. But I'm not on the banks of the Liffey, I'm in a hotel-room on the shores of Lake Ontario. It's a sign, I guess, of the degree to which my social and personal life is paying second fiddle to my work. I haven't been to a single party this year. Every time I've been asked, I've said yes and then found myself sat by my computer when the appointed hour came around. Now I'm leaving an old friend in the lurch. My excuse to him – which happens to be true – is that I simply can't afford the cost of two last-minute airfares to Ireland. The more significant truth, though, is that I've chosen to make another, far longer journey. Because it's business. And business always wins.

What happened was, I got a call from Microsoft.

'Come to Canada,' they said. 'Oasis are playing a show in Toronto and we've got a Business Class seat with your name on it.'

Well, you can't say fairer than that. I got on the plane and set off for the land of the maple-leaf, the moose and the French-speaking separatist. Now, I've been trailing British rock groups around North American concert halls for the best part of twenty years. But for the first time ever, I've got no desire whatever to interview the group. Because I've not come to Toronto as a music-writer. I'm here as a wannabe Net tycoon. So it's not Liam and Noel I care about, it's all the gadgets and gizmos that are going to be turning their latest show into a global webcast.

Webcasts are going to be the next big thing. Last year, Paul McCartney played to three hundred people at the Cavern in Liverpool – and one million on the World Wide Web. The Spice Girls have announced a massive deal for a series of online shows. And a few weeks ago, the manager of one of the world's biggest rock stars, to whom my lawyer Nigel Parker was pitching sho-biz.com asked him bluntly, 'If we gave you a world-exclusive interview and concert webcast, how much would you give us?'

The correct answer, according to Niall MacAnna, the Special Events Producer at MSN (Microsoft Network), the people who put McCartney on the Web and are doing the same for Oasis, should have been, 'Nothing.' Because MSN don't (yet) pay their artists any actual cash. Instead, they pick up all the production costs for the webcast, and then guarantee an online marketing blitz of banner-ads, e-mails and front-page stories on MSN that delivers – according to MacAnna, at any rate – twenty million pairs of eyeballs a day, every day for the two weeks leading up to the show.

Sooner or later, that sort of coverage is going to make webcasts a commercial proposition, which is why the days of free shows are as numbered as the days of free TV. As MacAnna said to me: 'When the money-men start moving in, you know it's because they've seen the potential of what's going on.'

To prove the point, our conversation was followed almost immediately by a call from a banker in New York. He said he'd heard about my plans for sho-biz.com. He was working on a website that was going to feature live, celebrity transmissions. He knew that sho-biz was going to be in the celeb-trade, too: maybe we should do a deal?

The synchronicity level was rising fast. A few hours later, I was talking to 28 year-old Giles English, the President of a British firm called Virtue TV. It sets up international webcasts for everyone from corporate chairmen, who want to address all their workers and shareholders simultaneously, to websites like BOL, who stage global online interviews with authors, whose new books you can then buy with a single click of the mouse.

English believes the next few years are going to see a host of different media meld together. Telephones, TV and the Internet will all come into homes from a single cable and the set-top box will be a thing of the past. In his words, 'There are going to be corporations that have spent billions setting up digital TV services turning around to shareholders and saying, "Sorry, we took the wrong decision."'

And thereby hangs the tale. Because on Saturday night, as Oasis are playing in Toronto, and sending their show to the world's computers via Bill Gates's MSN, Lennox Lewis will be boxing in New York and sending his victory to fee-paying TV-watchers via Rupert Murdoch's Sky satellites. So the massive question hanging over the Net is this: which screen is going to win, the PC... or the TV?

Will our computers get hooked up to super-speed modems, enabling them to handle live events, movies and videos instantly? Or will our TVs pick up the Internet as easily as they pick up BBC1? Both of those two things are happening now – but only for the few who have broadband Internet access, or subscribe to digital TV. Simon Hochhauser, the boss of Homechoice, told me that he thought the online option was the one to go for, because you could never build satellites big enough to handle the sheer weight of digital traffic that broadband services would generate. But twenty years on the Street of Shame have led me to the conclusion that Uncle Rupert very seldom backs the wrong horse. Then again, Bill Gates isn't known for being a moron, either...

So that's why I'm in Toronto. I've been given an expenses-paid chance to see how the webcast business works, and to make friends with Microsoft. The fact that a man I've known for more than twenty years is getting married just can't compete with that. But I've been fair. I've promised him some sho-biz.com shares, by way of a wedding present.

29 April

Toronto: The Maple Leaf Garden is a typical, old-fashioned downtown sports arena. It's a big concrete toilet, with peeling paint and plastic seats, named after the Toronto Maple Leafs ice-hockey team, whose banners still hang from the ceilings. The Leafs, however, have moved out to the swanky new Air Canada Arena, down on the lake shore, next to the astounding Toronto Skydome – a 50,000-seater baseball stadium that has a retractable, shell-like roof and a hotel built into one of the walls. Now the only people who play at the Garden are the local lacrosse team. But don't mock. They pull in around 14–15,000 people a time for a game played in England by girls who go to Blyton-esque boarding schools. Strange people, these Canadians.

At the back of the arena, there's a whopping great Outside Broadcast truck, filled with around £2 million's worth of state-of-the-art audio-video-telly-o kit, that's going to be the nerve-centre of the whole webcast. The signals from half-a-dozen cameras will come in here, be edited by the director, then fed by land line to a satellite up-station which will beam the show across to Derby where it'll then be converted into a web-compatible format and placed on servers which will whack it out onto the Web. That's the theory, anyway, and as the afternoon wears on there seems little reason to doubt that it will be the practice, too.

Oasis turn up for the soundcheck minus Liam and run through a long instrumental jam. After ten or fifteen minutes, Liam finally appears at the far end of the hall – a tall, shades-wearing, imperiously sullen figure who strides across the floor of the arena, stops in front of the stage and just stands there, glowering at the rest of the band. Then he walks off. It is, in its way, a magnificent performance.

Three hours later, the show is under way. Oasis are being supported by Travis. At home, that double-bill would fill any stadium in the country. But on the far side of the Atlantic, Travis don't yet mean anything and Oasis are on the wane. With their latest album, *Standing on the Shoulder of Giants* dropping from the Billboard album charts having barely troubled the scorer, they've been playing auditoriums, rather than stadiums, to crowds of around 5,000 a night and the Garden is the biggest venue on the itinerary. It's about half-full when Travis come on. They play all the hits (the Canadians don't know that they're hits, of course, not having been hit by them), Fran Healey sings like a wee Scots angel and chats to the punters like a beard and joke-free Billy Connolly, and the perform-ance is rewarded with applause that verges from the polite to the warm without ever getting over-enthusiastic.

As I watch Travis do their thing, I'm struck by how old-fashioned it all seems. Just as the Maple Leaf Garden has been superseded by the Air

Canada Arena, so the idea of blokes-with-guitars, just standing on-stage singing their songs, seems drab and uninteresting when people like Britney and Ricky Martin are doing full-on spectaculars with costume changes, sexy dancers, flashing lights and special effects. It's like the difference between Test cricket and the one-day game: more satisfying to the connoisseur, perhaps, but a lot less interesting to the general public. And that feeling of redundancy doesn't change much when Oasis come on and start working their way through a bunch of tracks from the new album.

There are probably about ten or eleven thousand people in the hall. It's hard to tell how many more could have got in: there's a lot of space on the floor, for example, but that's because people are standing and you often find that safety regulations limit the numbers. Most of the seats are taken, but there are two big blocks on either side of the stage that are completely empty: they don't have the greatest view in the world, but if this had been a hot ticket, they'd have been put on sale for sure.

So it's quite full, and the crowd quite like the show. Liam Gallagher stands in his usual posture, hands clasped behind his back, head tilted up to a high mike, a permanent snarl on his face. Whereas most lead singers exude energy, using their own charisma to kick-start the crowd's enthusiasm, Liam is just the reverse. He's a sort of black hole, utterly motionless, sucking the electricity into him.

But when I go round to the OB truck, the effect is completely different. Liam's stillness looks fantastic on camera. He has real screen presence. And the sound, which is being taken straight from the mixing-desk, is far cleaner than what you hear in the hall. The Director, an Englishman called Cliff, is chewing gun like a maniac and bawling instructions to his cameramen as he cuts from shot to shot. In front of him, a bank of screens shows all the options from which he can choose. There's a permanent wide-shot of the stage, close-ups on Liam and Noel and three or four constantly-changing images from the guys with the handheld cameras actually standing on stage with the band.

This is, without a doubt, the best possible way of seeing the show and I suddenly understand why people have been banging on for years about the way that digital TV is going to change everything by giving viewers more than one camera-angle from which to choose. So my first reaction (score one to Rupert) is to think, 'Christ, I must get Sky Digital.' I've developed a powerful hunger to watch football via the Playercam, or the cameras behind the goals. The basic overview isn't going to be enough any more.

My second reaction is to figure that everyone's going to feel the same way. Multiple cameras enable viewers to do on screen what they do in real life, which is to flit from one sight to another, concentrating on the ones they want. If you've got half-a-dozen girls in a row at a Boyzone concert, they don't all want to watch the same boy at the same time. Each will have a different heart-throb on which they want to shower their devotion. Well… now they can.

So just imagine a time – and it isn't very far from now – when the stuff that NowTV are doing, mixing broadcast images with online connectivity, melds with Sky Digital's technology… and it's all being put down hyper-fast broadband cables. Images will come through on enormous, but completely flat TV screens and you'll click on any one of several options in the corner of the screen to create your main image, while e-chatting to a pal on the other side of the world about the show that you are both simultaneously watching. That may sound too much like hard work to an awful lot of people. But to the generation that grew up with a PlayStation handset glued to their mitts, it will all be second-nature.

At least, it will be… if they can get the damn thing to work, which is more than the guys from MSN are currently able to do. Just to Cliff's right, there's a laptop which should, in theory, be providing a monitor of what is actually going out on MSN. Except that it isn't. The screen is completely blank. Cliff does his best to stay chilled, telling his cameramen, 'Okay, I have no idea whether anyone is seeing any of this. But we're just going to pretend that they are and keep going anyway.'

Not everyone, however, is quite so laid-back. If you want to see a living definition of sheer horror, mixed with mounting panic, just watch the face of a senior Microsoft executive whose globally-advertised webcast appears to be disappearing down the great e-plughole.

Mice are clicked. Keyboards are bashed. Nothing happens. Desperate e-mails are sent to Microsoft Network's London HQ. In a tragic admission of in-house systems failure, a telephone is used to make contact. Finally, contact is established… and back comes the news. Not only are they getting a signal, they've got a broadband connection, a video-projector wired up to their computer and a comfy settee. So they're sitting back in luxury, chugging down the odd beery beverage and watching a show that's being beamed across an entire wall of the office. Brilliant!

So why the hell aren't we getting anything, when we're fifty yards from Noel and Liam, inside the truck that is sending all the signals that are getting through to everyone on the planet except us? More desperate laptop-bashing reveals the cause of the problem: someone had loaded the wrong application. The computer is using an old Microsoft program called NetShow when it should have the current Microsoft program MediaPlayer. So it can't speak the same cyber-language as the webcast, and we can't see a thing until we get online, and download the appropriate player.

Even then the only Net feed into the truck is coming via AOL. And on peak-time Saturday nights, AOL is about as fast as a sloth on Mogadon. So while the happy dudes at Microsoft HQ are chilling out with wall-size, full-motion action, all we get is a postage-stamp-sized series of slowly-changing images, a bit like an Oasis slideshow. As the band launch into a supercharged version of 'Cigarettes and Alcohol' that comes as close to excitement as anything tonight, I slip out of the truck and head back to the real live show to check out the last twenty minutes from the floor.

So has my journey been wasted? No way. Because what I saw in that video-truck was the future of Internet entertainment. It took TV forty years to get from tiny black-and-white pictures of the Queen's Coronation, to giant colour screens, multi-speaker surround-sound and a zillion satellite channels. It will take the Net about one-tenth as long to get to the point where we're all getting as good an experience as the people at MSN HQ.

But before that happens, the glitches have to go. Someone has to decide on a single, agreed system, so that users can turn on the Net as easily as they turn on their TVs. If you speak to the techies who have so far dominated the development of the Internet, they're all fascinated by obscure bits of software, and they love bitching among themselves as to which is the better, or (far more fun) the more riddled with bugs and glitches. It genuinely doesn't occur to them that out here in Punterland, we don't give a fuck about any of that. We truly do not care whether we see moving pictures on MediaPlayer... or RealPlayer... or Flash... Quicktime... or anything else. We just want to be able to log on and watch. Instantly.

So one of two things has to happen. Either some bright spark comes up with a way than anyone can watch anything, regardless of the way it's been sent to them. Or the powers-that-be (Hello Rupert! Hello Bill!) have to agree on a single system. Whatever the outcome, I want sho-biz.com to be ready for it, because if we aren't, we'll be dead. Then again, Niall MacAnna's next big project is a live webcast of the Eurovision Song Contest, complete with instant user-polls on the Worst Haircut and Most Incomprehensible Lyric. Which may be one aspect of the future I can afford to miss...

30 April

Straight off the plane, and into my VAT return. This is for the first quarter of 2000. The gross income – including all expenses and before any deductions – generated by my writing is down to £19,000. That's barely one-third of what it was six months ago. I still have not drawn one penny from the Sho-Corp Ltd account. This has simply got to work, or I'm stuffed.

MAY

1 May

Another bunch of covers comes beaming in from the designer. There's Cazza looking sophisticated on French *Vogue*, sexy on *GQ*, kooky on *Just 17*, cute on *MP-3*, and confidently female on *New Woman*. All completely different. All from one day's shooting. And there's another dozen still to come. When people get a sight of this, they're going to get the point of sho-biz.com, and no mistake.

3 May

Golden Square, London W1: Another meeting with Michael Magoulias at Britannica. He hasn't, sadly, been able to deliver his billionaire boss as the purchaser of sho-biz.com: the man has bigger fish to fry. But that's the only disappointment. Michael loves the sho-biz.com demo site and is dead keen to press ahead with plans for making us the entertainment news and information suppliers to Britannica.co.uk. We talk through what that would entail and decide on a daily news-page, two or three weekly features, a big weekly interview and occasional special features which would virtually be sites of their own.

If we'd been in business now, for example, we could have done a sensational joint package on the release of Ridley Scott's new movie *Gladiator*, using Britannica's vast amounts of information on Ancient Rome and true-life gladiators, then melding that material with more light-hearted stuff about the way Rome has been treated by Hollywood. Michael, it transpires, really is a kid who likes gladiator movies.

4 May

The City of London: A major pow-wow with Kit and Zac at Summit's Broadgate HQ. They still don't think that sho-biz.com is ready to be presented to investors. They've just had a bad experience trying to punt another start-up (not an Internet one this time) and it's left them feeling that investors are in an extremely picky mood. Fear has overtaken greed as the dominant emotion in the market-place. The days when you could turn up at a venture capitalist's office, pull out an oboe, play Ave Maria and pick up a cheque from the receptionist on the way out are long-gone. If you want to get investment from the post-crash marketplace, you'd better have everything absolutely perfect, with i's dotted t's crossed and all your ducks in a row.

Kit's major concern is still that we don't have a properly thought-through marketing strategy. We need to demonstrate how we're going to sell sho-biz.com to both clients and customers. That means defining exactly how much we intend to spend, when, on what and with whom. And while we're at it, he needs an elevator pitch – a one-page corporate summary so-called because it must be short enough to be read in a single elevator-ride. It's also got to be good enough to persuade a company chairman, because that's the only bit he's ever going to read.

Speaking of chairmen, Kit tells me he had a meeting with Geoffrey Chamberlain at Durlacher, a few days ago. 'So, like a good boy, I raised the subject of sho-biz.com, and Chamberlain opened up his briefcase to prove that he had your business-plan sitting there. He promised that it was on his reading-list.'

Clearly, however, the plan remains unread.

Fact: Durlacher's share-price ended the day at 106. I doubt whether Geoffrey Chamberlain's worth much more than fifty or sixty million quid. Hah!

The elevator-pitch is written as soon as I get home and e-mailed to Kit Hunter Gordon at 7.22 pm.

5 May

At 11.46 am I send Kit a marketing plan, covering twelve different aspects of sho-biz.com's promotion, from PR, to viral marketing, to customer service, to affiliate relationships. It details the cost of every category, plus the staff needed to handle it. A second copy is sent to Lucien King, with instructions to find the best possible companies to provide every one of the services we need.

Lucien sends me an e-mail, too. It contains...

Cazza on French *Elle* (denim), Cazza on an Italian mag called *Chi* (vest and knickers) – and on German *GQ*, British *Marie Claire*, *Loaded* and American *Maxim*, all in the same kit (or lack of it). Cazza cuddling her boyfriend on the cover of *Hola!* and showing us around their gorgeous apartment for *OK!* and the *National Enquirer*. Cazza on the front of *Gala*, in Germany, *Officiel* in France and *Bazaar* in Russia. A really gorgeous couple of shots from the hotel sessions for *Rolling Stone* and *Cosmopolitan*. Enough Cazza, already! Is this girl publicity-crazed, or what?

8 May

Kit didn't get my marketing plan until today and he has a problem with it, to wit: 'It's not a plan. It's a budget.'

He doesn't want a category-by-category list of functions and costs. He wants a month-by-month strategy. He wants investors to know that if they give us money on Day One, then certain things will categorically have been achieved by Days Thirty, Sixty, Ninety and so on. That's what he calls a plan.

It's what I call a pain in the arse, but never mind...

9 May

Michael Magoulias calls. He sounds depressed and I soon discover why. Britannica.co.uk has just been closed down. They didn't even make it to launch. As he talks, a story slowly emerges. It seems that Britannica.com, like so many websites, simply wasn't ready for the Net.

Encyclopaedia Britannica went online in mid-October last year, hoping to end a decade-long decline. Back in 1989, there were 7,500 door-to-door salespeople shifting $650 million's worth of chunky books. Then the CD-ROM came along and killed the traditional multi-volume encyclopaedia stone dead. Who needed a shelf-full of hand-tooled hardbacks when you could get it all on a couple of little discs, complete with sound and vision? Over the next ten years, the company's staff had shrunk to just 280, before rising back up to 400 when they went into online development.

So the plan was: turn Britannica into this fantastic portal, go online in the Fall of '99 and then go for a mega-IPO (short for: 'Initial Public Offering', the American term for floatation) in the first quarter of 2000. With the markets rocketing, it seemed like a sure-fire thing: a fantastic brand, a killer site – the perfect e-commercial combination.

So Britannica.com opened for business, a gazillion people tried to log on... and the site crashed. It took two weeks to be back up and running, by which time the IPO plans had taken a terrible beating. By the time Britannica was ready to go to the market, the market had gone to pot. All of a sudden, the idea of a free encyclopaedia that cost the best part of ten million quid to keep going every month, and didn't have any obvious revenue-stream beyond the promise of advertising income, didn't seem quite so appealing. The company's bankers told its executives to concentrate on their core business in the US and forget the rest of the world. So bye-bye Britannica.co.uk .. and my hopes of a first content-provision deal for sho-biz.com.

Still, my problems are nothing compared to Michael's. He and his wife both work for Britannica. It sounds like they've been offered jobs in the States, but he's still feeling pretty bruised. As I know from bitter personal experience that it's tough to work on the creative side of a business when you feel the business-people don't fully understand what you do, completely under-value the benefit of your work and regard you just as a cost.

Meet the new media. Same as the old media. Let's just hope things are a bit different if you actually run the show.

11 May

Holland Park, London, W11: Britannica may be lost, but we are slowly, tenuously, painfully edging towards an actual deal with Homechoice. Today we go to see Hugh Williams at the company's new offices in Holland Park. He has one of his production executives Sarah Bentley with him at the meeting as we go through the various services that sho-biz.com might provide. It turns out that because Homechoice use all their own in-house technology, it's not going to be as easy as I had imagined to stream our material across, around or over theirs.

We'll have to start with simple, bog-standard stuff like scrolling information running along the bottom of the screen. Once that's in place we can think about making it HTML-compatible (i.e. Internet-friendly) so that customers can interact with it, clicking on certain points to call up boxes, just like they will be able to do on sho-biz.com itself. It's going to be a slow process, but it's good news in a way, too. I'm glad that Homechoice are still having to figure things out and find their feet. If they were already up, running and super-slick they'd be a lot less willing to take a chance on a new company like sho-biz.com. With any luck, we can grow together.

Over lunch, Lucien and I discuss the dreaded marketing-plan and the demands of the City. Lucien is typically forthright. 'They're all arseholes! They're the people you don't want to be. They sit there in the City, working away in their glass boxes, caning the cash. You don't need to be shy of them.'

Besides which, we have more important matters to worry about. What City types don't know, but Lucien does, is that anything we put up for sale on sho-biz.com is almost certain to be hacked within hours, decrypted and given away for free on so-called 'warez' sites. These places have got every game, software program and porn pic you can imagine, all for free, if you know how to get to them.

But, just as the porn boys were the first to crack the question of selling content online, so they're going to be the first to make that content unhackable. And the reason, says Lucien, can be found in Jenna Jameson's bottom.

Ms Jameson is an all-American porn star, and the golden girl of WickedWeb.com, a $25-a-month porn site that makes the Playboy Cyber-Club look like amateur hour at the scout hut. These guys are streaming full-length porn-flicks online, as well as flogging every single item of nookie-related mechanise you can possibly imagine, plus quite a few you probably can't. And Jenna is their prize commodity.

But, says Lucien, there's one special treat which Jenna has not, as yet, given her legions of adoring admirers. She's never done anal. So the whole hard-core community is waiting for Jenna to agree to let some lucky professional penis to penetrate her perfectly-formed butt, in the certain knowledge that this single event will be a webcast opportunity that will dwarf anything. The world's wankers will pay untold millions to watch Jenna take it like a man… but only if they can't see it for free on a warez site. So the boffins of Internet pornography are hard at work (as I guess they would be, really), trying to devise an uncrackable, as it were, means of encrypting Jenna's big moment. 'However they fix it, man, that's the solution we want,' enthuses Lucien. 'That's the prize item in fifteen years of online porn.'

12 May

And now those Cazza games – minor amusements intended for children's play. Can you put Cazza's picture back together? Can you save poor Cazza from the hangman's noose by giving the correct answer to Cazza-related trivia questions? Can you race Cazza's pink knickers against the hordes of onrushing Y-fronts? (No, really, it's a lot more innocent than it sounds!).

14 May

The Sunday papers are full of stories saying that the online clothing retailers Boo.com – the company whose gorgeous Swedish founders were exhibited at the National Portrait Gallery – are in serious trouble. They've been trying to raise $30 million without success – not surprising, really, since it transpires they've already blown $135 million on blurry ads that no one could understand and a website so sophisticated that only a tiny proportion of online customers were able to use it properly. Even if they get the money, they're going to have to lay off more than half their 400 staff and close most of their offices around the world.

I wonder how many air-hockey tables they have?

16 May

Chiswick, London W4: Here's a moral dilemma. I'm Neil Storey's friend. So if Neil's having difficulty with anyone, I will happily buy him a pint and tell him they're all bastards. And for the past couple of months, rightly or wrongly, Neil feels he's been having difficulties with the Board of TVO… when he stops to think about them, at any rate.

But, on the other hand, as a businessman, I think that TVO's product is just as sensational now as when I first heard about it, almost a year ago. I want TVO backing-tracks on sho-biz.com because they would fit perfectly with the whole vibe and purpose of the site. It would be great if kids could download backing-tracks by their favourite artists, sing along and e-mail them to their friends, relations… and us. We could have song contests, judged by the actual stars, charts of the most popular tracks, all sorts of interactive, audience-building fun.

So do I talk to TVO, or not? Sure, says Neil, why not? He's still a shareholder. He's happy for the company to get another prospective client. Which is just as well, because I'd probably have called TVO regardless. We have, after all, established the relative significance of friendship and business in the sho-biz.com universe.

I call Steve Thomas, with a view to having serious TVO/sho-biz.com negotiations, and he puts me in touch with his new Chief Executive, a 34 year-old woman called Francesca d'Arcangeli about whom Steve is extremely upbeat, not to say excited. Ms d'Arcangeli is currently splitting her time between TVO and her current employers, prior to taking up her new post full-time. She suggests we meet for lunch today at a restaurant near her office, which is in Camberley… less than a mile from the house where Neil Storey lives, works, and tears his hair out.

As things work out, I get stuck in meetings in London and can't make lunch. We meet instead at All Bar One on the Chiswick High Road in West London, where I discover that Francesca d'Arcangeli is a very different proposition from the middle-aged men who have so far been my only connections with The Virtual Orchestra. Half-Italian, but educated in England, she is an extremely elegant, slender blonde, whose stunning looks must have been an enormous advantage to her in every respect save the fact that they automatically make men think about pleasure, rather than business. So her manner, at least to begin with, compensates by being cool and super-competent.

When I saw Neil, Malcolm Messiter and John Lenehan, that day at Malcolm's house in Barnet, they talked about emotion and excitement. But Francesca is an experienced marketing executive who prefers to describe the whole project in terms of dispassionate professionalism. She has a product – Malcolm's Play software, plus the backing tracks that can be used on it – that is of obvious appeal to a large number of business-users, as well as consumers. She wants to apply it through the maximum number of media, and she's perfectly happy to make sho-biz.com one of them. 'This is an opportunity to be first-to-market with an innovative set of tools. We want to be the Number One web-based tool for the enjoyment, participation and study of music. Our plan is very focused and I think it will be successful.'

Her role, she knows, is to bring a dash of reality to the dream. 'Efficiency is very important. Around very creative people, you need highly organised people to do all the boring stuff.'

As the meeting progresses, Francesca relaxes a bit and a jollier side to her personality comes through. Malcolm Messiter, she tells me, is still involved in the project, still playing his oboe at vital presentations. 'His energy makes him a great advocate,' she says. 'The first time he played me Ave Maria, it was very emotional. Of course, now I know Ave Maria off by heart, I've heard it so many times. He does a few other pieces now, thank goodness!'

18 May

Carnaby Street, London W1: Boo.com calls in the receivers. Every e-commercial head-hunter in London promptly puts a fat cheque behind the bar at the local pub and starts recruiting the newly-redundant Boo-folk for their own clients. As always on these occasions, there's a gag on the Internet in minutes, viz: 'Q: How do you frighten a venture capitalist? A: Walk up behind him and go, "Boo!"'

From where I'm sitting, the collapse of the company has absolutely nothing to do with the long-term viability or lack of it, of the Internet, and everything to do with the lunacy of spending tens of millions of dollars when you're only earning hundreds of thousands. In the end, the basic Dickensian rules of economics apply: Annual income twenty pounds, annual expenditure nineteen pounds nineteen shillings and sixpence, result happiness. Annual income twenty pounds, annual expenditure twenty pounds ought and six, result misery.

There is, however, one new wrinkle which Charles Dickens did not anticipate and which I should like to name, 'Thomas's Law of Blondes.'

Inspired by the examples of both Boo and Lastminute, this states that no sane investor should ever buy shares in a company whose principal public spokesperson is an attractive blonde woman – particularly if that woman is under thirty.

The law, incidentally, has nothing whatever to do with the competence of the blondes. I'm sure that Martha is as bright as Brett and Kajsa is as canny as Leander. I'm absolutely certain that Francesca d'Arcangeli is as sharp as any of the men who appointed her. Nor does it have anything to do with the basic soundness, or otherwise, of their business. It's purely a pricing issue, and here's why ...

Most institutional investors are heterosexual males aged twenty-five to forty. Faced with an attractive blonde, they tend to get over-excited. They delude themselves that if they pump enough money into the blonde's company, they'll somehow be able to pump themselves into her knickers as well. Their valuations rise as inexorably as their dicks. Result ...the companies are over-hyped, the shares are over-priced. And they don't even get laid.

No, if you want top-quality investment opportunities, at value-for-money prices, avoid expensive blonde stock. Stick to companies run by nondescript middle-aged bald blokes. Like sho-biz.com, for example.

21 May

Sunbury-on-Thames: Summit meet and greet the rich and powerful at a flash mini-tower in the City. But the hard work is done at a back office on an industrial estate in Sunbury-on-Thames, which is where I have to go to start crunching numbers with Zac Barratt. First, though, I meet Adam Precious at a nearby pub. He shows me the latest gizmo he's been developing with Steve, Martin and the rest of the bearded wonders. Essentially, it's an application that will enable anyone who can work a keyboard to create sho-biz.com pages, just by filling in a spreadsheet with words and, if necessary, pictures (or audio, or video-clips). The program then assigns the content to the appropriate boxes on our page-templates; automatically generates links to all relevant lists, just by picking up keywords in the text; up-dates the lists themselves and bungs the finished page online. So the days of the £1,200 per diem HTML programmer look well and truly numbered.

I'm so thrilled and impressed by this toy (which seems to me like a decent business in its own right) that I insist on taking Adam back to the Summit building to show Messrs Hunter Gordon and Barratt. As I do so, I'm conscious of the contrast between Adam's no-nonsense Grimsby-ness and Kit's posh drawl. So when I get home, having spent a skull-pounding afternoon setting up financial spreadsheet parameters with Zac (not a subject on which we need to waste any space here), I mail Adam …

> **Don't be fooled by Kit Hunter Gordon's Bertie Wooster act. Take it from a middle–class boy who was educated among the posh... there's a reason the ruling classes have ruled for so long, and it's mostly that they're not half as dumb as they look. But I guess you knew that already...**

While all this is going on, YesTV, the video-on-demand company last seen wondering whether to postpone their floatation, back in April, have called it off entirely. They simply couldn't find enough investors and are therefore left looking like chumps. Elsewhere, a report states that 90% of Internet companies floated on the London Stock Exchange will run out of money within the next fifteen months. And Dame Barbara Cartland, the great romantic novelist and wearer of pink chiffon dies, having asked to be buried in a cardboard coffin beneath an oak tree in the grounds of her Hertfordshire home.

22 May

I get a reply from Adam, posted at 2.00 am (this, incidentally, is not unusual: Precious may yet break Keith Richards' records for long-term sleep deprivation – the man never rests). It reads…

> Cabbage crates coming over the briney, etc. Tis cool. I understand the problem more than you know. GY boy @Oxford...regs The Adman.

I reply at once:

> What did you mean by GY boy at Oxford? Does this mean I have to pity you for going to the wrong university, as well as for coming from Grimsby?

To which he zings back:

> Fuck off and NO

So I call him up and discover that Adam Precious has a Psychology degree from St John's College, Oxford. It is, I guess, a mark of both my social and intellectual snobbery that this piece of information makes me look at him in a whole new light.

Some people, of course, you just know are beyond the pale. At 12.14pm Mitchell Symons e-mails his friends to discuss the effect of Miss Cartland's demise on standings of the Dead Pool which has been running on their behalf since 1 January. The way the Dead Pool works is simple. Every player nominates ten celebrities whom he or she deems unlikely to survive the next twelve months. Any player who has correctly predicted a dead celebrity gets a points-score calculated by subtracting the celeb's age from 100. Cartland was a much-fancied choice among pool-members (who do not include me, though I take a keen interest in the others' progress), but being 98 she only scored two points. Had, say, a teenage pop super-starlet met a tragic end in a shock silicone explosion, she might have netted in excess of 80 points, giving anyone wise enough to have nominated her (or mad enough to have blown up her implants) an all-but unbeatable position in the Pool.

This year, being the first, has involved a very basic Pool. The only real rule is that no one is allowed to nominate a celebrity known to be suffering from a terminal disease, although celebs who are just sick, drug-addicted or non-specifically fucked-up are allowed, indeed encouraged.

Personally, I think there should be a few more subtle, complicating factors. You should, for example, be able to have each-way bets on groups of people – 'any Beatle', say, or 'any member of the Redgrave family' – in which the points scored would be divided by the number of people contained within the category. Also, being a cheery sort of soul, I think contestants should be able to pink one 'Surprise Survivor' – a star so sick that they would actually be disqualified from the Dead Pool, but who, in the opinion of any Pool-member, may surprise us all by staggering on past 31 December.

No sooner has the Cartland e-mail done the rounds than the news of Sir John Gielgud's death is announced. Now there was a man. I met him when I was a cub presenter on *Film '82*, doing location reports on movies being made in Britain. One week I was sent to a churchyard in Buckinghamshire where Gielgud and Sir Ralph Richardson were playing cameo-roles in a film about a society wedding (it was never, in the end, released, so far as I am aware). I had to interview the two great theatrical knights together, which would have been nerve-wracking enough without the fact that Sir Ralph was either slightly ga-ga, or merrily taking the piss. Whenever I asked him a question, he would gaze off into the middle-distance, pausing for minutes at a time, before giving an entirely irrelevant answer. I became increasingly panic-stricken, fluffing my lines and calling Sir John 'Mr Gielgud' as all semblance of coherence fled from my mind and all the questions I had so carefully memorised vanished from my brain. We had barely got a single second of usable conversation on film before Sir Ralph – who was wearing black motor-bike leathers and bright yellow socks – staggered to his feet, said, 'Terribly nice to meet you, but I really must be going,' and started wandering off towards the set. He looked terribly frail, I remember, as if he was walking into an exceptionally strong wind, his legs slightly apart, his arms sticking out from the side of his black-clad body, like a child's stick-man drawing.

Gielgud turned in his chair, caught his retreating chum by the wrist and said, 'Now, now Ralph. I really think we ought to give this nice young man just a little bit more of our time,' and steered him back to his seat. Ten minutes later, the interview was done and Gielgud had earned my gratitude for life, a gratitude which was mixed with affection when he spent the rest of the afternoon entertaining me and the rest of the BBC crew with anecdotes from his amazing career.

Now he's an anecdote in my less remarkable life. And speaking of those, Hugh Grant and Liz Hurley have just announced their 'temporary' separation as a couple. What a bloody nuisance. This could really bugger up my chances of getting either or both of them involved with sho-biz.com. Still, at least it explains why Karin Smith still hasn't read my business-plan. She's been to the Cannes Festival, she's had Liz Hurley acting in *Bedazzled*, she's got Hugh Grant in *Bridget Jones* and now this has all blown up. So she's had much, much better things to think about. Oh well, I guess we'll get there in the end...

24 May

Pall Mall, London SW1: The morning is spent at the Institute of Directors, talking about marketing plans with a man named Jonathan Fingerhut. Here is a terrible example of the way the world is biased against men. If he had been called Jane Fingerhut, he, or rather she could have gone out and found a nice boy called Smith, Jones or Brown. Instead, being a man, he has to carry the burden of a name that has (and I know this from his former schoolboy friend M Symons) caused him grief from his earliest youth. Consider, if you will, the four-letter word – second letter 'u' – that replaced 'hut' as the suffix to his name, when chanted by adolescent meanies.

'You'll easily recognise Fingerhut,' says Mitch before I set off for our appointment. 'He's got his pubic hair on his head.'

Fingerhut is, indeed, short and curly on top. But what does he care? For he took his revenge on his schoolboy tormentors. Knowing that nothing he did could make him any naffer than he already was, he took out his first endowment policy when he was eighteen While his pals were out roistering, he was thinking about pension-plans. A quarter of a century later, he has had the last laugh. All around him, savings plans are maturing like gorgeous golden flowers coming into bloom. Fingerhut is rich.

He is also a very smart cookie. Fingerhut has spent his working life working in marketing, first as an executive, then as a consultant. A few years back, he saw the Internet coming and began specialising in e-marketing. This makes him virtually the only person over thirty to have any clue at all about how to market websites.

As our conversation goes on, Fingerhut's powers of perception come to the fore. 'I've suddenly realised what motivates you,' he says, towards the end of our meeting. 'It's fear. You're absolutely petrified of financial insecurity.'

Bullseye. He's absolutely right. It's not greed, nor a lust for power, nor an urge to attract shapely young maidens that gets me up in the morning (though the money and the maidens would be nice: power I really couldn't give a stuff about). It's the terror of being unable to provide for myself and my family. That will have become overwhelmingly obvious by now, of course. But you've had an entire diary to work it out. Fingerhut got there in an hour. I am, naturally, as flattered by his interest as I am impressed by his perception. Fingerhut is appointed our Marketing Consultant without further ado.

25 May

There's a story in the papers about a new EU ruling called the Distance Sales Directive. The idea is that anyone who buys anything from any source other than a face-to-face sale in a shop has got seven days in which to cancel the deal... and the supplier has to inform them of this right. Which is something that could only be thought up by some moronic Brussels bureaucrat who has no conception of how the Internet actually works. What happens if a kid downloads a bunch of star pictures from sho-biz.com, prints them all up, makes a T-shirt and a mug, passes a few snaps on to his mates... and then calls up sho-biz.com and says, 'I've decided I don't want them pictures after all'? He's had the use of the pics, but we have to give the money back.

And that isn't all. In seven days you can receive and read a book, then give it back. Or you can buy a CD and record it, let alone download an MP3. According to Ian Ivory, the lawyer who wrote the article, 'The directive is aimed at protecting consumers. However, the potential cost implications to e-tailers are enormous and the directive will inevitably place further strain on the efficiency (and perhaps even the viability) of many online retailing operations.'

Which is exactly the sort of thing that makes me Eurosceptic. In theory, the new Directive protects consumers. In practice it acts as a massive disincentive to anyone thinking of providing new products or services... so they don't start their new company, don't hire new workers, don't give customers new products. So the economy is stifled and the only people who do well out of it are bureaucrats who've never had to worry about a profit-margin in their lives... and the big old companies that can afford to fill in all the forms that the new rules demand, and regard the extra work as a small price to pay for squeezing upstart competitors out of the market and reinforcing their position. Which is why, incidentally, chairmen of big corporations tend to be pro-EU and pro-Euro, while small business people and entrepreneurs are much more likely to be sceptical. The EU is basically a fat-cats club.

The practical question is what difference the new directive will make to sho-biz.com. I call up Ian Ivory and ask him what the rules are likely to be for things like downloads. Will they count as perishable commodities, which are outside the scope of the agreement? 'It's not clear,' he says. 'In fact, defining what is or is not perishable is one of the big questions the government will have for the EU regulators. One hopes that when the British regulations are issued they'll make it all clearer. Otherwise, there will probably have to be a test-case.'

Oh great. I'll have to take some snot-nosed little fourteen-year-old to the High Court because he's downloaded fifty snaps of Britney Spears and then decided he can't be arsed to pay for them. That *will* be good for my public image.

I'm seriously pondering whether to jack the whole consumer side of the business on the head and just concentrate on syndication and content-provision – low risk, low costs, and the rules don't apply to business transactions – when I get an e-mail from Dawn Garner at Summit House, Sunbury. She and Zac have finished the calculations of profit and loss for sho-biz.com. They've input my downwardly-revised sales-expectations, and then deducted production costs, manufacturing, artists' royalties, Rocket Fuel discounts, £1.5m per annum promotional budget and all the overheads of staff, rent, professional services... everything down to telephones, postage and office-cleaning – all of which has been worked out in detail for the next six years.

It turns out that if we can sell as many downloads, CD-ROMs and DVDs as I have said we can (and that is a mighty big 'if'), we are on course to make £25 million profit by 2005/6. Which, on a traditional valuation of twenty-times-profits would value the company at £500 million. And if you take the New Economy model which, in the absence of any actual profits, doubles the number you first thought of and adds a couple of noughts, it could be worth billions. By way of example, eBay makes profits of $10 million, or £6.7 million and its founder Pierre Omidyar is worth around $11 billion. With a 'b'.

If I've got a company whose profits are almost four times as large as eBay's, I'll be worth… No, best not think about that. But perhaps I will stick with consumer sales, after all.

Except that there's suddenly another, more immediate problem. It suddenly occurs to me, with a sickening jolt – a bit like the realisation that struck me on the evening before I was due to sit my university entrance exams and suddenly realised (as if in some terrible anxiety dream) that I had not done a single scrap of revision – that I have not given a moment's thought to registering shobiz, without the hyphen. I race to register.com and discover that shobiz.co.uk has already been taken… by a hairdressing salon called ShoBiz, run by Mr or Ms Shobie Quinn at 189 Lewisham High Street (open 9.00 am – 6.00 pm every working day except Wednesday, Thursday and Friday when it stays open till 9.00. Women's cut-and-blow-dries cost £39.50 if done by the salon director with reductions for less experienced staff).

Pantspantspantspantspantspants…What am I going to do? If I call up and ask for the name, they'll sense my desperation and demand a fortune. Perhaps I could buy shobizhair, shobizbeauty and shobizsalon, then offer to give them those names, plus a fab write-up in the papers, in exchange for shobiz.co.uk. I call up that eminent psychologist Mr Adam Precious for advice.

'Well,' he says, 'I could get it closed down, if you want.' I get the point: his tame geeks could flame and spam any site on earth to smithereens if they put their mind to it. But it would hardly be good publicity.

'In that case,' he says, 'How about a bag of cement? Put it down the drains and it'll take two weeks for them to work out what's happened.

By that time there'll be turds floating in the basins and they'll say yes to anything.'

Alternatively, he suggests, bringing a more reasoned tone to the debate, how about calming down, sleeping on it, and then letting him go and use his not-inconsiderable negotiating skills, should they be needed. Which they will... but not for a bunch of innocent hairdressers in Lewisham. Because I've also by now noticed the presence of shobiz.com, which is some sort of entertainment industry consultancy in the States, whose site has already had 1.3 million hits.

Bollocksbollocksbollocksbollocksbollocks... How in God's name did I miss this? How could I have spent 24 hours a day, seven days a week, for six sodding months, thinking about virtually nothing but sho-biz.com ... and never for one second pause to think what would happen if I just removed the hyphen?

I call Zac and tell him to revise his figures. Sho-biz.com is a total non-starter. We're all going to go bust. 'I don't think that's a particular problem,' he says, calm as you like. 'We're trying to get investment for a company. The company is called Sho-Corp Ltd. So that's what we'll sell them.'

So I buy sho-corp.com, sho-corp.net and sho-corp.co.uk. Then I call Mitch. He takes a similarly soothing line. The way he sees it, neither one of my panics are justified. EU-wise you just have to make it so inconvenient to go to the hassle of getting something returned and re-paid that people just can't be bothered to do it. As for the name, well, there were always bound to be lots of names that sounded the same. Kids are smart. They'll work it out. So how about chilling out and going to lunch at I-hate-you-Butlers?

Sadly, I have spreadsheets to go through, so I'll have to take a raincheck on Butlers and Sacha. Instead, I call Stacy Mann. She's spent the past week on the set of *Bridget Jones*, where they've been doing a series of night shoots. For obvious reasons, it's all been a tad more intense than anyone had expected. Hugh Grant arrived for work on Monday night, just after the split with Elizabeth had gone public, having had his car chased, Diana-style, by paparazzi who were banging on the doors and windows. Stacy's main role is just to be his on-set friend. They sit up all night waiting for dawn, preparing for the moment when Hugh has to go home and run the gauntlet again.

So calm down David. Cease your panic. Get a bloody grip. Think how much worse things could be. You could actually be famous. Far better just to make money out of people who already are. That way, you don't get chased by photographers. You just sell the photographs instead.

26 May

Central London: I've been doing this since October, and this is the best day yet. Not that you'd guess it from the way it begins.

I set off from Sussex first thing in the morning. It's the usual London route: up to Gatwick Airport by car, then into town on the Gatwick Express and I've got the journey-time calculated down to the last minute. I've given myself plenty of time... but not, it transpires, enough to allow for a main road blocked by cop-cars, a diversion via Brighton, a total absence of parking-spaces at the airport and a technical problem that delays all trains into Victoria.

My first meeting is with Associated New Media. This is the Internet arm of the *Daily Mail* and Ted Verity – who originally commissioned my e-Mail column – has become one of its senior players. I've held off going to see him before now because the plan has been to steer clear of any big media corporations until sho-biz.com is up and running – at which point our price will be much, much higher. But in the present market, you need all the help you can get. If I can go to investors with a partner like Associated already in the bag, that'll act as a major reassurance and they'll feel far less nervous about having a punt for themselves.

So this is not a good time for me to be late. Or to get caught in the rain between Warren Street tube and the ANM offices in Charlotte Street. Or to get there and discover they haven't got my e-mail requesting a flip-chart. All they can muster is a big A1 pad, which I try to prop on the sofa in Ted Verity's office. It flops back down onto the floor like a great big dead flatfish, so I have to do my drawings on the floor.

Ted Verity's boss Kevin Beatty has come to the meeting. 'Are you always this professional?' he asks. But the more he hears about sho-biz.com, the more he pays attention. And when I fire up Ted's computer and get into the demo site, Kevin seems genuinely impressed. He leaves for another meeting, but not before saying that he wants to meet again soon. Ted is delighted. 'I told him this was either going to be completely mad, or completely brilliant,' he says.

While he's filled with enthusiasm, I tell him what I'm after. I don't just want cash – though that would be nice – I want a proper partnership. The Associated name can give my project credibility and the *Mail* papers can add enormous power to my marketing effort. If they're with me, sho-biz.com will work. If it works, then it will be well-placed to get its pick of the biggest entertainment exclusives. They'll be one step ahead of the rest of Fleet Street. And ANM will have the best entertainment website around.

Ted gets the point. Now he wants to get the project in front of the ANM board. I ask him to hang on for a few days. I'm about to get the finished financial projections from Summit. Once I've got those, I'll do the definitive business-plan. It won't take me more than a day or two. I should have everything he needs by the end of next week. We shake on that – a great start to the day.

Next stop: TalkLoud PR. I have lunch with Addie Churchill at a Japanese noodle-bar in Soho. Addie runs a PR company called TalkLoud. A few weeks ago, they sent me a press-release which I was just about to bin when my eye happened to catch the name of the American company with which TalkLoud is associated: Baker Winokur Ryder.

BWR is one of Hollywood's elite PR agencies. They look after Brad, and Leo and sundry other stars too brilliant to need a surname. They are, therefore, people I very much want to know, which is why (apart from the pleasure of her company, obviously) I'm thrilled to be paying for Addie's noodles.

She makes the same point that Jonathan Fingerhut did last week: that 90% of the people pitching Internet start-ups that she gets to see (and a lot of wannabe millionaires seem to come TalkLoud's way) still don't have any idea of how they're actually going to generate money. I, on the other hand, do. Addie can see just what sho-biz.com wants to do and thinks stars will love it. Better yet, she offers to get in touch with Baker Winokur Ryder. So by 3.00pm I've got myself an enthusiastic potential business-partner and access to one of Hollywood's biggest PR agencies.

Now I've got a journalistic assignment for my column. I'm going to see an Internet incubator called Illuminator. It provides all the seed-finance and support – site-design, technology, marketing and recruitment

– that e-commerce start-ups need before they can approach major investors for the serious funding required to create a fully-functioning business. So the idea is that I'll go to see them, pitch sho-biz.com and write about the experience. Meanwhile, an Illuminator exec called Ben Freeman will write about his experience of meeting me. That way, the theory goes, readers will get an understanding of how the whole process works, and pick up a few tips if they ever need to sell an idea of their own.

When I take sho-biz.com to the City, I'll be armed with a full-on multi-media presentation. I'll have the site, the Cazza magazine covers, the games, and the video. I'll have Kit Hunter Gordon going through the numbers, and I'll have the full force of Adam Precious doing a knock-out technological demo. But most people who go to see incubators are at the very first stages of their projects. They may have a proper business-plan. But equally, they may just have an idea on a few sheets of paper, or a website they've knocked together in the garage at home. So all I'm allowing myself with Illuminator is a single-sheet description of my business-idea, a list of the people working with Sho-Biz and, of course, my trusty flip-chart diagrams.

I turned up at Illuminator's address, right by Trafalgar Square, to find a typical e-location: a rented suite in a building filled with short-term, fully-furnished offices. This is a good sign. Any Net-biz that's investing in property and fancy decorations is almost certainly burning its money too fast. A slinky Russian PA called Natalya asks me what I want to drink and I asked for my usual still water (better for you than coffee or tea – and less likely to make you want to dash for the loo, especially if you're doing several presentations per day).

At the meeting, there are three Illuminator staffers: Ben Freeman, a burly Irishman called Keith Temple, and a cool, fair-haired chap called Simon Freethy. I begin with my one-page intro: I want everyone to understand, right from the off, the basic proposition I'm trying to sell. Then I stand by the flip-chart, draw a few diagrams and launch into my pitch.

Which goes fine, until I do something really dumb. One thing I've learned by now: don't expect to be able to give your presentation in a nice, uninterrupted flow. People will have questions, they won't be shy of butting in, and they'll expect you to give confident, well-informed answers. But they won't expect you to be rude.

Half-way through Simon Freethy's first question, I realise that he's going to make the standard objection that everybody makes when I talk about the syndication side of the business, which is: 'Editors will refuse to buy material from you. They'll insist on using their own writer.' I have three answers to this...

1   Yes, editors will object – for a while. But if the choice is between accepting what we have to offer, and not getting a star interview, they'll take what we've got... especially if it means that their competitors don't get it.

2   It doesn't really matter what editors think. One thing I've learned over the past decades – as both an editor and a writer – is that editors don't run publications. Accountants do. And accountants see editorial purely as a cost. So they want the cost to be as low as possible. So if we give them top-quality material at reasonable prices, without the need for them to pay for journalists' airfares, hotel bills and mini-bars, they'll be only too happy.

3   Magazines already buy syndicated material. And even when they use their own writers, they accept outrageous limitations on editorial freedom imposed by Hollywood PRs. The pass has already been sold.

So, there I am, about to give this reply to Simon Freethy when something strikes me. And I'm so excited by my new thought that I don't even wait for Freethy to finish his sentence. I just barge in: 'I know what you're going to say, because there's only been one company I've seen that *hasn't* asked the same question. That company was Associated New Media, and they didn't ask me, because they're journalists and they already knew the answer. No one gives a damn where the stories come from, just so long as they get them ahead of the competition.'

So I've interrupted this guy and then I've cut off his dick in front of his colleagues. This is not a smart thing to do. And what makes it doubly not smart is that I've neglected to read the job-title on Freethy's business-card. Which is, 'Chief Operating Officer.' So he's the power in the room. And I've made him look like a jerk.

Freethy, understandably, is not best-pleased. For the next half-hour, he puts me through the wringer. This turns out not to be such a bad thing after all. It forces me to demonstrate three vital things: that I've thought about my project in-depth, that I really care about it, and that I know my business in the way that only comes from long years of experience.

By the time the meeting is over, Freethy has given me a hard enough time to re-establish his position and is feeling a lot more mellow. The way he sees it, the big issue for sho-biz.com is acquiring stars. If we can get the talent, we'll certainly have a business. So our number one priority has to be to persuade the people who control access to those stars – 'gate-keepers' as he calls them.

As for his own business, he tells me that Illuminator are planning a funding-round of their own. The aim is to get enough money to be able to step up a gear and take companies right through from incubation to floatation. So they're looking for opportunities to invest at the first-round funding stage. And, not to put too fine a point upon it, he's very interested in pursuing the possibility of investing in sho-biz.com.

So make that a partner, a PR and an investor. Not bad for a day's work. And it gets better, because I round it all off by meeting Zac Barratt at the Groucho, where we both try very hard not to get too excited about the prospects for Sho-Biz … and fail miserably. I don't get home till 11.00 at night and everyone's gone to bed, but I'm still way too fired-up to sleep. I hardly dare believe I can pull it off. But it really does look like I've got a shot this time.

27 May

I wake up shattered, with an overpowering emotional hangover. I was high as a kite yesterday, I'm knackered and depressed today. Clare, poor thing, has got a filthy cold, complete with a rasping, chest-rattling cough. Real life has returned with a vengeance.

30 May

Neil calls, with some interesting information. Steve Thomas just called him out of the blue – the first time they've communicated in months – and asked whether he was doing okay, financially. Because, Steve said, he happened to know some people who might be interested in buying Neil's TVO shares. He then mentioned a substantial six-figure sum.

So what's that all about? Neil's already spent a night talking it over with his wife: what do I think? Neil is feeling somewhat insecure and although there is nothing to substantiate this, has even considered the possibility that the TVO people might reckon he has run out of cash, and are hoping to use that weakness to get his stock at a lower price. Because, as we both agree, they're worth an awful lot more than the figure that has just been mentioned.

This is all very strange. I've spoken to Francesca d'Arcangeli since our meeting and she's not said anything about Neil at all, except that she'd like to meet him one day. She's certainly got no axe to grind with him. Then again, she wasn't around when he quit the Board. Whatever the ins and outs of it all, there's one thing, I tell Neil, he's absolutely got to do ... take a lawyer with him to any meeting with Steve or TVO. Meanwhile he still owns a substantial chunk of the company. That's the one big weapon he has, and he shouldn't give that up unless there's a very good reason to do so, or a very, very good price.

JUNE

1 June

Business-plan day. Having promised Kit Hunter Gordon that I'd definitely have it ready for him by Friday, 19 May, I'm way behind schedule. But the way I see it, this shouldn't be too strenuous a job. Writing, after all, is the one bit of this whole process I really know how to do.

Except that I don't. Or can't. Because here I am, several months into the most important project of my life, just about to compose the document that will have to persuade hard-headed business people to invest in my business... and I can't even decide what to call the bloody thing. I'm determined not to go with sho-biz.com, because that makes it look like a simple Internet start-up, which is commercial death these days. But if I go with Zac Barratt's suggestion, and call it Sho-Corp, you lose the whole point of the name... i.e. the abbreviation of 'showbusiness'.

So I make my first decision. From now on – in this diary, as well as everywhere else – the entity formerly known as sho-biz.com will henceforth be referred to as Sho-Biz, plain and simple. Which is the glaringly obvious solution, except for one thing: you can never write a sentence containing the phrase 'Sho-Biz is ...' It just looks, and sounds, appalling.

I spend about three hours wrestling with this dilemma, endlessly writing and re-writing the Executive Summary which will start the plan and set the tone. Eventually, I settle on a solution. I will use Sho-Biz as the project's working name... and then I'll put everything into the future tense. So I'll never write 'Sho-Biz is,' but always, 'Sho-Biz will be.' This has the bonus of making it sound much more purposeful. This is not what we want to do, or hope to do, or aim to do. It's what we will do.

So buy it, you venture-capitalist bastards.

Once I've wrestled with the wording, I start thinking about type-faces and colours. You might think this is all pretty trivial stuff, but it isn't. If you ever go on TV, the way you look, your gestures and the tone of your voice are far more influential in determining the audience response than anything you say. And the same applies in print. A document that looks professional and elegant conveys a positive image before anyone's read a word.

That's why, when I first started sending plans out to people, I was obsessive about putting them in natty little transparent folders... and not just any transparent folders, but one particular type of miniature ring-binder. And that's why, having spent the first half of the day wrestling with the problem of 'Sho-Biz is', I spend the next several hours going over and over the same couple of pages, changing fonts, type-sizes and colours.

By the end of the day, I've cracked it. The headings are in 18-point Franklin Gothic Condensed Italics – as opposed to 24-point Bold Italics, which they were in before. I've also changed the colour from bright red to teal – a kind of greeny-blue. So the effect at the top of every section is much more subtle than the screaming scarlet frenzy that I had before.

Since I'm now selling Sho-Biz, with capital letters, as opposed to sho-biz.com, all in lower-case, I'll put capital letters back on the chapter-headings, too. And I'm going to group the chapters within specific, numbered sections – Marketing, Finance, etc – which means that the chapters will themselves be numbered within the sections: 1.1, 1.2, 2.1 etc.

Next change: in every version of the plan this year, I've had headlines at the top of every section, letting people know what's coming up. This time, though, I'm taking them off the top of the chapter, and scattering them through the text, to introduce each new paragraph. So you could skim through the plan, just look at the paragraph headings and get a pretty good idea of what the whole thing is about. These sub-heads are going to be in 10-pt Helvetica Bold Itals, coloured Dark Blue. Again, that's smaller and lighter than the previous headings, which were in 12-pointt black type.

Finally, there's the body-type, which is 10-point Palatino – down a size from all previous versions of the plan. So I'll get more content into fewer pages. I want to be able to go into things in depth: it's important that people know that I've got answers for all the questions they're ever likely to have. But I don't want a fifty-page tome that looks like *War and Peace*: they'll never bother to read a word. So the trick is to con them into reading far more than they realise. Hence the nice colours, the regular headings, and the pages that contain far more words than readers think they do.

The only exception to the rules is the Executive Summary itself, which is in bigger, bolder type, which basically says, 'Cop this.' I fax versions back and forth to the long-suffering Fingerhut all day. Finally I end up with something with which we're both happy. So by the end of the day I've got a name, a style and a basic proposition. Which seems oddly reminiscent of where I was about six months ago. But I suppose I've made progress since then … haven't I?

2 June

I'm supposed to be going to London today to meet Eric Fellner, one of the two founders of Working Title Films. With his partner, Tim Bevan, he's produced *Four Weddings and a Funeral*, then *Notting Hill* and is now doing *Bridget Jones*. Their basic movie-making formula is Cute, very English script by Richard Curtis + Hugh Grant playing dithery posh bloke + Winsome American actress = Vast Sums of Money…and a pretty hot formula it is, too.

They've got other ideas as well, of course. *Bean* and *Elizabeth* were both Working Title pictures, and you couldn't have two more different films that those two: a Twentieth-century gurning spectacular and a Sixteenth-century costume epic. They've got a production deal with Universal that basically means they can fund pretty much any film they ever want to make. That makes Working Title by far the biggest players in the British film industry… and probably the only London-based company anyone in Hollywood takes seriously. So they're gatekeepers to the max, and I want to make Fellner a three-stage proposal (with a bonus at the end).

Stacy Mann knows him really well from *Notting Hill* days – being the PR for *Bridget Jones* doesn't hurt, either – and she has set up the meeting. Fellner, she says, isn't any more enamoured by junkets than anyone else and would be interested to hear of any alternative. He has a reputation as one of the movie-business's nicer guys. But he's also known as a man who likes to keep meetings short and sharp. If I can't make my point in twenty minutes or less, he'll be gone.

No problem. I'll take a big pad and a fat-tipped felt-pen, do my Rolf Harris act, rip through the concept and take a guided tour through the site on his office PC. Then I'll hit him with my one-two-three.

1   If he likes Sho-Biz, but doesn't want to make any serious commitment, I want him to write a nice, encouraging memo that I can show to investors.

2   If he seriously thinks it's a good idea, I want him to set up a second date to talk about doing some work on one of his productions.

3   If he can see a few bob in it for himself, I want to sell him on the possibility of being an investor (at super cut-rate prices, naturally). And the bonus at the end is that if I like him, too, I'm going to offer him a Non-Executive Directorship, because the truth is that I've had my eye on Fellner for that slot, ever since Stacy first mentioned him two or three months ago.

Except that none of this happens, because just as I'm about to set off for London, I get a message saying that Fellner's son has got a big cricket-match and dad wants to go and watch it. Deep breath, David. Don't lose your temper. Get back to the business-plan.

It pisses with rain all day. If Fellner Junior played a minute of cricket, it'll have been a bloody miracle. Bollocks.

3–4 June

I probably ought to be working over the weekend. But there are things to do in the garden, the Monaco Grand Prix on the box and a family with whom to regain contact. Besides which, Ted Verity rings up saying he's been called in to pull together a Euro 2000 special for the *Mail* and can he have 500 words of beautifully-crafted prose on how the whole nation is looking forward to this feast of football, etc, etc… on his desk by 9.00 am Sunday morning? So of course I say yes. I settle down at the i-Mac at 8.00 on Sunday, polish off the words on time and bask in the simplicity of the working freelance journalist's life: you work, you earn… that's it. I've got 400 quid I didn't have before. And, frankly, I can't be bothered to do any more today.

5 June

Had an amazing day, pitching Sho-Biz to David Bowie and Tom Hanks. Bowie recognised me and greeted me by name, which I suppose wasn't too surprising, given that I've interviewed him three times. But I was still insanely nervous talking to him, anyway. The chat with Hanks went a bit better, though I never had time to ask him the one question to which I really want an answer: how come he always manages to pick films that turn out to be hits? Then I woke up. It was 4.20am. This is getting stupid.

When I get down to breakfast, there's a story in the paper about Kylie Minogue. She's just done the cover of *GQ*. It's a parody of that (in)famous Seventies poster: the girl on a tennis court, scratching her naked rump. The sight of the cover makes me think about all those e-mails I sent to Terry Blamey, back in January. I'd always assumed I'd be up and running by now, but here we are, almost six months later, and I'm still dealing in hypotheticals and future tenses. Kylie really has a new single. She's really doing publicity. I'm still making promises.

There's no point feeling sorry for myself, I've got to get to work on the business-plan. But when I open up my e-mails I find the following message from an investment banker called Jeremy Young. Two weeks ago, I was put in touch with him by a contact of Adam Precious's. I sent a jaunty e-mail, by way of introduction, expecting to give a serious presentation, plus business-plan, at a later date. Today I get his answer:

> > Sorry to be a bit tardy in responding here, but I've been
> > syndicating views around the office. I think our consensus view is

that whilst your plan has some merit, we see it hard to build a
sustainable business big enough for a fund such as ours ($500mm),
so do not wish to proceed.

> I would like to wish you the best of luck, however, and thank you
for thinking of WP.

Why is it that one rejection can overwhelm so many positive responses?
I'm devastated by Young's dismissal, all the more because my original
message to him was so casual. To me, it was just an introduction, prior to
a proper meeting. If I'd thought he was going to show the bloody thing
to all his chums, I'd have written it very differently.

I send him a message pointing this out, but a bit more politely. I don't
get any response. Oh well, the Fellner meeting that was scheduled for
Friday has been re-arranged for tomorrow. So maybe there's hope yet.

6 June

Oxford Street, London WC1: On the way into town, Nigel Parker calls. He's
set up meetings with Madonna's accountant, who handles all her business affairs. And he's got the Simply Red gang to agree to a proper presentation. They're both next week: Madonna on Tuesday and Simply Red
on Thursday. He'd arranged to see the Spice Girls' people on the
Wednesday ages ago, so that'll be three-in-a-row. We'd originally
planned to have all these meetings in the week beginning 12 April. So
we're exactly two months behind schedule. And I still haven't finished
the plan.

The Fellner meeting goes well. He comes across as a decent bloke:
forty, slim, thinning sandy hair. He's also half-an-hour late, because a
team from Universal are in town, taking up time. Stacy and I wait while
Fellner finishes off his previous meeting with Johnny Vaughan, who
emerges in an untucked purple shirt, being very confident and take-
charge about some upcoming TV project. There are a couple of people
waiting for the meeting after us, like courtiers craving an audience with
a medieval king. Fellner tells them – in the nicest possible way – to come
back some other time.

The meeting is due to start at noon. By the time I begin my spiel it's 12.35. I ask Fellner if he's got the e-mail I sent, giving the URL of the Sho-Biz demo site. If he can just click on that, it'll take us straight onto the homepage. Fellner doesn't know if he's got the e-mail, because he never reads e-mails – 'If people really need to speak to me, they'll phone' – and he can't get online at all easily, because his computer's hooked up to a network. He tells me he'll check out the site when he gets home: why don't I just tell him what it's all about?

I figure Fellner must have a lunch appointment, so I race into the patter, desperate to get through it before he or his mind drifts off elsewhere. Because I'm rushing, I'm not really putting it over quite as well as I like to. Plus, there isn't a flipchart or board in the room, which means I'm having to do my drawings in a pad on Fellner's desk, sitting next to him, which isn't half as effective as standing up and commanding the room.

As I talk, Fellner asks tough, searching, sceptical questions. I get the feeling I'm behind on points. But then I realise that twenty, thirty … forty minutes have gone by and he hasn't kicked me out yet. At the end, he asks me what I want, so I give him my three options. Fellner says he thinks it's an interesting idea. He won't commit himself to anything right now, but if I send him a business-plan, he'll read it over the weekend and get back to me early next week.

Then he adds something else: if Working Title get behind Sho-Biz, they'll really be able to help the project along, not just by passing work our way, but also by getting us in with Universal. And if we can get them on our side, we'll get the rest of Hollywood too. We say our goodbyes and I leave him in for a couple of minutes with Stacy, doing Bridget Jones business, while I wait outside in reception: I want to have a quick chat with Stacy, just to get her feeling about how things went. As I'm sitting there, Fellner emerges, grins rather sheepishly and says, 'How embarrassing. I've just been saying nice things about you.'

Does that mean I've got him? Surely he wouldn't say that, or make a point of emphasising how much Working Title could help, if he was just going to give me the brush-off. He's spent long enough telling script-writers that their movie ideas are shit to know how to say, 'Thanks, but no thanks'… hasn't he?

I really hope so. Stacy reckons we're definitely in with a chance. Which is just as well, because things are looking a bit ropey on the Hugh Grant front. Karin hasn't yet had the chance to read the last version of the plan. I ask Stacy to tell her to bin it – I'll send her the new version instead. Better yet, I'll go and present to her, because that's always what works best. I may be wasting my time. But if I can't be arsed to go up to London on the off-chance of snaring an international movie-star, I'm in the wrong business.

I get home by 4.00, determined to work on the plan. Then the phone rings. Once that's started, it never stops. So another evening goes missing… and still no bloody business-plan.

7 June

A minor problem: I'd promised a Sunday magazine that I'd finally finish an article that was due in months ago. I swore they'd have it by lunchtime today. So I don't start work on the plan till early afternoon, and nothing much is achieved.

8 June

Finally get down to serious work. I start at 5.30 am and don't finish till gone 8.00 in the evening. My brain has been reduced to cream-cheese and I've missed the last post, which means no one's going to get anything from me this week.

9 June

The plan is finally finished – thirty-three pages of tightly-knit argument, backed by an incredible array of statistical information. It is, of course, a work of the purest fantasy. I have no idea whether we will actually be able to sell £49,000's worth of downloads in November 2001. The confident assertion that the establishment costs for the same month will be £12,700 is, in fact, nothing more than guess-work. By the time we get to the budget for 2005-6, we might as well be in la-la-land. I am, however, assured that investors will be greatly reassured by the sheer barrage of numbers.

'This bloke may be talking cobblers,' they'll think. 'But it's incredibly thorough, professional cobblers. So with any luck he'll be just as thorough and professional when he starts spending our money.' Or, of course, he'll just talk even more beguiling cobblers and take even more of their money.

That's all for the future. For now, all I care about is that the plan is written. By way of celebration, I knock off at 4.00 in the afternoon – four hours earlier than any other working day this year – and take Clare off to see *Gladiator*. I've spent the past few months thinking of nothing but how to make money out of movie-stars... and this is the first time we've been to the pictures this year.

10 June

Terrible news for Sho-Biz ... Euro 2000 has begun. I work in an office that has a 28-inch, surround-sound TV stuck in one corner. From now until the end of the tournament, it's going to be on whenever there's a game ... irrespective of the teams involved.

Televised football has always been my fatal weakness. I went up to university to study Philosophy, convinced that I was going to be the next Bertrand Russell. I come from a family of egg-heads. My dad had got a First at Oxford in the days when they were still hard to come by. My mum, who met my father in a university History lecture, got a scholarship to both Oxford and Cambridge, picked Oxford and has never in her entire life got over the shame of being the first Senior Scholar of Lady Margaret Hall not to get a First. So I grew up believing that anything other than an Oxbridge First was a total failure.

Cut to June 1978. It's the afternoon before my first Part One Philosophy exam. Am I hard at work, revising my notes? No. Is my nose pressed between the leaves of some dusty philosophical tract? Hell no. I'm not doing any of that. I'm sat in my room watching Iran vs Peru on a tiny black-and-white portable.

Two weeks later I had a miserable 2:2, they'd stripped me of my scholarship and I was applying to do History of Art on the basis that I no longer gave a monkey's about my degree. I liked paintings and the History of Art faculty was notable for the number of women it contained, and its proximity to the best café in Cambridge. It turned out, ironically, to be a subject I loved and a course that taught me to how to make informed judgements about art and design – a qualification that has come in handy in a career that has involved a fair number of conversations with pretentious designers. But that's not the point. The point is that I can't resist an international football match. I'm almost as feeble in the face of a cricket Test Match. And Wimbledon's just around the corner. How the hell am I going to get any work done over the next two months?

12 June

England lose 3–2 to Portugal – a completely predictable result, as anyone who's been on the end of my recent barrage of e-mails berating Keegan for his outdated obsessions with (a) 4-4-2 and (b) Alan Shearer will know. I spend the first half of the game being driven mad by spreadsheets. I'm trying to put together a presentation for the Spice Girls management. Nigel Parker and I are meeting them in a couple of days' time and I'm creating a proposal for a possible shoot that makes it look as though I know what the hell I'm doing. It begins with a creative outline, which specifies what photo-shoot and interview time we'd need, along with the different types of story and product we'd expect to create. Then there's a budget, divided into sections: 'Pre-Shoot Costs', 'Artists' Costs', 'Production Costs' and 'Post-Production Costs'. But every time I print the sheets out, I spot another mistake. And every single tiny error ripples through the spreadsheets, sending my calculations further and further out as it goes.

I'm probably wasting my time. There's virtually no chance that an actual Spice Girl will ever read a single word or number. But the band's affairs are supervised by Andrew Thompson, Nigel Parker's ex-boss at Lee and Thompson. He's a lawyer, which means that he loves going through paperwork, looking for discrepancies. If I want to persuade him I can do a job for his girls, I've got to get everything absolutely right.

But as with the business-plan, the more specific the detail becomes, the more overwhelming the feeling of unreality becomes. More than ever I fear that Sho-Biz is nothing but an impertinent fantasy. How dare I suppose that I can actually turn it into a functioning business? How can I possibly pretend that it will make millions of pounds... or that anyone at all will want to buy a single thing we try to sell?

It's not even as if I really want to become as rich as Sho-Biz would make me if it ever in a million years worked. Obviously, I wouldn't say no to a bumper pay-day, but … Look: I was in the garden on Saturday afternoon. It was a lovely day, with the sun shining and clouds scudding across the sky. I was doing some planting in one of the herbacious borders. Clare was in the chicken-run, tending to the hens while Fred pottered around her looking for 'gugs', which is what he calls slugs. Every time he found one of the disgusting, slimy creatures, with its black back, orange flanks and sticky underbelly, Fred would proudly show it off, letting it slide across his hand as he squeaked with delight.

I looked across my garden, with all the flowers just coming into bloom and the roses nodding in the wind as they climbed up the cottage walls and I thought: 'This is enough.' All I want is to keep what I've got and to know that my children will be able to grow up in some degree of financial security. But these days, with the economy as insane as it is, the only way I can do that is to try and become obscenely wealthy. Because that's the Twenty-first-century way: you're either a triumph or a disaster – cosy security, somewhere in between, isn't an option any more.

As if to illustrate the point, Clare says she wants to do some work on the raised pond that sits on the patio outside our living-room. All she wants to do is change the shape and make it a little bigger. A decent brickie could do the job in a couple of days. Add a bit extra for the cost of a new lining and you're probably looking at £250, tops. Under normal circumstances, we could easily afford that. But as things are, there are only two possibilities…

First Possibility: Sho-Biz will work, in which case I cannot only afford £250 to change the pond, I can afford £250,000 to put in a swimming-pool, build the conservatory we've always dreamed of and finish all the renovations and decorations we have planned for the house.

Or…

Second Possibility: Sho-Biz won't work, in which case I can't afford £250 to fix the pond, because I can't afford the pond at all, because I'll probably have to sell the house.

I am, in short, equidistantly poised between triumph and disaster. I will do my very best, like Kipling says, to treat those two impostors both the same. But Kipling wasn't trying to run a business. Apart from the bakery, obviously…

14 June

Somewhere in West London: The Spice Girls' office is hidden away behind an unmarked door in a small side street in a nondescript area of London, just north of the Westway. This is not a sign of any dip in their fortunes, so much as an example of the anonymity with which stars like to operate (Robbie Williams, for example, has his office behind a garage door). Most of Spice HQ is actually in the basement, where they've fixed up a couple of offices, a nice kitchen-cum-bar area and a big meeting-room under a skylight. The walls are covered in posters and signed mementoes, and wherever you look there are shelves crammed with Spice memorabilia, including more variations of Spice dolls than you could ever have imagined possible. There is no sign whatever of the existence of Geri Halliwell. Odd that.

The girls' day-to-day affairs are looked after by a small team led by a woman called Nancy Phillips. Nigel's never met her and has no idea what she's like. I'm worried that she may be the kind of neurotic, insecure, annoyingly aggressive individual – all-too common in the entertainment industry – whose chief satisfaction in life is to demonstrate their own supposed power by making life as hellish as possible for anyone who wants to get anywhere near the stars whom they serve. I'm ready for a confrontational encounter, in which I spend most of my time answering objections to everything I suggest, along with constant reasons why none of it would work.

How wrong I am. Nancy Phillips is a blonde, upmarket, thirtysomething Englishwoman who used to manage the Undertones. She asks tough, relevant questions, but makes no effort whatever to impress me with her vast importance. This, of course, makes her genuinely impressive. Or perhaps I'm just a sucker for flattery, because she understands Sho-Biz, right off the bat. The idea that the Girls could condense all their media work into a few days is far more appealing to her than the prospect of making money. I show her the production budget for a four-day shoot (roughly £180,000, excluding the band's own costs and another 150K's worth of post-production) and apologise for the size of the bill. Nancy just smiles and says, 'You should see what our videos cost.'

The meeting goes incredibly well, despite my being in total motor-mouth mode (I talk so much and so loudly that I actually give myself a sore throat). It is only after we've all said goodbye, amidst many hand-shakes and smiles, that I realise I have forgotten to set any sort of agenda for follow-up meetings or work. That shouldn't be a problem... should it?

15 June

Swiss Cottage, London NW5: I couldn't sleep last night, so at two in the morning I gulped down 15mg of Temazepam. As a result, I spend the day in a chemical haze, feeling like there is a thick mist between me and the outside world. This afternoon, I'm presenting Sho-Biz to David Ravden, an accountant whose partnership Martin Greene Ravden handles a substantial chunk of the rock aristocracy. Just to give some idea, Madonna is one of his clients.

If Ravden decides that he likes Sho-Biz, he can put us next to some seriously big names. So I stand at his flip-chart, draw my diagram and do my thing. Only much, much more sedately than yesterday. There's a snoozing slug where my brain should be. Sometimes I lose so much momentum I feel I'm going to nod off, right there and then. All the while, Ravden just sits there, paying attention, barely saying a word. It's like the Geoffrey Chamberlain disaster all over again. I'd panic ... if I had the energy.

After a while, I peter to a close. Silence falls across the MGR board-room. Eventually, I look at Ravden and say, 'What do you think?'

'It's a no-brainer,' he replies.

Oh Jesus, he thinks it's the most stupid idea he's ever heard. 'Er... no-brainer in what sense?' I ask.

'In the sense that it's obviously going to work,' he says. 'So... what are your plans?'

I talk him through the money-raising strategy: we'll go to the City for £2 million now, just to get ourselves up and running, and come back for another chunk of £4 million in April/May next year, to finance the full-on launch.

Ravden looks at me like it's just become a no-brainer in the 'lacking-a-brain' sense. 'How much of the company are you expecting to give away?' he asks.

'No more than 25%, preferably 20,' I say.

Ravden shrugs his shoulders as if to say, 'You'll be lucky.' Then he gives me a quick reality-check. As he knows, from personal experience, venture capitalists faced with new media start-ups are currently demanding 65% of the equity before they'll even think of investing. Even then, they make you jump through impossible hoops to get a bean out of them.

There's no point bothering with those people. It would be far better just to start the business, no matter how modestly, and get some sort of trading history. The moment the company earns its first penny it stops being a start-up and becomes a proper business. At that point, money is much easier to find, and comes at a much more reasonable price.

Well, I say, we have been thinking about a Plan B. In fact, we've just put a proposal to a Major Girl Group which offers them two options. Either we act as risk-taking producers – i.e. pay for all costs, give them an advance against royalties – and then recoup the majority of the money for ourselves. Or we just act as service-providers, managing a job that the client pays for, in which case we just get a fee and they keep most of the loot. The second option severely limits our possible profits, but it removes any risk because we get paid no matter what. If we were going to go into business without up-front capital, that would be the way to go.

Ravden agrees. In fact, he might even invest in Sho-Biz. If he does, I'm going to give him terms which make this a no-risk no-brainer. As far as I'm concerned, he can basically have his shares for free, and for one extremely simple reason. If David Ravden has a stake in the success of Sho-Biz, he has a stake in calling up Madonna and telling her what a fabulous idea it is. And that's worth a point of anyone's company.

16 June

Soho, London WC1: I present Sho-Biz to Sony Records, paying particular attention to the fact that Sho-Biz can save them the fortune they currently pay to schlep music journalists all over the world to interview artists in hotel rooms for 20 minutes at a time (or five minutes if you are granted an audience with Celine Dion, as I was last year. Mind you, she does speak *very* fast). I also soothe their corporate paranoia by stressing the degree to which I am interested in co-operation, rather than competition. I can generate content for their sites. They can sell CDs on mine.

They love it. Of course they love it. Everybody loves it. You'd have to be an idiot not to love it.

Now just give me some money for it... Somebody... Please.

19 June

North Kensington, Soho and Holland Park, London: On the hottest day of the year so far, with the temperature way into the eighties, my tube gets stuck in Queen's Park and I have to walk two miles to my meeting with Simply Red's management. I arrive at their office looking like a losing entrant in a wet T-shirt contest (I am not, it must be said, flattered by having my shirt stuck to my nipples with my own sweat) only to find that, while they love the idea of Sho-Biz (naturally), Mick Hucknall has just begun a prolonged career hiatus and has no interest in talking to the press, or anyone else, for the next eighteen months.

I lunch at the Groucho with a couple of guys from Bath who have a demon application which creates multi-dimensional cyber-cards. They've been recommended to me by a man who has an online credit-system that might be perfect as the basis for Rocket Fuel, whom I met last week. I was put on to him by Ben Freeman at Illuminator. In both cases, the person who passed me on said that they couldn't tell me exactly what the next chap down the line was actually doing, because they were tied by confidentiality agreements... but if I gave him a call, it would be worth my while. (In both cases, the person I was calling had been told the same about me). It's almost as if there's an underground economy being created in total secrecy, right under the eyes of established companies, filled with revolutionaries conspiring to bring down the existing order of things.

The Bath guys pull out a laptop and show me what they've got. Imagine one of those picture cards they used to give away in fag-packets and bubblegum, or a Pokémon trading-card. Only it has an infinite number of sides, contains an unlimited amount of information, and has both audio and video capacity. Now imagine you're a teenage subscriber to sho-biz.com and we send you one of these babies every week, filled with great stuff about your favourite stars. You'd be a happy bunny… wouldn't you?

My lunch is a delicious stew of lamb and beans. It's tender. It's tasty. And it makes me fart like an over-excited whoopee-cushion all the way through my afternoon meeting with Pat Savage. An Irishman with a forgiving disposition – he's tact itself in the face of my overpowering flat-ulence – he's another accountant and he echoes David Ravden's opinion that while Sho-Biz may be a very good idea, going to the City is a very bad one. He is also the third artists' representative in a row to say that the money isn't important. And if the man who minds the money for U2, Radiohead, Van Morrison, Tina Turner, Oasis and Bryan Adams says that, who am I to argue?

21 June

Covent Garden, London WC2: Bernard Doherty is the Rolling Stones PR (he's Shania Twain, Tina Turner and Janet Jackson's UK spokesperson, too). Every time you see an item in the press about 'a friend' of Mick Jagger, telling the world about Mick's reaction to the latest divorce case or palimony action, Bernard's the friend. He's the doyen of rock PRs. He's also the first person who starts to give me chapter and verse about various people, in various parts of London, New York and LA, who are trying to do the same thing as I am – or bits of the same thing. There's a husband-and-wife team in LA, for example, who are doing big-time celebrity profiles (he shoots, she writes) and syndicating them through their own website.

Fair enough, I say, but they aren't doing all the other stuff that Sho-Biz will do – the online goodies, the consumer website, the video-on-demand. Bernard says there's a reason for that. If you try to do everything, you end up bumping up against other people who already own part of the rights. He gives an example. A big star had their tour sponsored by an Internet company. To promote the tour, the same star made a TV documentary. The TV company agreed to pay for the documentary, but slipped a clause into their contract saying they could put extracts from the documentary onto their website. It was only later that anyone noticed that the Internet company had already bagged exclusive online rights to the star for the duration of the tour. M'learned friends were, even now, trying to sort it out.

All the more reason, I say, to have one single company handling the whole thing. That way there's no confusion.

Bernard is semi-convinced. He's not so blown away he's biting my hand off... but then again, he's convinced enough to suggest that we should pitch for the right to run the wesbite for an awards ceremony he helps organise. There is, though, one subject on which he's 100% behind the general consensus: the dosh. 'It's just peanuts to these people,' he says. Then he tells me about a big rock concert that was going to be shown live in the States. It was one of those tribute events, with a lot of 'surprise' special guests, popping on stage to sing duets with the main attraction. The network wanted Mick Jagger to be one of the guests. All he'd have to do was drive across London, do a quick rehearsal at the sound-check in the afternoon, then get up and sing one number that night. He said, 'No thanks.'

So they started offering him money. Fifty grand. A hundred grand. It got up to £250,000 for five minutes' work. Mick still said no. The thing was, he told Bernard, it was just going to wreck his day. And the fact that he'd get a quarter of a million wouldn't make the day any less wrecked.

I walk from Bernard's office in Soho down to Covent Garden to meet Amanda Bross. She's a razor-sharp Canadian lawyer who works at an agency called Eclipse that represents actors and models including Kevin Spacey, John Malkovich, Claudia Schiffer and Naomi Campbell. She says that Sho-Biz sounds like a nice idea, but frankly, if she takes it to her clients, there's only one thing they'll want to know: 'How much?'

This comes as a bit of a shock. There I was, thinking that stars were going to be attracted to Sho-Biz by the promise of an easier, more ordered life and suddenly mammon rears its ugly head. But it only takes a few minutes of conversation with Amanda to figure out the difference.

Musicians make their own records and sing their own songs. They and their representatives are obsessed by issues of copyright ownership, for the very simple reason that their long-term incomes can be radically affected by whether or not they actually own the songwriting and publishing rights to their own work. You never know when an old track might not be picked for a jeans ad, or a film soundtrack, or a cover by a hot new star. At that point, you either rake in vast amounts of money… or sit there going nuts while someone else, who owns your rights, picks up the cash instead. If you don't think that matters, just ask Sir Paul McCartney how he feels about Michael Jackson owning the publishing rights to all his old Beatles songs. For songs, read 'interviews'. Musicians will happily invest now, if it means owning in the future.

Actors and models are completely different. Aside from the very few people, like Clint Eastwood or Woody Allen, who direct and produce the films in which they star, actors do all their work for other people. And they get paid up-front. You want a superstar, you write a cheque for $20 million. Then maybe he'll talk to you.

It's the same with models. A cover-girl doesn't care how many copies the magazine sells. She's paid a daily rate for the shoot and that's it. The 'face' of a giant cosmetics company has only a marginal interest in how many lipsticks or bottles of scent are sold as a result of the ads in which she appears. Of course, she wants the campaign to do well so that she gets asked back again, at an even higher fee. But she's not picking up a royalty on the lippy. So if you want her looking beautiful in front of your camera, you'd better have deep pockets. Linda Evangelista famously wouldn't get out of bed for less than $10,000… and that was a decade ago.

So Amanda Bross has a very simple question: how much can I pay? And forget about the Internet. She's not interested in downloads and DVDs. She wants to deal with what actually exists now – the conventional press media as we know and love 'em. Just to be specific, she lists four possible photo-stories involving her clients. Put a price on them, persuade her that she can get her clients involved in a new project without risk to their careers or reputations and she might just be interested in doing business.

I tell her I'll get right back to her.

23 June

Wall Street, New York, USA: Two investment banks cast doubt on Amazon.com's revenue forecasts, saying that the company is going to make less money than it currently claims. A third warns that Amazon is in danger of running out of money by mid-2001. In a research note for Lehman Brothers, an analyst called Ravi Suria warns that 'In its current situation of high debt load, high interest costs, spiralling inventory and rising expansion costs we believe that the current cash balances will last the company through to the first quarter of 2001 in a best case scenario.'

The company answers that it's got a billion bucks in the bank. But here's the problem: Amazon's top executives sold £15 million's worth of shares in the past month. Most of those were flogged by the company's founder, Jeff Bezos, who pocketed around £12.7 million on 12 May. Good thing he got out when he did – for him at any rate. Because today Amazon's share-price promptly drops 24%, pulling the NASDAQ market down by 90 points. Now, Amazon is the boss of e-commerce. It has by far the best brand recognition of any online retailer. It's the big kahuna and *le grand fromage*. And if neither its, nor my prospects improve, we are both going to run out of cash at exactly the same time. Maybe I should find some other business in which to try to make my fortune. Because this one's looking dodgier by the day.

24 June

Kylie Minogue goes straight in at Number One with her new single, 'Spinning Around'.

26 June

After Friday's jitters in New York, London's tech stocks take another hit. QXL, the online auction site, loses 11.8% at the start of the day, though it later recovers. When I wrote about QXL in February the stock was over £14. Now it's down at £1.09. That's somewhat misleading, because they had a rights-issue in the meantime, which effectively halved the price of any individual share. But even so, it's still worth about one-seventh of what it used to be… and the other sixth-sevenths have evaporated in about four months flat.

Meanwhile Freeserve pulls out of a deal in which it was going to be bought by the German Internet service provider T-Online and promptly drops 17%. If you'd bought Freeserve at the top of the market, each share would have cost 921 pence. You could pick them up today for 365. Frankly, a mattress, under which to stick your money, would have been a far, far better investment.

Back amongst the minnows, an e-mail arrives from hardbastard@ tough.com. It reads:

> Me and the management are sorting out these gits with your domain name…u know the bastards in south London….anyway we have set them up with a new email it is showbiz@hairdresser.com we intend to visit and make this part of an offer they can't and should not refuse….Cheers HB (aka Slasher, CodWar, MBD, Adam, Pruce, Presh, Oi Bollock Brain).

The man who sent this e-mail is an Oxford graduate with a senior job at a multi-national corporation. He is also my Technology Consultant. Perhaps I should have one of those naff Seventies stickers above my computer which reads, 'You don't have to be mad to work here. But it helps.' As the day goes on, evidence of rampant corporate insanity mounts by the hour.

Jonathan Fingerhut calls. He sounds a little morose. In part this is because he is sitting amidst the filth and frenzy of his local casualty department, waiting to have a suspected broken leg examined. But I have added insult to injury, as he discovered when reading my business-plan this morning. In the page listing all the high-powered people associated with Sho-Biz I have called him Jonathan Fingergut.

It's bad enough having a mockable name without people getting it wrong. And it appears that I have made another mistake, as Mitchell Symons swiftly informs me. When I said that his school-mates replaced Jonathan's 'hut' with a four-letter word, second letter 'u', I got the wrong word. It was, in fact, even worse than I had imagined. So much worse, in fact, that I couldn't possibly tell you what it was.

That, though, is not why Mitch is calling. It's more a matter of current affairs. The papers have just revealed that multi-millionaire Labour peer Lord Levy paid £5,000 tax last year. Mitch is outraged by this scandalous deed allegedly committed by a member of his own faith. 'He paid £5,000 in tax? We're ashamed of him. ' A perfectly timed pause… 'That much?'

Next up is Lucien, whose news intake has focused on the aftermath of Mike Tyson's latest fight. 'Did you see what Tyson said? How he was going to rip the hearts out of Lennox Lewis's children and eat them? That's the spirit we want on sho-biz.com. We need to get some of that jungle action. You can't do better than that.'

Lucien has a plan to fly to India and score some serious Sho-Biz money off his sub-continental relations. So he needs to know what the deal is: how much we're prepared to give away for what.

'It's simple,' I say. 'Either Sho-Biz is a complete piece of shit which is never going to work, in which case it isn't worth anything at all. Or it is going to have at least some success, in which case the absolute minimum it's worth is five million quid. If anyone offers to invest at a valuation below five, they can fuck off. If they offer more than ten, I'll bite their hand off. Between five and ten, it's as long as a piece of string. I'm open to negotiation.'

Lucien seems fine with that. Next point: How are the shares divvied up at the moment?

'Okay,' I start, 'Kit and Zac…'

'The little weasels,' Lucien interrupts.

' … have 17.5% between them…' I continue.

'For what?!' he exclaims, his voice fired by righteous indignation.

'For everything they've done so far.'

'Yeah? And where's that got us, exactly?'

The man is a total lunatic. His opinions of other people are as irrational as they are scurrilous. But I have to admit, that's a very fair question.

27 June

I call Eric Fellner at Working Title. He's in a meeting. I call Bernard Doherty at LD Publicity. He's just popped out. I call Amanda Bross at Eclipse. Her phone is temporarily out of order.. I call Nancy at the Spice

Girls office. Not in yet... then on the phone. I call Stacy Mann, Nigel Parker and Ben Freeman: voicemail every time I call Bernard Doherty again. The place he popped out to was Switzerland.

I want to bang my head against the wall.

This combination of impotence and frustration is crushingly depressing. I know I have a good idea. I know people like it. I just can't cross that gap between interest and action. If we can just get one deal – any deal at all – the rest will fall like ninepins. But we've got to get that first deal.

In the meantime, all I can do is sit... and wait... and pray... Please, someone, call me back. And say, 'yes.'

28 June

Fingerhut to the rescue. He calls to talk about my business-plan which he's just about to show to the managing director of a very major bank, who happens to have a discretionary fund of £3 million to invest exactly as he pleases, and who seems interested in Sho-Biz. This seems like a great opportunity to grab the half-million or so that would keep us going until we are earning decent money and can go back to the City for serious amounts of cash.

In the meantime, the absence of response is plunging me into depression. I'm convinced the whole thing is going to be a disaster. Tell me, I ask Fingerhut, is this normal?

'Absolutely normal,' he replies, in the comforting tones of a family GP. 'If you didn't feel like that from time to time I'd be worried. When my clients are permanently optimistic it only tells me that they aren't properly based in reality. There are bound to be banana-skins and you're inevitably going to feel that the glass is half-empty, or even completely empty. But trust me, it will work.'

This, I realise, is the kind of wisdom that can only be acquired if – like Fingerhut – you have spent eight years as the man Kellogg's turn to when they want enticing goodies to give away in their packets of Frosties and Coco Pops. The search for the ultimate miniature *Toy Story* figurine, or lifelike midget gorilla prepares a man for the vicissitudes of life. Nothing can phase him. 'It's all right,' he says, when I apologise for burdening him with my troubles, 'I'm a bit like a therapist to all my clients.'

So I ask him another question, while the asking's good: How many times can you call a person who doesn't call you back before you become irritating and faintly pathetic?

Even Fingerhut knows that this is a tricky one. He just can't define the point at which eagerness becomes desperation. His solution, he says, is to send out letters: bright, breezy, single-page notes on crisp, clean paper, outlining all the fabulous things that are going on in his company's life. He knows that the recipients skim through them, at best, before dumping them in the bin. But at least it keeps him fresh in their minds.

Then he asks a question of his own: 'Do you know the single most important contribution to public transport in London over the past twenty years.'

I confess that I do not.

'Timed announcement boards,' he says. Then he explains... A few years ago, London Transport did some research on people waiting for trains on Tube platforms. They asked the punters how long they had been waiting. Invariably, their perceptions were way out of line with reality. Customers would say they had been waiting for ten or twelve minutes when they'd actually only been there for three or four. But of course the wait felt longer because it seemed open-ended: you just never knew when the train would arrive. As soon as the electronic noticeboards went up telling people how long it would be before the next train came along, the perception of waiting-time dropped dramatically.

Exactly the same principle applies in business. If you don't know when a potential client is going to get back to you, the wait seems to stretch on forever. But the moment you have some information, you can relax. He's so right. It wouldn't bother me in the slightest if any of the people I'm currently hassling told me that they couldn't do a follow-up meeting till September: once I knew it was going to happen, I'd be fine.

Later in the day I ask the same question to Neil Storey: how many calls? My view, I tell him, is that if your first call results in being told that the person you want to speak to is out, engaged or in a meeting, you're entitled to one more call. After that, you're a loser.

Storey disagrees. He goes for three calls, plus an e-mail.

You know what I think? I think people should return their fucking calls.

29 June

I have misjudged the mighty Fingerhut. He is neither embittered nor downcast by his name. On the contrary, he says, 'All the teasing at school was worth it. My name has proved to be one of the biggest boons in my business. It's not talent or ability to which I owe my success, it's being called Fingerhut. I can meet people I've only ever seen once in my life, years before, and they always remember me. They say, "How could I ever forget that name?" People I'm trying to get as clients have been known to take a meeting just to meet the person behind the extraordinary name.'

Now there's accentuating the positive for you. And, what's more, Fingerhut's been busy on my behalf. He's found another old contact – who remembered his name, of course – whose massive law firm, specialising in the movie industry, has just set up a venture capital fund, specialising in new media start-ups. He has, like a latterday Jeeves, taken the liberty of arranging an appointment at which I can present Sho-Biz.

In the meantime, he has had lunch with his MD friend, discussed Sho-Biz and handed over the plan. Oddly enough, the next people coming into the bank as Fingerhut was leaving were an American company called Broadband Studios (slogan: 'Games without frontiers'), which is a partnership between an Israeli company and Rockstar Games. Fingerhut just had time to direct the MD's attention to the fact that Sho-Biz and Rockstar were (and still are, from everything Lucien tells me about his ongoing confabs with Sam) intending to do business together, trading our entertainment content for their gaming expertise.

Well played, Fingerhut!

30 June

I get a call from a vet called Bruce Fogle, who has a weekend cottage near me in Sussex. We'd first talked a couple of months ago because Bruce was another middle-aged web-dweller. He's a vet by profession, and an extremely successful vet at that, the author of world-renowned books on dog and cat behaviour, published by Dorling Kindersley. So when people started setting up pet-related websites, they all beat a path to his door. And Bruce always said, 'No.'

Most of these outfits were using content as a sales-tool – their real business was shifting petfood. Petfood is a fantastically stupid thing to sell online. It's bulky, for one thing, so it costs a fortune to deliver, and the person on the far end has to be in to collect it. It's also a low-profit product. In the States, especially, the supermarkets work on such tight margins that there just isn't any room for significant savings. And finally, who the hell wants to waste their time ordering dogfood online?

So Bruce stayed clear and very smart he was, too, because the four big Internet pet-plays blew a billion bucks between them and still show no sign whatever of making any money. In fact, they're classic burn-rate casualties that are liable to blow all their cash on self-promotion, fail to create a sensible business and then be unable to get any more.

Pogopet, though, was different. Pogopet was based on the idea that the most valuable thing on the Internet is information. It wanted to use the editorial content and expertise that Bruce Fogle had accumulated over the years as the basis of a genuine content proposition. Pet owners would sign up, register the name, breed and distinguishing features of their pooch or moggy, and then come to Pogopet whenever they needed advice, or wanted to chat about their pet's behaviour, its favourite foods, or the way it was being treated by its vet.

Pet owners would do this because the majority are women, and women are the Internet's great chatters. As they logged onto Pogopet and yacked away, giving more and more details about themselves and their pets, they would be pouring data into Pogopet. This could then be sold at a high price to pet-food and pharmaceutical companies, ad agencies and goodness knows who else.

Bruce liked the concept and got involved. Pogopet hired a cool designer in San Francisco and she gave them a great-looking site. Bruce found himself sitting up late at night answering 100 online questions a week. The day we spoke, he'd just helped Selena from Belgrade deal with her dog's bad breath, and given advice to a German Shepherd-owner from Lake Hiawatha, USA. It wasn't how he'd planned to spend his 57th year, but what the heck. He was having a great time and he stood to make a fortune. Not that he needed the cash, but it never hurt to have more.

So a few months go by, and we promise to have a beer together some time, but never do. Then, today, Bruce calls again. He has good news, and he has bad news. The good news is that Pogopet was given a Best of the Best award by Forbes magazine. The bad news is it's been caught up in the general financial crisis currently gripping the Web. The venture capitalists that were hoping to back its next funding round have run short of cash, and Pogopet is having to go in search of new sugar-daddies.

'We had a contract,' says Bruce, 'but I've realised that doesn't mean anything. You have to have other salivating VCs to fall back on. Continue negotiations 'till the money's in the bank.'

Looking back, he says, he should have seen the signs of trouble way in advance. 'We'd agreed the deal, done the due diligence and they were saying, "Don't go anywhere else." But we could never get the final signature from the man at the top. We kept being told things like, "He's gone skiing. But don't worry, he'll deal with it when he gets back."'

It turned out that the VCs had been trying to raise their own finance. But they were too late. By the time they came to market the bubble had burst. They wanted £40 million but only got £5 million, and all of that was spoken for by people further up the queue than Pogopet.

I ask why they don't go somewhere else for the cash. He says they have had approaches – he names one merchant bank that still has £400 million of private money to spend on technology stocks – but the poor performance of other pet sites has made a lot of people nervous: 'Pet's become a pejorative word.'

Bruce is okay. As he explains, 'This has been enormous fun as far as I'm concerned. I can't say I ever took it too seriously.' But I think of all the people like Michael Magoulias who've felt the cold wind of collapse and haven't had million-selling books to fall back on. I think of John Hyslop, the Telinco sales executive. The last time I saw him, back in March, he told me that Telinco had just been taken over by an company called World Online, run by an amazing Dutchwoman called Nina Brink. World Online were about to float and John had invested his life savings to buy up shares. 'If this goes under,' he'd joked, 'I've blown four hundred grand.'

Well, World Online launched onto the Amsterdam exchange that month, priced at 43 Euros. By 1 June it was down to 12.85 Euros, a loss of 70%. Investors lost a total of 1.6 billion Euros and the wonderful Nina Brink found herself embroiled in a storm of controversy when it emerged that she had sold the bulk of her stake in the company months before the floatation although she denied making any profit as a result. Three weeks ago, World Online announced that the company was going to reimburse all its staff, giving them the full 43 Euros for every share they bought, but I wonder whether that news came in time for John Hyslop? I haven't heard a word out of him in months.

Then there's Neil Storey, whose TVO dream turned sour. How does he feel now, looking back on it all? Not too bad, is the answer. After all the agonising over Steve Thomas's call, asking if he wanted to sell some shares, it turns out that the question was an entirely straightforward, hidden-agenda-free offer to let him make some money, if he wanted or needed to.

More significantly, he's just had a call from John Lenehan and a couple of e-mails from Malcolm Messiter. His former partners have talked to Neil about him playing an active role again. He tells me that John began the conversation by saying, 'We're both a bit nervous. You've every right to tell us to fuck off.' But that's not what he's going to do.

There are other people involved with TVO – which has, incidentally, just changed its name to Rhythmica.com – who may have to work a bit harder to get back on his Christmas card list. But John and Malcolm are friends. Shit may happen, water may flow beneath the bridge, but the friendship remains. 'Knowing that makes me feel a lot happier,' says Neil.

So how does he feel about the whole TVO saga? Is he glad he ever got involved?

'Oh yeah, no question. I've only ever been on a roller-coaster once in my life and it was unbelievably terrifying. TVO was as close to that roller-coaster as anything I've ever done, but I wouldn't have missed it for the world.

'It was a big adventure, without a map. We knew we had an idea, and the more we lay awake in the middle of the night dissecting it, the more we thought that there really was something there – a product people would enjoy. Then it gets turned into buzzwords and stupid amounts of money and people get seduced, and that's when they start to fall over. The thing I've learned is that you've got to stay true to the reasons why you started the project in the first place.

'I have a friend called Scott Sunderland, an Australian, who's a professional racing cyclist. In the late-Eighties he moved halfway round the world and settled in Belgium because he thought he had enough ability to make the grade in what I reckon is one of the toughest professions on this planet. He's ridden the Tour de France and he's acknowledged as one of the most experienced riders in the world. Two years ago, he was almost killed in a race in Holland. He was hit by a team car towards the end of the Amstel Gold Race – I was watching, live on Eurosport, completely freaking out – he was just lying there in the middle of the road, motionless... as the entire race rode past. He had horrific injuries, a double brain-haemorrhage and he was within a hair's breadth of losing his life, but the way he pulled himself back was an unbelievable example of triumph over adversity. He'd had everything taken away and he had to start all over again. But he always believed in himself and what he did. And he was winning races within a year of the crash.

'I relate to that. You can't get caught up in all the shit that surrounds what you do. You've just got to focus on what matters, no matter how much it hurts. Scotty's worked harder than anyone I know to get himself back. In the end, it all comes down to hard work and self-belief. '

JULY

---

1 July

Today was the day when sho-biz.com was supposed to launch. Or so, at any rate, I thought on that rainy morning in December, when I sat with Joanna Jordan in a Greenwich Village café and she asked me whether I thought that Charlie's Angels would be a good project to start with. My schedule went roughly as follows...

January:
Write business-plan, get seed capital.

February/March:
Create winning package of people, partners and demo site.

April:
Hit the City hard and get a couple of million quid, a la Virtual Orchestra.
Hit the entertainment industry equally hard and get a whole bunch of clients.

May/June:
Prepare site.

July:
Launch.

It didn't take me too long to see that I was being a tad unrealistic. By mid-March it had become apparent that there was no way at all that I was ever going to meet that schedule. And even if, by some miracle, I had been able to get the techies and the Attik designers and the video gang all to deliver the goods by the end of the month, as I had intended, I would then have gone to the City at the exact moment when the market for technology and Internet stocks was plummeting fastest. On the other hand, my initial worries that the crash of bad ideas would take all the good ones down with it seemed unduly pessimistic. Everyone I spoke to reassured me that there was still plenty of money available for the right ideas. Since 'right' meant ideas that had business-to-business sales and strong revenue-streams – both of which were built into sho-biz.com, I remained confident that I would be able to get my cash. It was just going to take a little while longer.

So I moderated my expectations. I reckoned to have all my preparations done by the beginning of May. I then allowed two months for the whole process of going to see investors, making presentations, taking follow-up meetings, finding people who were interested, going through the process of due diligence and finally cashing my cheques. By this second schedule, the beginning of July should have seen me with three million in the sho-biz.com account, newly installed in a groovy suite of offices somewhere close to Victoria Station, frantically conducting job interviews for my putative staff, while the techies worked on database construction and Mitch wrote out his 200 star biographies.

But that's not what has happened. I'm still sitting at the exact same desk I was sitting at when I began this diary. I have no more money than I had in February – in fact, I have a great deal less. After six months of constant effort I have not one major investor, not one confirmed client. So you could say that the whole thing has been an utter failure.

But if you did, I would vehemently disagree. It's not just that I'm convinced that we are really, really close to getting both money and contracts. It's not even that I'm still expecting to be in business soon, but without having to give away huge chunks of my company to venture capitalists. It's because I've come to understand that I had been thinking about this business in completely the wrong way.

At the height of the Internet boom, people treated business like a lottery in which the odds were massively stacked in favour of the players. You chose your numbers by having a bright idea. Or even a not-very-bright-idea – just about any idea would do. Then you bought your ticket with a few million pounds handed over by a bunch of rich, private investors. Then you waited for a bit while the stock market balls tumbled around – or rather, tumbled up, which was all they ever seemed to do. Then you gave yourself an IPO and watched in delight as huge waves of money came crashing into your bank account.

When people think like that, they presume that a start-up is like a story with a beginning, a middle and a very happy end. But here's what I now understand: it isn't.

A few smart people got there before me. I remember talking to Neil Storey, some time in January, when the Virtual Orchestra had got their dosh and it looked as though nothing could go wrong. I kept being told by people close to the company that it was going to float by the autumn and be worth £200 million. That would have given Neil a paper fortune of £30 million-plus, so I was teasing him about the life of gross self-indulgence he would now be able to lead. But Neil was refusing to become the least bit over-excited, let alone complacent or smug. 'The thing is,' he said, 'I've just realised that the hard work's only just begun.'

In then end, the work went on without him. But he was still absolutely right. Unless you manage to become one of the tiny minority of people who are either bought out, or get out while the getting's good, there's never a point where you can relax, pour a drink and say, 'There … that's it.'

Starting a business isn't a story with a final full stop. It's not a piece of work, so much as a process. At any one time, you can take a snapshot of where that process is at, but it's an entirely arbitrary view. Suppose, for example, I had written a magazine article about Boo.com in mid-February 2000. I might, as an individual, have been sceptical about the idea of selling fashions online. But, as a reporter, I would have noted the buzz of activity in Boo's many offices and I'm sure I would have been told (accurately) that Boo was doing more business in February alone than in the whole of the previous quarter. I would have been aware that my editor (whoever he or she might have been) would have been fascinated by the fact that one of the company's founders was an ex-model. And since the mood – not just in the Internet business or the City, but also the media – was still relentlessly upbeat, I would have felt obliged to write a glowing report, tempered only by a couple of modestly-expressed doubts, just to give a sense of balance and objectivity.

So I would have got it totally wrong, just as all the pre-launch hype around Lastminute turned out to be completely inappropriate – the envious attacks on Brent and Martha were as misguided as the praise – or just as the *Vanity Fair* special feature on the glories of e-entrepreneurs coincided with their imminent demise. In all those cases, the presumption of success turned out to have been premature. But exactly the same applies to the presumption of failure.

There are thousands of little businesses, just like mine, trying to survive in an Internet environment that has suddenly become far tougher. Most of them – or rather, most of us – will fail. They'll be devoured by predators, catch a terminal financial sickness, or simply starve to death. But some of them won't. Some of the people you might write off today will be heroes tomorrow. And, just as a biological death always produces new life, so the death of companies will act as springboards for some of the individuals within those companies. Their first shot might have failed, but they'll have learned enough to make it, second time around. Or third. Or fourth. Or as many times as it takes.

Which brings me back to Sho-Biz. I would love to believe that an idea that has been greeted so positively by so many people will be able to survive and even flourish. I know that if I don't make it work, someone will eventually create something just like it. Every time I step into my garden and look at my house I wonder if I'll still be living here in twelve months' time. I've spent all my savings. I've broken contacts with editors that have taken years to create. As I realise every time I pick up a magazine and see some other writer's by-line on a story that should, and otherwise would have been mine, I've let my competitors pass me by and, in the fiendishly competitive marketplace of freelance journalism, I may find it impossible to regain the ground I've lost.

So I fear for my wife and children and I dread the shame and over-whelming sense of failure that I would feel were we forced to sell and move out. It may be old-fashioned, but I judge myself by my ability to provide – most men, I suspect, still do – and I would feel far, far less of a man if that ability were to be diminished, or even disappear. I try very hard to imagine a better, simpler life in which we live on far less money, but have far more time for the things that count... and all I see is a loser. I will not take a backward step.

But then again, maybe I won't have to. I've not yet taken a penny out of Sho-Corp Ltd. I've kept the development costs down to £75,000 or so, which means that Mitch and I have still got more than 80% of the company between us. If Sho-Biz has any value at all, which I remain convinced that it does, my stake has to be worth at least £3 million. This is all just pretend. I can't go to the bank and try to borrow money against that virtual fortune. I certainly can't go to Sainsbury's and try to buy groceries with it, let alone pay the mortgage. But the moment that Sho-Biz does its first job with its first real star, then reality starts to bite and that valuation becomes meaningful. I really could be worth a fortune.

Even if I'm not, there simply has to be a way in which everything I've learned can be put to use. I've spent the past twelve months getting a crash-course in new media technology, business practice and commercial finance – none of which I had the first idea about when I started. The Web is still so new that no one really knows yet how it's actually going to impact on our lives. And the people who best understand the technology often have the least comprehension of how normal human beings are actually going to react to it or interact with it. Even if you only know a little bit about that, you're still well ahead of the game.

I guess what I'm trying to say is that I'm glad I did it. Just when I'd reached a point in my career where I knew too well how to do what I did, I've been forced to confront and overcome my utter ignorance. If you're a typical middle-class fortysomething, deeply settled in your routines and prejudices, that kind of challenge can be very frightening. But it's also exciting, invigorating and even inspirational.

It's only prejudice that makes people suppose that the young have a monopoly on the understanding of new technology. If I had started this business at 25, rather than 40, I would never have come as far as fast as I actually have done. The whole idea for sho-biz.com rose originally from two things. First, that Mitchell Symons and I had a vast amount of material which we wanted to turn to profitable use. Second, that I knew, from personal experience and observation, that the business of celebrity journalism was hopelessly inefficient and ripe for reform. Both those conditions depended upon being around for long enough to get the material and really understand the industry in which I worked.

Once I'd had the idea, my age enabled me to pick up the phone and call people who could hugely increase my chances of success. As I've compiled my diary, the writer in me has been painfully aware that a certain tension has been lacking. It was just too easy for me to find people who could give me money, or get me in to see the Spice Girls' management, supply an ambitious little telly-babe to be my cyber-star. If I was just starting out, it might have been more exciting. I'd have been knocking on doors, pulling stunts, camping outside people's offices, begging for appointments. But a full address-book is what you get for staying in a business for two decades without upsetting too many people too badly – and it saves an awful lot of time and grief.

So here I am, biting my nails, waiting for the phone to ring and that first all-important job to be commissioned. One call, that's all it will take. Just to say that one of Amanda Bross's beautiful people is open to a big enough offer, or that the Spices are willing to chuck us even a sliver of their PR campaign, or that – glory be – David Ravden's spoken to Madonna, and she wants to talk about those baby pics that someone's going to be taking any day now.

Or maybe the call will come from the other end. Maybe we'll get the gig to cover the awards show online… or to supply information to Homechoice… or to be the entertainment partner when Adam Precious's multinational employers launch their massive Japanese Internet service in the UK and Europe. Perhaps one of Jonathan Fingerhut's big-time bankers will come through with his half-mill… or Lucien's Indian connections will pay off… or I'll resurrect the Illuminator deal… or

Associated will decide to do business. All it takes is just one call... and then another, and another, and another.

Once it starts, it won't stop. There may be an unhappy ending, but there can't be a happy ending, because the happiness will come from the fact that it doesn't end. Not unless someone comes along with an open cheque-book and buys me right out. I wonder what it would take. This business could be so big if it works. Just think of James Dyson: bust at 45, but a half-billionaire at 52. That could be me.

So if somebody came along tomorrow and offered me a couple of mill to sell all my shares, get out of Sho-Biz and never come back, would I take it? Would I sell out my dreams, abandon everything I've worked so hard for, just for the easy option?

I know what the answer should be. But what do you think? Would you take the money, if you were in my shoes? Yeah, of course you would. Absolutely. Like a shot.

I'd take the money and go for a long lazy holiday. Then I'd redecorate the house and learn to windsurf and play golf. And then I'd think of another daft idea ... and start all over again.

For the latest update on what has happened to the Sho-Biz project since this book was completed, go to www.fujitsu.co.uk/sho-biznews. Or just try www.sho-biz.com and discover the answer to the big question: has it been www ... or bust?